A Portrait of the Artist

IN

DIFFERENT PERSPECTIVE

A Portrait of the Artist

—— IN ——
DIFFERENT
PERSPECTIVE

JOSEPH A. BUTTIGIEG

Ohio University Press
Athens, Ohio
London

Library of Congress Cataloging-in-Publication Data

Buttigieg, Joseph A.
  A portrait of the artist in different perspective.

  Bibliography: p.
  Includes index.
  1. Joyce, James, 1882–1941. Portrait of the artist
as a young man.   2. Modernism (Literature)   I. Title.
PR6019.09P6435   1987   823′.912   87-1730
ISBN 0-8214-0857-7

for Anne

CONTENTS

ACKNOWLEDGMENTS

From *A Portrait of the Artist as a Young Man by James Joyce.* © Copyright 1916 by B. W. Huebsch. © Copyright renewed 1944 by Nora Joyce. Definitive text Copyright © 1964 by the Estate of James Joyce: Reprinted by permission of Viking Penguin, Inc.

From *Dubliners* by James Joyce. © Copyright 1916 by B. W. Huebsch. Definitive text Copyright © 1967 by the Estate of James Joyce. Reprinted by permission of Viking Penguin Inc.

From *Proust* by Samuel Beckett. © Copyright 1931 by Grove Press. Reprinted by permission of Grove Press Inc.

From *Concluding Unscientific Postscript* by Soren Kierkegaard, translated by David F. Swenson and Walter Lowrie. © Copyright 1941 by Princeton University Press. Reprinted by permission of Princeton University Press.

PREFACE

Had this been a sufficiently lengthy book to justify a substantial preface, I would have used the occasion to provide a detailed account of its genealogy. A leisurely evocation of my formative years in a small Catholic nation under British rule and of my Jesuit education would have helped explain my initial interest in James Joyce's work, particularly *A Portrait of the Artist as a Young Man*. In a retrospective account of my formal training in philosophy I could have shown why I find many aspects of Heidegger, Nietzsche and Kierkegaard especially attractive. Through an extensive description of my graduate studies and subsequent academic career in the United States I would have traced the development of certain concerns regarding aesthetics, criticism and literary history. Instead, I will detain the reader only briefly with a few introductory remarks.

At this very moment while I'm writing these sentences in South Bend, Indiana, the Tenth International James Joyce Symposium is in full swing far away in Copenhagen. This year, apart from taking the obligatory trip to the bastions of Kronborg Castle in Elsinore, viewing some cinematic versions of Joyce's works and attending a speech by Joyce *petit-fils*, the Symposium participants expect to direct some of their attention to the relations between Joycean studies and contemporary literary theory and criticism. This is not the first time exponents of postmodernism will have addressed large gatherings of Joyce devotees. Still, the proceedings at the Copenhagen Symposium may provide further encouragement to those who feel impelled to move Joyce studies in new directions. Already during the past few years some valuable essays and books on Joyce have appeared that not only take cognizance of contemporary critical preoccupations but also signal significant breaks from the generally predictable and outworn practices that have dominated Joyce criticism for over three decades. These new departures are important not so much because they will give new impetus to Joyce scholarship per se, but rather because they have the potential to make the critical study of Joyce's texts interesting and relevant to an audience that extends far beyond the restricted circle of Joyce experts.

There have been a few eminent Joycean critics and scholars whose writings, while "traditional" in a general sense, forcefully demonstrated how overwhelmingly important the careful study of Joyce's corpus can be for any serious consideration of broader questions concerning the history and critical analysis of narrative fiction and of Modernism. The impressive contributions of Hugh Kenner, for instance, come readily to mind. Too much Joyce criticism, though, has failed to elicit significant attention, much less enthusiasm, beyond the narrow confines of the Joyce-industry. Now that the inherited version of Modernism and many of the long-lived basic assumptions about the nature of narrative are being put to question, the time is opportune for a reconsideration of the frequently unexamined presuppositions and critical-theoretical stances that inform the greater part of the immense body of scholarship and commentary that engulfs Joyce's works. A revisionary history of Modernism cannot help having as one of it salient features a critical reexamination of Joyce and Joycean scholarship. Similarly, a thorough critique of the literary theories and critical practices that have conditioned the most influential, authoritative interpretations and evaluations of the Modernist canon must attach special significance to the peculiar character of Joycean studies.

In this volume I have sought—without any ambition of being comprehensive—to provide some indication of how a critical reconsideration of Joyce's work, and specifically *A Portrait of the Artist as a Young Man*, can contribute to the larger task of reevaluating the widespread, orthodox version of Modernism. I have also tried to point out that in *A Portrait* one can locate the point of departure for a severe critique of the central tenets of that very same critical movement—i.e., the New Criticism—that formulated the most pervasive fundamental definitions of Modernism and that helped fashion the basic contours of mainstream Joycean studies. Above all, I hope that what follows will become part of a larger effort to prevent Joyce's work from being overtaken by the paralysis that reverential monumentalism and arid antiquarianism normally induce and thus make it more readily available to contemporary readers. In pressing my argument for a critical revitalization of Joycean studies I have relied heavily upon Nietzsche's views on history and although I lack the boldness to follow his example and philosophize with a hammer, I did purposefully employ a polemical (and, at times, satirical) tone for a substantial part of my discussion.

Some of the contents of this book have been previously published. The second chapter is a modified version of an essay with the same title that formed part of the collection edited by Leonard Orr, *De-Structing the Novel: Essays in Applied Hermeneutics* (New York: Whitston, 1982). The first section of Chapter 3 appeared as "The Interest of Irony" in the *Notre Dame English Journal* (1983). For the opening pages of the final chapter I have revised an earlier essay published under the title "Aesthetics and Religion in *A Portrait of the Artist as a Young Man*" in *Christianity and Literature* (1979). At some points in the present text I have also incorporated a few paragraphs from my essay "The Struggle Against Meta(Phantasma)–physics: Nietzsche,

Joyce and the excess of history' " which was included in *Why Nietzsche Now?*, a special issue of *boundary 2* (1981), edited by Daniel O'Hara. I gratefully acknowledge the editors' permissions to republish these items.

The number of friends who directly or indirectly helped me in the course of writing this book is much too large to list here. To my friend and colleague John Matthias, however, I owe special thanks for his constant encouragement and support. My indebtedness to J. Anne Montgomery for her intellectual companionship, selflessness and trust cannot be adequately described. The dedication of this book to her is a reflection of my thankfulness. Our son Peter Paul has contributed an uncommon measure of patience and tolerance.

The writing of this book was aided, in part, by the award of a Jesse Jones Research Grant which is administered by Dr. Robert Gordon, the vice-president for advanced studies at the University of Notre Dame.

1

A Modernist Classic in a Postmodern Age

The Case of *A Portrait of the Artist as a Young Man*

The classic is a problem in any age. An ambitious newcomer to the literary scene encounters the classic as an insurmountable barrier or unshakable burden. Even the writer who has the highest regard for the classic and readily accords it an especially prominent place in the pantheon of literary history, feels the necessity at times to correct, circumscribe or qualify the admiration frequently bestowed upon it. Thus, for example, Alexander Pope in his "Imitations of Horace: Ep. II i":

> Authors, like Coins, grow dear as they grow old;
> It is the rust we value, not the gold.

And:

> I lose my patience, and I own it too,
> When works are censur'd, not as bad, but new;
> While if our Elders break all Reason's Laws,
> These fools demand not Pardon, but Applause.

And again:

> He, who to seem more deep than you or I,
> Extols old Bards, or Merlin's Prophecy,
> Mistake him not; he envies not admires,
> And to debase the Sons, exalts the Sires.[1]

Pope is expressing here his sense of what Walter Jackson Bate has called "the burden of the past," and his exasperation can probably be explained in accordance with Harold Bloom's theory of "the anxiety of influence." Clearly, however, it is not so much the classic text that oppresses Pope—after all, he is composing these verses in imitation of a classic—but the normative use to which the classic is put by the critic.

From among the many thoughts Pope provokes by these lines, two especially poignant ideas merit particular attention. First, the high esteem for the classic text may be based on false, extraliterary grounds. Second, the classic may be so highly revered as to deprive the belated writer of a chance to be heard seriously. In both cases one detects the same underlying impulse: to extol the past as a golden age in which all great things have already been achieved. The classic, in this context, is great by virtue of its antiquity; its apparent flaws are regarded as admirable characteristics; it is a monument against which the work of the new writer is measured and found wanting. The classic, then, becomes a god erected by the worshipers of the past—a monstrous god to whom are sacrificed the aspirations of the living. It is important to note here that Pope is not engaging in literary parricide. Instead, he inveighs against those worshipers of the past who have invested their monuments or idols—the classics—with the power to murder or, at least, paralyze the living.

It is instructive to juxtapose Pope's verses and some of the observations and opinions set forth by Harry Levin in his essay "What Was Modernism?"[2] In many respects, our contemporary writers have cause to fear Mr. Levin for some of the same reasons that Pope disliked certain critics of his time. Harry Levin's essay celebrates the magnificence of a golden age which, though not nearly so far removed from us as the Age of Augustus was from Pope and his contemporaries, he nonetheless treats with similar reverential awe. Looking back on a period stretching from the last decade of the nineteenth century to the outbreak of the Second World War, Harry Levin considers himself sufficiently distanced to "perceive, with increasing clarity, that the modernistic movement comprises one of the most remarkable constellations of genius in the history of the West" (*WWM*, 284). That movement has now come to an end as the "Modern Age" has given way to the "Post-Modern Period," according to Levin. That was a time of great creativity whereas ours is a time for retrospection, admiration and appreciation. "Looking back toward the Moderns, we may feel as Dryden did when he looked back from the Restoration to the Elizabethans, contrasting earlier strength with later refinement. 'Theirs was the giant race before the Flood . . . The Second Temple was not like the First' " (*WWM*, 277).

Harry Levin quotes selectively from John Dryden's "To My Dear Friend, Mr. Congreve" and masks the fact that his sentiments are markedly different from Dryden's. These are the opening lines of Dryden's poem:

Well then, the promis'd hour is come at last;
The present Age of Wit obscures the past:
Strong were our Syres; and as they Fought they Writ,
Conqu'ring with force of Arms, and dint of Wit:
Theirs was the Gyant Race, before the Flood;
And thus, when Charles Return'd, our Empire stood.
Like Janus he the stubborn Soil manur'd,
With Rules of Husbandry the rankness cur'd;
Tam'd us to manners, when the Stage was rude;
And boist'rous English Wit with Art indu'd.
Our Age was cultivated thus at length;
But what we gain'd in skill we lost in strength.
Our Builders were, with want of Genius curst;
The second Temple was not like the first:
Till You, the best Vitruvius, come at length;
Our Beauties equal, but excel our strength.
Firm Dorique Pillars found Your solid Base;
The Fair Corinthian Crowns the higher Space:
Thus all below is Strength, and all above is Grace.[3]

Dryden's poem praises the giants of an earlier age in order to eulogize the success of his competitor and contemporary Congreve in emulating their greatness. Harry Levin, by contrast, evokes the greatness of the past, the magnificence of the Modernist classics, only to mock the mediocrity of the present. The Moderns possessed strength and genius; they responded to their belatedness with vigorous experimentation and proceeded to establish a new order. The "Post-Moderns," on the other hand, incapable of similar innovation, manage only to squander and dilute their precious patrimony. "Lacking the courage of their [i.e., the Moderns'] convictions, much in our arts and letters simply exploits and diffuses, on a large scale and at a popular level, the results of their experimentalism" (WWM, 277).

Like the critics satirized by Pope, Harry Levin "extols old Bards" and "exalts the Sires" in order that he may "debase the Sons." He praises Joyce so that he may belittle Beckett. He highlights the "uncompromising intellectuality" and the "single-minded detachment" of the race of giants so that he can pour scorn on the inferiority, the ignorance and the Philistinism of their successors. "Beckett, after Joyce, seems thin and strident and monotonous" to Harry Levin, who cruelly characterizes Beckett as Joyce's "dishevelled disciple" (WWM, 273, 278).

Harry Levin's denigration of the postmoderns appears to be a necessary corollary of his glowing description of Modernism. His recollection of the literary past is steeped in nostalgia as becomes most evident when he directs his attention to the *annus mirabilis* of his golden age. He chronicles at some length the great literary events of 1922, the year in which "English letters had . . . to absorb the twofold shock of *Ulysses* and *The Waste Land*" (*WWM*, 283)—the two classics nonpareil of Modern literature. After such monumental achievements there is nowhere to go but down. In Mr. Levin's view, Joyce has written the novel to end all novels. All subsequent novelists, then, have to labor with the despairing knowledge that no matter how high the peaks they manage to scale, there will always be Joyce waiting for them.

Yet, Harry Levin discourages despair and offers instead the pleasures of untrammeled aesthetic contemplation. "But we may console ourselves by reflecting, there are times of change and times that seek stability; a time for exploring and innovating may well lead into a time for assimilating and consolidating. We may well count ourselves fortunate in that we can so effortlessly enjoy those gains secured by the pangs of our forerunners" (*WWM*, 277). In other words, since we cannot hope to match the remarkable feats of our forebears, we should devote our energies to writing dissertations about them. And that is precisely what has been done under the direction of scholars like Mr. Levin. Nonetheless, he himself writes contemptuously of the generation which has made of Joyce's books "a happy hunting ground for doctoral candidates" (*WWM*, 278) and he is appalled even more by the appearance in *PMLA* of an article on Beckett.

Pope censures those critics who invoke the classics to downgrade the new writer. Dryden eulogizes the achievements of the past in order to magnify the success of his contemporary, William Congreve. Harry Levin celebrates the giants of Modernism; he bestows upon James Joyce and T. S. Eliot the stature of a twin colossus and then he invites the Lilliputians of the "Post-Modern" age to recognize the puniness of their own productions. In this polemical essay, Levin plays the role of what Nietzsche calls the "monumental historian." In fact, Nietzsche's definition of monumental history aptly illustrates the underlying nature of Levin's endeavor. "Monumental history is the cloak under which their hatred of present power and greatness masquerades as an extreme admiration of the past. The real meaning of this way of viewing history is disguised as its opposite; whether they wish it or no, they are acting as though their motto were: 'Let the dead bury the—living.' "[4] In addition to being a historian, Harry Levin is also a critic (although he is not, by any means, what Nietzsche would call a "critical historian") and much as he bemoans the postmodern emphasis on criticism, his own position, if taken seriously, can have only two consequences: to breed more laudatory criticism of the past and to paralyze the creators of our own time. It is in this regard that Harry Levin differs most from Pope and Dryden. The critic and monumental historian can afford to give himself over completely to the monuments of a dead past, but the poets cannot do so without rendering themselves impotent.

But what about the giants of Modernism, on whom Levin writes so eloquently? How did *they* overcome the paralyzing influence of *their* forebears? Herein lies the most intriguing aspect of Harry Levin's argument; for while he exhorts the latecomers of the "Post-Modern" age to "effortlessly enjoy" the Modernist classics, he also writes in eulogistic terms about the image-breaking and the innovations of the Moderns. However, according to Levin's version of the story, the Moderns were not iconoclasts, but renovators; they did not destroy; they metamorphosed the past. Levin considers the metamorphic impetus to be at the very heart of Modernism and, not surprisingly, the paradigms of metamorphosis are James Joyce's *A Portrait of the Artist as a Young Man* and *Ulysses*. (It will be recalled that for an epigraph to *A Portrait*, Joyce chose a line from Ovid's *Metamorphoses*.) These two Modernist classics embody all the major elements of Harry Levin's definition of Modernism, a definition which has for its center the concept of metamorphosis. What Levin means by *metamorphosis* is the transformation of the past into a new order—an order which simultaneously embraces the inherited sense of the past and the exhilaration of a new beginning. In his own words: "What I have called the metamorphic impetus seems to have resulted from this paradoxical state of feeling belated and up-to-date simultaneously, and of working experimental transformations into traditional continuities" (*WWM*, 287).

Harry Levin admires the Moderns for being innovative without severing their links with tradition. James Joyce's novels are, for him, classics of Modernism because they exemplify unity, order, and continuity in this regard. "Joyce's use of myth," writes Levin echoing T. S. Eliot, "makes the past a key to the present" (*WWM*, 290). Joyce's texts serve as models for emulation because in them Joyce gives form to the formless, he endows with meaning what would otherwise remain meaningless, and he does this through a method which subsequent writers must adopt for themselves. This view is all too familiar since it is derived from T. S. Eliot's frequently quoted essay "*Ulysses*, Order, and Myth." "In using myth, in manipulating a continuous parallel between contemporaneity and antiquity, Mr. Joyce is pursuing a method which others must pursue after him. . . . It is simply a way of controlling, of ordering, of giving a shape and a significance to the immense panorama of futility which is contemporary history."[5]

Much attention has been lavished on the importance of Joyce's supposedly new method. T. S. Eliot, for his part, was interested mostly in what Joyce's method made possible: control, order, shape, significance. His essay, in fact, sets out to rebut Richard Aldington's assessment of Joyce as a "great undisciplined talent." Eliot wants to show that Joyce exhibits great discipline and mastery over his material and that Joyce's novel constitutes an endorsement of "classicism." Eliot considers "classicism . . . a goal toward which all good literature strives."[6] He understands the term much as T. E. Hulme does. "Classicism" attributes supreme importance to order and form and is the cornerstone of most of the orthodox versions of Modernism. The Modernist text attains the status of a classic when it can be shown to be a paradigm of "classicism"; that is, when it is taken to be a magnificent example of order, control, unity, form, and significance. Thus, for example, when Cleanth Brooks wishes to demonstrate the Modernity of T. S. Eliot in his essay "T. S. Eliot as a 'Modernist' Poet," he concludes with the categorical assertion: "For Eliot, poetry was order."[7] Similarly, ever since Eliot pointed out how Joyce through his mythic method achieved mastery over chaos by imposing order and form on his material, countless critics have produced mountains of books and essays to confirm the orthodox belief that beneath the apparent confusion and proliferation of detail in *Ulysses* there lies an intricate and well-wrought design. These critics have been determined to prove that behind or beyond or above the mass of heterogeneous material confronting the reader of *Ulysses* one can detect the presence of a controlling imagination, and that the multiplicity and chaos on the surface of the text are ultimately governed by a stable ironic vision. Many of the productions of Joycean scholarship are, in effect, repetitive rejections of Richard Aldington's evaluation of *Ulysses* as an invitation to chaos and of Joyce as a capable but undisciplined artist.

The voluminous criticism and analysis produced in the seventy years since the appearance of Joyce's first novel have also helped to restrict and to dull the impact (on the student of literature) of *A Portrait of the Artist as a Young Man*. A similar and, perhaps, even worse fate has attended *Ulysses* and *Finnegans Wake*. Serious readers can hardly approach Joyce's works without a sense of paralyzing awe, or without the guilty feeling that they are intruding upon hallowed ground reserved for the extremely erudite few. The daunting mass of scholarship dealing with allusions, references, influences, complex and subtle symbolic patterns, structure and architecture, leitmotifs, autobiographical echoes, and a plethora of other matters makes the actual texts virtually inaccessible. Nonetheless, numerous scholars have continued to venture into the territory of Joycean studies. Some of them have made valuable contributions to the understanding of Joyce's fiction but many more have only swelled the ranks of the Joyce-industry. A considerable amount of the attention lavished on *A Portrait* has been, as in the case of Joyce's later novels, generated by the critical impulse to lay bare and to explicate its allusive richness and complex structure. The reader of *A Portrait*, laboring in the shadow of the mass of scholarship surrounding the text, is led to ask with R. P. Blackmur: "How is it that the vice of scholarship should replace the élan of reading?"[8]

The necessity of breaking through these artificial barriers in order to approach the text anew is obvious. It would, however, be unforgivably naive simply to ignore what has already been written and stated. For no reading of a literary text ever occurs in a vacuum; rather, it takes place in a historical context. This context provides the reader's frame of reference, it delineates his horizon, and it marks the boundaries of the questions he asks as well as the answers he expects. The reader inevitably approaches a text with certain a priori notions of what he is likely to find in it and of how he should go about finding it. What Gadamer writes about the human sciences in general is true of literary studies in particular, namely that "the interest in tradition is motivated in a special way by the present and its interests. The theme and the area of research are actually constituted by the motivation of the enquiry."[9] The reader's response to the literary work is intimately related to the extent to which the work confirms or disappoints his expectations and to the procedures with which his approach discloses the work's conformity to or departure from his presuppositions. A major source of these expectations and presuppositions is literary scholarship: critical theory, literary history, biography, theories of aesthetics and aesthetic evaluation, and so on. It is this vast corpus of scholarship and tradition that frames the questions a reader addresses or formulates a propos of a text. Blindness to these shaping elements would be tantamount to a blindness to one's own limitations.

A careful exploration of the inescapable literary critical context within which the most influential treatments of *A Portrait* have been carried out must be a task of the highest priority. At no time could there possibly have been a reader of Joyce's novel who first confronted a text with a tabula rasa. Even the very earliest reviewers of Joyce's *kunstlerroman* must have had their expectations and presuppositions which they brought to bear on the text. Their encounter with *A Portrait* was no more in a vacuum than that of today's readers. They received the work in a literary historical context: it was a text belonging to a particular genre, within a tradition which possessed certain identifiable characteristics. The *bildungsroman* tradition, for example, as it had developed and as it was perceived at the time of the appearance of *A Portrait*, shaped the frame of reference within which several of the earliest reviewers of Joyce's novel responded to it. As Hans Robert Jauss explains, the "frame of reference for each work develops in the historical moment of its appearance from a previous understanding of the genre, from the form and themes of already familiar works, and from the contrast between poetic and practical language."[10]

The study of the criticism surrounding *A Portrait* necessarily entails an examination of the tradition within which that criticism was produced. This, in turn, involves an inquiry into the way in which the tradition was approached: the methods and yardsticks used to analyze and evaluate works within it. It is not enough, for example, to show that *A Portrait* is a descendant of Goethe's *Wilhelm Meister* and *The Sorrows of Young Werther* or that it shares various characteristics with Meredith's *The Ordeal of Richard Feverel*, Butler's *The Way of All Flesh*, Wilde's *The Picture of Dorian Gray*, Moore's *Confessions of a Young Man*, and Pater's *Marius the Epicurean*. Nor is it enough to demonstrate that Joyce's novel differs from all its predecessors and the manner in which it does. One must also consider how such similarities and divergencies were significant or otherwise within the literary critical milieu in which they first appeared. It is noteworthy, for instance, that the aesthetic theories and critical procedures prevalent during the early part of the twentieth century made recognition in the book of some of the elements more recognizable today very difficult for the earlier readers of *A Portrait*. "It can happen that the potential significance of a work may remain unrecognized until the evolution of a newer form widens the horizon and only then open up the understanding of the misunderstood earlier forms."[11]

At the same time, though, one must guard against the illusion that the passage of time and the widening of horizons will make possible, even if only theoretically, an objective and definitive interpretation of a particular work. A reading of *A Portrait*, or any other text, *sub specie aeternitatis* will never be possible. What remains possible, indeed necessary, is the constant rewriting or revision of literary history. In other words, the version of literary history or tradition that has been handed down needs always to be confronted critically. In the absence of a revisionist (i.e., critical) history, the monuments erected by a dead past will exercise control over the living present and become an obstacle to a vital future. That is why Nietzsche, in the *Use and Abuse of History*, enjoins the historian to summon all his critical resources "to help him revolt against secondhand thought, secondhand learning, secondhand action" (*UAH*, 21). This revolt will not produce "the truth" or "true" knowledge, for our vantage point is no more privileged than that of our ancestors. Nor will it constitute a clean break with the past. "For as we are merely the resultant of past generations, we are also the resultant of their errors, passions, and crimes; it is impossible to shake off this chain. Though we condemn the errors and think we have escaped them, we cannot escape the fact that we sprang from them. At best, it comes to a conflict between our innate inherited nature and our knowledge, between a stern, new discipline and an ancient tradition" (*UAH*, 21). Nonetheless, one must engage in this conflict or else condemn oneself to paralysis. On this matter Joyce has written as eloquently as Nietzsche.

The motto "Let the dead bury the—living" would have been the most appropriate epigraph for James Joyce's *Dubliners*. The collection of stories consists of a veritable gallery of characters paralyzed by their uncritical allegiance to tradition. They allow the past which is dead and exists only in their foggy memories to exercise such a powerful influence over their lives as to deprive them of all vitality. Received notions, secondhand ideas, vague distorted memories, nostalgia, perverted patriotism, and superstition pervade the thoughts and conversations of the characters and prevent them from taking hold of their own lives and fashioning their own futures. Joyce's Dubliners pay homage to the monuments of the past with a fervor so intense and a devotion so complete that it would be sacrilegious for them to allow any present needs or accomplishments to challenge the supremacy of the dead, no matter how stifling or paralyzing that supremacy might prove to be. The loss of the past causes them greater grief than the oppressiveness of the present. By their fond recollection, the worshipers of tradition invite the ghosts of the dead to deprive them of life. Joyce's Dubliners are dead because they fail or refuse to summon "the strength to break up the past, and apply it, too, in order to live" (*UAH*, 21).

"Excess of history," Nietzsche wrote, "has attacked the plastic power of life that no more understands how to use the past as a means of strength and nourishment" (*UAH*, 69). This is especially true of the Irish scene described by Joyce. In "Ivy Day in the Committee Room" history/ memory emerges as the great pacifier, the convenient alternative to revolutionary action. Just when political differences threaten to lead to disagreement and shatter the lazy bonhomie of a group of undistinguished Dubliners, just when the situation calls for an assertion of principles and a commitment to a cause, the past is evoked; it is evoked precisely because it is dead and so can deaden any spark of passion. The Parnellites and the royalists bury their differences in an empty, nostalgic recollection of a ghost. They all approve of Hynes's verses on "The Death of Parnell" because Parnell no longer calls for a course of action but has become a safe and convenient monument by virtue of his passage into history. Parnell is dead and gone, and the men in the committee room, like most other Dubliners, are also dead, buried under their heaps of history and memories.

Joyce's stories are not merely studies in the nature and effects of nostalgia. The stories which make up *Dubliners* are, among other things, elaborations on the Nietzschean insight that "the historical sense makes its servants passive and retrospective" (*UAH*, 49). Joyce examines the ways in which life can be so debilitated by an excess of history as to cease to desire itself. Furthermore, if the stories in *Dubliners* are epiphanies, they are epiphanies in a most unusual way. Whereas a bright star guided the three legendary kings to the site of a birth that marked the end of an old dispensation and the inauguration of a new order, Joyce invites his readers to behold a series of mummified Dubliners, all victims of their complacency in confronting the obduracy of their own dead legacies.

The earliest readers of *Dubliners* were struck by what they considered to be the morbidity of Joyce's vision. While almost uniform in their admiration of Joyce's stylistic mastery, the reviewers found the author wanting in another important respect: his stories contained no hint of a higher, or even merely better, order to which the characters could attain, nor did his stories offer the reader an alternative vision. "The book," according to the *Everyman* reviewer, "may be styled the records of an inferno in which neither pity nor remorse can enter. Wonderfully written, the power of genius is in every line, but it is a genius that, blind to the blue of the heavens, seeks inspiration in the hell of despair." The *Athenaeum* reviewer expressed the hope that Joyce might learn "to enlarge his outlook and eliminate such scenes and details as can only shock, without in any useful way impressing or elevating the reader."[12] What these and many other readers expected from fiction, Joyce could never provide. Indeed, how could Joyce offer the heavens as a consoling and uplifting counterforce while at the same time showing that those heavens are populated only by ghosts and monuments for the dead? Joyce's Dubliners, like Nietzsche's modern man, need to destroy the monuments to the dead past, dispel the ghosts, stop looking backward and start creating the very world in which they are solidly anchored. First it is necessary to destroy, and only then would it be possible to engage in a new creation— the new creation, however, would be so radically new, so manifestly a creation, so divested of any privilege that it could not be mistaken for yet another variation on what has been lost or displaced.

Stephen Dedalus recognizes early in his life the need to escape the murderous burden placed upon him by a sacrosanct tradition. In both *A Portrait of the Artist as a Young Man* and *Ulysses* we find him struggling against the nets which constrain him and the ghosts that haunt him. In both novels Joyce traces the progress of Stephen as he moves willfully toward fulfilling his self-imposed artistic vocation. Yet, it must be stressed, Joyce never produces a picture of Stephen as creator but only of Stephen in the throes of becoming a creator. Whatever Stephen might think of himself,

there should be little doubt that in *A Portrait* and in *Ulysses* he is still struggling against those forces which prevent him from attaining the status of
a genuine, as opposed to a self-styled, artist. The forces which campaign
against Stephen's emergence as artist, in the full Nietzschean sense of
creator, are the ghosts of history, the phantasms of his own past as well
as the phantasms foisted upon him by his country and his religion. The
two are hardly separable. Stephen is not unaware of these ghosts nor is
he blind to their pervasive influence. He knows he has to free himself
from the excess of history in order to become the creator of a new order.
"—History, Stephen said, is a nightmare from which I am trying to
awake."[13] Nevertheless, Stephen often fails to realize fully the extent to
which he is enmeshed in that nightmare, and consequently his declarations of freedom are, with possibly one exception, premature. (The possible exception occurs when Stephen smashes the lamp with his ashplant
in the phantasmagoric "Circe" chapter.) There is one thing, however,
which Stephen thoroughly understands and about which he is certain: in
order to escape paralysis he must "bring the past to the bar of judgement,
interrogate it remorselessly, and finally condemn it" (*UAH*, 21).

In our time, the conflict with the inherited tradition in literary and
critical studies must likewise take the form of a remorseless interroga-
tion which should result in a *critical* (in the Nietzschean sense) history of
Modernism. The classics of Modernism present the postmodern age with
a problem not entirely different from the one which for Pope and Dryden
was posed by the Greek and Roman classics—they threaten to become a
debilitating force, they might induce paralysis. Hence, one of the most
pressing needs of postmodernism is to produce a critical history, as opposed to a monumental history, of Modernism. The postmodern age
must construct its own definition of Modernism. In a sense, of course,
Modernism has already been defined and its monuments identified; but
the prevailing definitions of Modernism and the privilege conferred upon
certain texts deemed central to it come to us as part of that very same
tradition which we must now confront critically and "interrogate remorselessly." For this reason, the construction of a postmodern definition of Modernism is inseparable from the "destruction" of the received
tradition. "Destruction" here derives its special meaning from Martin
Heidegger who, like Nietzsche, has made clear the problem that arises
from the uncritical acceptance and transmission of tradition. "When tradition thus becomes master, it does so in such a way that what it 'trans-
mits' is made so inaccessible, proximally and for the most part, that it
rather becomes concealed. Tradition takes what has come down to us and
delivers it over to self-evidence; it blocks our access to those primordial
'sources' from which the categories and concepts handed down to us have

been in part quite genuinely drawn. Indeed it makes us forget that they have had such an origin. . . ." To overcome this forgetfulness Heidegger proposes the critical method of "destruction." As he hastens to make clear, "to bury the past in nullity . . . is not the purpose of this destruction; its aim is *positive*." Destruction enables the interpreter "to go back to the Past in a positive manner and make it productively [his] own."[14]

The critical or revisionist historian sets about the task of defining Modernism by scrutinizing the Modernist tradition as it has been articulated, represented and delivered over by its self-proclaimed adherents or by those monumental historians who upon looking at the past could discern enough novels, poems, plays, and critical writings which share a sufficient number of salient characteristics to justify their being classified all together as Modernist. What are the characteristics that have been singled out as the major feature of Modernism? How have certain novels, poems, plays, and so on been interpreted and explicated so that they could be inducted into the Modernist pantheon? What are the fundamental presuppositions and the central ideas on which and around which the whole edifice of Modernism has been constructed? In what ways have the major monuments of Modernism been construed to yield those very same critical approaches and evaluative criteria which were used to confer upon them the status of classics?

The importance of Joyce's texts in the Modernist pantheon is so great that any attempt to understand Modernism must include a careful consideration of Joyce's novels and the preeminent—one might even say paradigmatic or classic—status they enjoy. Yet, precisely because these texts are constitutive of Modernism as it has been habitually understood, it is especially difficult to examine them anew. They cannot be separated easily from the tradition which they both exemplify and constitute. It is quite hard to read them in a manner that differs significantly from the way in which they have already been read and presented. Still, any new beginning with regard to these texts must contend with the problem of extricating them from the authoritative critical and historical literary discourse that envelops them. In other words, if Joyce's *A Portrait of the Artist as a Young Man* and *Ulysses* are to be reappropriated for a postmodern readership, if they are not to be abandoned as the beautiful but ossified monuments of a dead past (i.e., a Modernism that once was and is no more), then their reappropriation will involve an analysis and critique of Modernism. Simultaneously, a critical or revisionary approach to Modernism necessarily entails a reconsideration of its canonical texts among which Joyce's novels occupy a very special place. These two tasks are one and the same and must be carried out concurrently because they cannot be separated effectively.

So, in trying to rediscover or, more accurately, to uncover *A Portrait*, that is to say in the course of making it available again to an audience that is not wedded to the supremacy or preferability of the received version of Modernism and to readers who are not addicted to the nostalgic recollection of a lost golden age, one inevitably becomes a participant in the postmodern endeavor to redefine Modernism. By making it possible for *A Portrait of the Artist* to be something other than the repository of orthodox Modernist principles and desires, one becomes engaged in a critique of the received version of Modernism. The production of a new critical description of Modernism seeks, in effect, to demythologize the authoritative tradition which thus far largely controls our understanding of many twentieth-century literary works.

Ever since its publication in 1916, *A Portrait of the Artist as a Young Man* has been absorbed ineluctably into what is generally assumed to be the mainstream of the Modernist tradition. There was, initially, some confusion as to its merits and some debate as to whether it belonged to the naturalist movement or whether it represented a move into more original territory. Gradually, however, critics and literary historians started to regard it as an early example of the symbolism and realism that characterize many Modernist classics, from the novels of Henry James to those of Virginia Woolf and E. M. Forster. Among the influential critics who placed *A Portrait* in the naturalist tradition was Wyndham Lewis. In Lewis's view, *Ulysses* is "the very nightmare of the naturalistic spirit" and *A Portrait of the Artist* a failed naturalistic novel.[15] In spite of these early associations of *A Portrait* with naturalism, though, it soon became evident to many critics that Stephen Dedalus's aesthetic theory which occupies such a central position in the novel does not embody the tenets of naturalism but works well as an expression of the emergent symbolist aesthetic. Quite predictably, Stephen's aesthetic theory was used to incorporate *A Portrait* into the postnaturalist orthodoxy. *A Portrait of the Artist as a Young Man* became a part of the orderly progress of literary history; a place was found for it in the Modernist canon. In the process, the novel was covered by the massive amount of explication lavished on it, by the uses to which the aesthetic theory it contains has been put, and by the incessant attention it attracted as the precursor of the more highly valued *Ulysses*.

In order to extricate *A Portrait* from the prisonhouse of the tradition within which it has been confined and in order to loosen the hold which the received version of Modernism exercises over *A Portrait*, one must necessarily touch upon those issues which are closest to the core of the dominant aspects of twentieth-century literary history and criticism. Thus, for example, since the aesthetic theory set forth by Stephen Dedalus has been among the most widely discussed items in twentieth-century literature, the relationship of this theory to New Critical theory is an unavoidable issue. A discussion of this matter leads one directly to the very heart of the New Critical version of Modernism and is a crucial element in the revisionary project of demythologizing the received tradition and demystifying its authoritativeness. Likewise, because the aesthetic theory in *A Portrait* is intertwined with various aspects of religion and because of the confusion that exists in the orthodox version of Modernism as well as in the mainstream of New Critical theory with respect to the relation of religion to aesthetics and art, one cannot avoid dealing with these thorny matters.

But why *A Portrait of the Artist as a Young Man?* Would *Ulysses* not be a more suitable starting point for a revisionist treatment of Modernism? The least important, but no less valid reason for focusing on *A Portrait* is that it is better known and more widely read than Joyce's later novels. Another reason is that many commentators have treated *A Portrait* as if it were the origin of Joyce's artistic progress; they have found in it, albeit in embryonic form, all that was to flourish subsequently in the Modernist classic par excellence, *Ulysses*.[16] The impetus for this approach comes from the incalculable influence exercised by the adoption of Stephen's ramblings on aesthetics as a source of insight not only into the whole Joycean corpus but also into the nature of literature and art in general. The attempts to adapt and even adopt Stephen's theories to serve as a kind of Modernist manifesto have been many and varied.

In his essay on "Poetry and Christian Thought," W. K. Wimsatt uses elements of Stephen Dedalus's aesthetic theory from *A Portrait* to demonstrate certain central tenets of "recent literary theory" which he compares and contrasts with "some aspects of the Christian tradition in thinking." He finds in Stephen's idea of *claritas* not only an expression of the kind of order and unity about which "recent criticism has much to say" but also the fundamental connection that exists between the formalist concerns of "recent critics" and the more traditional (i.e., Aristotelian, neo-Platonic and scholastic) "ideas about order, harmony, and unity." Wimsatt defines Stephen's *claritas* as "the radiant epiphany of the whole and structurally intelligible *individual* thing."[17]

Like many other critics, Wimsatt cannot resist inserting the notion of epiphany into his discussion of Stephen's aesthetics, even though Joyce left out all mention of epiphany when he revised *Stephen Hero* and transformed it into *A Portrait*. This is noteworthy because the literary concept of epiphany has been repeatedly invoked as an identifying feature of Modernist literature. Maurice Beja articulates a widely held view in *Epiphany in the Modern Novel*: "Just as epiphany is associated with the dominant themes of modern fiction, so it is one of its most useful and central tech-

niques."[18] Critics have used the concept of epiphany to connect Joyce
with Bergson[19] whose ideas on *"l'intuition philosophique," "durée réele,"* and
simultaneity have supplied the basis for a demonstration of how the
Modernist imagination constitutes a rejection of the positivism prevalent
in much late nineteenth and early twentieth-century literature. Ever
since T. E. Hulme expounded on the idea of the intensive manifold which
he derived from Bergson,[20] the epiphanic mode of handling the problem
of time has been found to characterize the writings of such central Modernist figures as Marcel Proust, Virginia Woolf, Dorothy Richardson,
William Faulkner, Sherwood Anderson, E. M. Forster as well as Joyce,
and to distinguish their works from those of H. G. Wells, Arnold Bennett,
John Galsworthy, and Theodore Dreiser.

Another facet of Stephen's aesthetic theory which traditional Modernist critics find irresistible is the insistence on the artist's detachment, indifference and distance. The ubiquitous references to Stephen's remark
about God paring his fingernails indicate, perhaps more than anything
else, the extent to which this idea is ingrained in criticism. Wimsatt traces
certain aspects of the doctrine of aesthetic distance to Aquinas's *apprehensio* and Kant's "disinterest." But for the modern understanding of disinterest he turns, once again, to Stephen Dedalus.

> One must apparently be content to say that the Thomist and Kantian doc-
> trines have their most manageable meaning in the fact that certain sensory
> experiences, those of sight and hearing, are more pervaded with the force
> of intelligence than others: they have pattern and form, are shaded by recol-
> lection, and induce contemplation—whereas the experience of the so-called
> lower senses is more restless from moment to moment, and notably incom-
> plete. But there is another and more special sense in which the doctrine of
> aesthetic detachment may be taken—and this, I believe, is the more usual
> modern sense—one which applies to works of art only in so far as they are
> references to something beyond themselves. It is this sense which is chiefly
> if not entirely operative in Stephen Dedalus' distinction between kinetic
> feeling (that excited by didactic and pornographic art) and static emotion
> (the truly dramatic and aesthetic). The painting looks like a landscape, but
> we rest in the looks and need not be moved to go outdoors. . . . In short,
> the aesthetic symbol absorbs the interest of its referents into itself and
> contains them in an impractical stasis. Recent poetic theory continually im-
> plies this doctrine—in part acquired from aestheticians and in part worked
> out by litterateurs for themselves.[21]

Among the most influential early twentieth-century aestheticians
who concerned themselves with the doctrine of aesthetic detachment
were A. C. Bradley, Clive Bell, and Roger Fry. Fry described the proper

aesthetic response as "disinterested intensity of contemplation."[22] All three also devoted much attention to the supreme importance of form in art. From them comes the famous phrase "significant form" which Clive Bell used most extensively in his widely discussed book *Art*.[23] "Significant form" has been regarded as a quintessentially Modernist term. So, when William York Tindall asserts that "the aesthetic theory in *A Portrait of the Artist* is a definition of significant form"[24] he is, in effect, inscribing Joyce's novel into the very core of the standard Modernist canon.

Many critics have found other ways to demonstrate the Modernist character of *A Portrait*. Frederick J. Hoffman, for instance, considers Stephen's aesthetic explorations similar to Yeats's reactions against the prevailing tradition. In his view, Stephen's difficulties with handling the complex reality which surrounds him typify the problems of modern youth. For Hoffman, therefore, "Stephen Dedalus has undergone an experience which all but identifies the twentieth century and him with it."[25] H. M. McLuhan, adopting a different approach, finds in *A Portrait* the evidence he needs to support his contention that "Joyce the artist . . . was able to complete the work of the symbolists."[26] According to McLuhan the aesthetic theory set forth in *A Portrait* puts Joyce in the front rank of Modernism (with T. S. Eliot) as the man who perfected the insights adumbrated in the works of Flaubert, Rimbaud, and Mallarmé. In a similar vein, Jane Jack in an essay on "Art and *A Portrait of the Artist*" proposes to show that Joyce's novel belongs to the Modernist rather than the naturalist novelistic tradition by emphasizing Joyce's "considerable use of the technique of symbolism."[27] Bernard Benstock adopts an almost identical approach. He elucidates at length and in detail the complex symbolic structure of *A Portrait* in order to justify his initial assertion that with the completion of Joyce's first novel "the nineteenth century was scrapped and the twentieth century ushered in."[28] In a much more original and sophisticated essay, Hugh Kenner suggests that "Joyce's *Portrait* may be the first piece of cubism in literary history."[29] Cubist painting has been used to exemplify one of the main achievements and identifying features of Modernism—the spatialization of time.[30]

There can be little doubt, of course, that in *A Portrait* Joyce, by way of Stephen Dedalus, touches upon matters of great interest and even crucial importance to the late nineteenth and early twentieth-century readership. Also, many of Stephen's problems are alive today and his perorations on aesthetics address issues which have yet to be satisfactorily resolved. Identifying various aspects of *A Portrait of the Artist* as typical of much that was being discussed and written during the time of its composition is a normal exercise of literary study and can only enhance one's appreciation of the work itself. Problems arise, however, when one approaches the novel with a predetermined set of standards. Thus, for example, if a complex symbolic structure is a necessary characteristic of a Modernist novel, then one may feel impelled to set about demonstrating that Joyce's novel possesses the required complex symbolic structure, and thus deserves its place in the Modernist novelistic tradition.

There has been a more serious problem and one that is specifically connected with *A Portrait*. That is the problem arising out of the very special attention accorded to Stephen Dedalus's aesthetic theory. Not only has Stephen's theory frequently been taken to represent Joyce's own position (and this even by critics who otherwise are careful to distinguish James Joyce from Stephen Dedalus), but it has also been taken to embody the main principles espoused by the main proponents of the dominant version of Modernism, the New Critics. As a consequence many readers have assumed that Stephen's aesthetic theory contains the key to *the* proper mode of reading *A Portrait*. The aesthetic theory thus becomes normative—if *A Portrait* (or *Ulysses*, or any other text in the Modernist canon) can be shown to fulfill its requirements, then it is a good/successful novel. Joyce's supposed theory of art is mistakenly located in his novels. Too many critics have remained blind to the fictionality of Joyce's fiction and they have lifted the aesthetic theory out of its fictional context and then used it to examine and evaluate the fiction from which they extracted it. According to William T. Noon, much of the attention accorded to *A Portrait* stems from the supposition that it provides the reader with a reliable guide for its own interpretation. "The continuing independent interest in this relatively simple story," writes Noon, "suggests that it can be read not just for its story but also for its built-in interpretation of that story, without further need of glosses from other works of fiction or from overmuch commentary by experts."[31] Thus, for instance, Grant H. Redford asserts quite categorically that *A Portrait of the Artist* is "the objectification of an artistic proposition and a method announced by the central character."[32] Seen in this way *A Portrait* becomes the perfect paradigm of the New Critical ideal: the fully autonomous or autotelic artifact.

There are many reasons why Stephen Dedalus's aesthetic proclamations have been taken so seriously and interpreted more or less straightforwardly, but two come most readily to mind. First of all, Stephen's ideas are in many ways anchored in traditional and orthodox principles. Second, much of what Stephen has to say coincides in large part and in the most important respects with the views propounded by the New Critics who dominated literary studies during the first half of our century. It is not surprising, then, that *A Portrait* "should serve with scriptural authority as a primary source of New Critical doctrine."[33] Because the New

Critics and their followers could find in *A Portrait* a reaffirmation of their theoretical position and a confirmation of their expectations, they appropriated the text and gave it a prominent place in their Modernist canon. Their limited horizons and their interest in buttressing their basic stance have prevented those with a New Critical orientation from seriously considering the possibility of discovering in *A Portrait* "a satire on the angelism of *fin de siecle* aestheticism"[34] or a serious critique (one might even say destruction) of that very same Modernist sensibility it supposedly exemplifies and articulates. These readers have been caught in a vicious circle of interpretation: their expectations have so governed their approach to *A Portrait* that their reading of the novel cannot help confirming their expectations.

The vicious circle of interpretation can be broken only by inaugurating a new beginning in the study of *A Portrait*. "A beginning," as Edward W. Said has shown, "is what . . . scholarship ought to see itself as, for in that light scholarship or criticism revitalizes itself." Any true beginning demystifies the authoritativeness of the received tradition; that is it makes the scholar "controvert the dynastic role thrust upon him by history or habit."[35] No authentically new interpretation of a text can take place unless some space is cleared for it first. To obtain that space one must confront the past critically; in other words, one must revise the inherited versions of history. Beginning anew with *A Portrait*, then, means liberating it from the boundaries within which traditional literary interpretation, and more specifically New Criticism, have confined it. In thus making *A Portrait* available to the postmodern reader one opens up new possibilities for the production of a literary history and a definition of Modernism which can compete with the orthodox and more authoritative versions that have been handed over. A related and equally exciting possibility is also opened up by a revisionist reading of *A Portrait*. While we recognize that Stephen Dedalus's aesthetics do indeed represent the culmination of the Western metaphysical tradition and reiterate the main tenets of New Criticism, it remains possible to insist that Joyce's implied criticism of Stephen in the novel constitutes a serious challenge to that tradition and those tenets. Rather than confirm the place of *A Portrait* in the traditional canon, the critical historian will show that Joyce's first novel lays bare the grounds upon which the prevailing myth of Modernism has been constructed.

2

Joyce *Redivivus*

A Meditation

Composition of Place I

Once upon a time (and I am not sure it was a good time) in a "dark gaunt house on Usher's Island"[1] on the south bank of the River Liffey slightly west of the centre of Dublin[2]—"the centre of paralysis"[3]—there was, as there always had been for "as long as anyone could remember" (D 176), a splendid Christmas dinner party. It was a great affair, for "it was always a great affair, the Misses Morkan's annual dance" (D 175). At this gathering the guests and their hosts entertained themselves dancing, singing, reminiscing nostalgically, gossiping. The annual reunion was capped by a sumptuous dinner, towards the end of which the guests were regaled by a speech by Gabriel Conroy, the Misses Morkan's favorite nephew.

> He began:
>   —Ladies and Gentlemen.
>   —It has fallen to my lot this evening, as in years past, to perform a very pleasing task for which I am afraid my poor reserves as a speaker are all too inadequate.
>   —No, no! said Mr. Browne.
>   . . .
>   —Ladies and Gentlemen. It is not the first time that we have gathered together under this hospitable roof, around this hospitable board. It is not the first time that we have been the recipients—or perhaps, I had better say, the victims—of the hospitality of certain good ladies.
>   . . .
>   —I feel more strongly with every recurring year that our country has no tradition which does it so much honour and which it should guard so jealously as that of its hospitality. . . . the tradition of genuine warm-hearted courteous Irish hospitality, which our forefathers have handed down to us and which we in turn must hand down to our descendants . . .
>   . . .
>   —Ladies and Gentlemen.
>   —A new generation is growing up in our midst, a generation actuated

by new ideas and new principles. It is serious and enthusiastic for these new ideas and its enthusiasm, even when it is misdirected, is, I believe, in the main sincere. But we are living in a sceptical and, if I may use the phrase, a thought-tormented age: and sometimes I fear that this new generation, educated or hypereducated as it is, will lack those qualities of humanity, of hospitality, of kindly humour which belonged to an older day. Listening tonight to the names of all those great singers of the past it seemed to me, I must confess, that we were living in a less spacious age. Those days might, without exaggeration, be called spacious days: and if they are gone beyond recall let us hope, at least, that in gatherings such as this we shall still speak of them with pride and affection, still cherish in our hearts the memory of those dead and gone great ones whose fame the world will not willingly let die.

    —Hear, hear! said Mr. Browne loudly.

    —But yet, continued Gabriel, his voice falling into a softer inflection, there are always in gatherings such as this sadder thoughts that will recur to our minds: thoughts of the past, of youth, of changes, of absent faces that we miss here tonight. Our path through life is strewn with many such sad memories: and were we to brood upon them always we could not find the heart to go on bravely with our work among the living. We have all of us living duties and living affections which claim, and rightly claim, our strenuous endeavours.

    —Therefore, I will not linger on the past. I will not let any gloomy moralising intrude upon us here to-night. Here we are gathered together for a brief moment from the bustle and rush of our everyday routine. We are met here as friends, in the spirit of good-fellowship, as colleagues, also to a certain extent, in the true spirit of *camaraderie* . . . . (D. 202–204)

Gabriel concluded his speech by proposing a toast in honor of the three hostesses. All the guests joined in an uproarious rendering of "For they are jolly gay fellows." Before very long the gathering started gradually to disperse; the merrymakers headed for home, while Gretta and Gabriel took a cab to the Gresham Hotel where they had planned to spend the night. As he prepared to go to bed Gabriel began to realize that the past, the faces of the dead, could indeed intrude upon him and interfere with his living duties and affections. Or rather, to put it more accurately, the dead burst into Gabriel's life and interjected themselves between him and the object of his desires—Gretta.

Composition of Place II

There is another version of this story. This version, too, is set in Dublin, but it does not unfold in the ahistorical "once upon a time" of myth and fairy tale. So this story is based on "real" events and "real" people; but then, the same is true of Joyce's novella. The fact that I am reconstructing historical occurrences does not make my account any less fictional. (I, therefore, can also claim the right to assert that all resemblances between the characters I describe and living individuals are purely accidental.) This story takes place during the summer of 1969 and the occasion is the Second International Joyce Symposium. Scholars and fellow enthusiasts gather from all over the world, but mostly from the United States. Acquaintances are renewed, vows of friendship reaffirmed; gossip is exchanged and nostalgia given free rein. Several papers are read and discussed in a spirit of camaraderie. There is much gaiety and merrymaking. The Irish tradition of warm-hearted conviviality is upheld as vast quantities of Guinness stout, Irish whiskey and Irish coffee are consumed. The bustle and rush of humdrum everyday life are briefly put aside. While the citizens of Dublin and the rest of Ireland go on with their normal occupations and the city carries on with its daily business, these partygoers visit the sites and spots and monuments.

Directed by maps and guides of a dead Dublin—a Dublin that once *was*—they retrace the steps of some long dead and of others who never lived. Armed with texts which have somehow acquired the status of sacred books, they try to bring the printed word to life. Forgetful of the writer's frustration at his inability to breathe life into his words and names, as a mythic god is supposed to have done in the *origin*-al and unrepeatable act of creating the universe out of nothing, these Joyce connoisseurs talk of Gabriel Conroy and Stephen Dedalus and Leopold Bloom with the same earnestness exhibited by Mr. Browne and Mr. D'Arcy in their discussion on the relative merits of Tietjens, Ilma de Murzka, Campanini, Trebelli, Giuglini, Ravelli, Aramburo and Caruso. They discuss and evoke a past which for the most part never even existed, one which they perceive as being eternally and pervasively present. Bloom remains forever living, roaming the streets of Dublin on a never-ending, never-changing June sixteenth. "History as her is harped. Too the toone your owldfrow lied of."[4] On Bloomsday of some future year the participants at the umpteenth International Joyce Symposium will probably walk around the same streets, look at the same things (or what will be left of them), recall the same details, and quote the same relevant passages as the participants of 1969.

In short, the party assumes, to a very large extent, the character of a tour. But what is being toured? Are these pilgrims looking at the living or the dead? Is this a voyage of repetition, or is it rather a tranquil exercise in recollection? In other words, are these latter-day voyagers discovering a new, mysterious, confusing city throbbing with life, or are they merely visiting the familiar? One suspects the latter is true. For even if some of

these visitors have never been to Dublin before, they are still likely to
perceive Dublin as a huge museum exhibit. Each item on display is cata-
logued and placed in the large scheme with which every true Joycean is
familiar. When these modern pilgrims visit Adam and Eve's they see the
church where Julia Morkan used to sing, or else the Eve and Adam's past
which the "riverrun." It is a place on the map and its significance is secured by that unique Dublin Baedeker, the Joycean text. And when they
inspect the Liffey, is it the ever-changing river they look at? Or is it the
Liffey captured by the text—the Liffey in which the Dublin women are
forever doing their laundry while gossiping; the Liffey which stands as a
symbol of the eternal woman? Does not this most unextraordinary river
always appear special to the Joycean tourists, special for reasons which
have nothing to do with the river itself? Its unimpressive ordinariness
escapes them. A cruel irony is at play here. Joyce's works deal with the
familiar and render it unfamiliar. The blindness of the fictional Dubliners
who populate his novels is repeated by Joyce in order to disclose a world
continuously encountered but never really experienced. Many of his
characters are paralyzed and dead even while going through the motions
of life because they are creatures of habit caught in the web of conven-
tions or in the mechanical routines of hollow rituals. But now Joyce's
texts have themselves become familiar; they have been tamed and neu-
tralized to a very significant degree. What is even more striking, these
same texts have become both the source and the tools of what Beckett
calls the "Baedeker consciousness."

Once the Joyce text has been domesticated, it serves the purpose of a
guidebook through which one can look at the world—not the world teem-
ing with difference and characterized by change, but the world as a centered text apprehended safely and indifferently from the vantage point of
aesthetic distance. The tourists look at and talk of a dead Dublin, a world
created once and for all and to which they are habituated. They are,
therefore, paralyzed by the grip of habit—a paralysis which, it must be
noted, is a protection from the "suffering of being."

> Because the pernicious devotion of habit paralyses our attention, drugs
> those handmaidens of perception whose co-operation is not absolutely es-
> sential. . . . But our current habit of living is as incapable of dealing with
> the mystery of a strange sky or a strange room, with any circumstance
> unforeseen in her curriculum, as [Proust's] Francois of conceiving or realis-
> ing the full horror of a Duval omelette. . . . when it [i.e., Habit] is opposed
> by a phenomenon that it cannot reduce to the condition of a comfortable
> and familiar concept, when, in a word, it betrays its trust as a screen to
> spare its victim the spectacle of reality, it disappears, and the victim, now an
> ex-victim, for a moment free, is exposed to that reality—an exposure that

has its advantages and disadvantages. It disappears—with wailing and gnashing of teeth. . . . What is taking place? . . . Between this death and that birth, reality, intolerable, absorbed feverishly by his consciousness at the extreme limit of its intensity, by his total consciousness organised to avert disaster, to create the new habit that will empty the mystery of its threat—and also of its beauty. "If Habit," writes Proust, "is a second nature, it keeps us in ignorance of the first, and is free of its cruelties and enchantments." . . . "Enchantments of reality" has the air of paradox. But when the object is perceived as particular and unique and not merely the member of a family, when it appears independent of any general notion and detached from the sanity of a cause, isolated and inexplicable in the light of ignorance, then and only then may it be a source of enchantment. Unfortunately, Habit has laid its veto on this form of perception, its action being precisely to hide the essence—the Idea—of the object in the haze of conception—preconception. Normally we are in the position of the tourist . . . whose aesthetic experience consists in a series of identifications and for whom Baedeker is the end rather than the means. . . . The creature of habit turns aside from the object that cannot be made to correspond with one or other of his intellectual prejudices, that resists the propositions of his team of syntheses, organized by Habit on labour-saving principles.[5]

The party of our Joycean tourists goes on for a few days. Then, to conclude it, a dinner is held and at this dinner there is to be a speech. This year it has fallen to Leslie Fiedler's lot to address the gathering. After the usual calls for silence all those present direct their attention to the speaker who is well-known even outside professional literary circles and needs little introduction. He launches into the speech with his normal verve and wit. Needless to say, his subject is Joyce and Joyce's work; the talk is entitled "Bloom as the Humanity of Joyce." In the course of his delivery Fiedler makes a very intriguing remark. "I have in the past several years become more and more aware, painfully aware, that the literary movement which we have agreed to call 'Modernism,' and at the center of which Joyce stands, is a literary movement which is now dead."[6] The speech and the dinner bring the festivities to an end. Gradually, the gathering disperses and everyone starts preparing to return home either directly or else after a swing through Europe. The ritual will be repeated two years later and on every alternate Bloomsday—the Joycean calendar dictates the month and the day.

I. Modernism is Dead: Joyce is Dead

The remarks Leslie Fiedler made in Dublin at the concluding session of the Joyce Symposium appeared not long afterwards in an essay, "Bloom on Joyce; or, Jokey for Jacob."[7] He chose to publish the essay in the inaugural issue of the *Journal of Modern Literature*, a journal dedicated to the study of Modernism as a historical phenomenon which has run its course and which, now that it is extinct, may conveniently be examined and analyzed with a modicum of objectivity and detachment. The editor of that journal, Maurice Beebe, himself a Joyce scholar of considerable stature, has on a number of occasions taken Leslie Fiedler's remarks as his starting point for a consideration of Joyce's position in the Modernist tradition and the ramifications of the death of that tradition. Beebe does not dispute Fiedler's assertions that Joyce stands at the center of the "literary movement we . . . call 'Modernism' " and that "Modernism . . . is a literary movement which is now dead."[8] Unlike Fiedler, however, he does not regard this death as a source of pain or regret; rather, he sees it as offering a good opportunity to launch a more lucid and coherent study than has hitherto been possible of Modernism—"an international current of sensibility which dominated art and literature from the last quarter of the nineteenth century until about 1945—from the exhibitions of the 1870s and the first writings of Henry James to about the time of the Second World War."[9] During this period, according to Beebe, immeasurable riches were amassed in the treasurehouse of literary history, and the need for an analysis and assessment of those riches is pressing. Now that, by Beebe's calculation, at least a quarter of a century has passed since Modernism faded away and about twice that long since it reached its peak, "it is as if we have stepped outside the gates of a walled city where for too long we were such baffled and busy citizens that we could never see the whole place singly and clearly." He, therefore, finds it "comfortably reassuring to know that it is now possible to look *back* on the modern period."[10]

One detects in Maurice Beebe's language more than just a trace of Stephen Dedalus's pronouncements on aesthetic apprehension and aesthetic distance. The suspicion that Beebe is adapting Stephen's ideas for his purposes is reinforced when one reads that he prefers "to see it [i.e., Modernism] as an island separate from the mainland,"[11] and when he discusses "Modernism . . . seen as a new and basically independent and autonomous phase in the literary history of the past two centuries."[12] Not only is Beebe's reliance on the metaphor of sight strongly reminiscent of one of the hallmarks of Stephen's formulations, but also, and more significantly, his insistence on separating and singling out Modernism from the confusing background of various literary traditions and crosscurrents is a direct echo of Stephen's explanation of the first stage of artistic apprehension.

—In order to see that basket, said Stephen, your mind first of all separates the basket from the rest of the visible universe which is not the basket. The first phase of apprehension is a bounding line drawn about the object to be apprehended. . . . the esthetic image is first luminously apprehended as selfbounded and selfcontained upon the immeasurable background of space or time which is not it. You apprehend it as *one* thing. You see it as one whole. You apprehend its wholeness. That is *integritas*.[13]

Stephen's task of explaining *integritas* to Lynch is not too difficult; he points to a real basket which a butcher's boy is playing with. Beebe's task is not so simple. He is pointing to something which is not there, or which, at least, is not obviously in front of him. He has to make us see it and then he has to persuade us that it is Modernism. Beebe attempts to show that Modernism is "selfbounded and selfcontained" by, first of all, separating it from that which precedes it (Romanticism) and that which follows it (postmodernism). It is not incidental that he appears to regard postmodernism as a form of neo-Romanticism. But that is not sufficient because several works produced during the period he calls "Modernist" have been shown to have affinities to Romanticism and have, in fact, been used to demonstrate the continuity of the Romantic sensibility through the twentieth century. Beebe does not seek to negate this continuity fully, but he wants to separate Modernism from it and demonstrate that Modernism was independent of the mainstream. So he draws a distinction. He segregates the sheep from the goats, as it were, by excluding from Modernism those writers whose Dionysiac tendencies betray a continuing allegiance to the Romantic tradition. In this manner, Frost, Lawrence (whose *Women in Love*, contrary to Beebe's chronology, did *not* first appear in the same year as *Ulysses* and *The Waste Land*), Hemingway and others are placed in one camp whereas Flaubert, James, Conrad, Ford, Pound, Woolf, Forster, Joyce and several others, including Williams, Stevens and Beckett, are placed in another camp, of which Joyce is the central representative.

This distinction, however, cannot be based on such vague grounds as the Dionysian inclination of one group and the Apollonianism of the other. So Beebe proceeds to look for those characteristics which distinguish the latter group from the former. He comes up with four characteristics which, in his opinion, "work quite well if Modernism is seen as a new and basically independent and autonomous phase in the literary history of the past two centuries."[14] The "if" in Beebe's statement looms large and renders his position dubious, for it suggests that one must first accept the fact that Modernism really existed before he is able to see it as distinct from that which it is not. Suppose we transpose Beebe's statement; it will become evident that the autonomy of Modernism depends on an a priori acceptance of what Beebe considers to be its characteristic traits. Modernism is seen as a new and basically independent and autonomous phase in literary history *if* these characteristics work well when applied to it. But from where did Beebe derive these characteristics? The Modernist texts, of course. And why did he find these characteristics and not others when he examined the Modernist texts? Because these are the characteristics which would show Modernism to be Modernism and not just another phase or aspect of Romanticism. Maurice Beebe might have led himself into a trap. He will find in his explorations only what his preconceptions told him he would, and then he will use his "discoveries" to prove the validity of those very preconceptions. (Beebe's presuppositions are, not incidentally, derived for the most part from New Critical theory.) He draws arbitrary boundaries on the map of literary history— for he sees literary history as a map with islands and mainlands—and then calls one of the territories "Modernism." The arbitrariness with which he draws his boundaries is illustrated by the fact that he lists writers such as Williams, Stevens and Beckett as belonging to Modernism. Yet, these three writers have been recognized by postmodern sympathizers as serious challengers to the particular variety of Modernism which Beebe thinks they exemplify. It may well be that Modernism is simply a convenient image created by the critic's imagination in order that he might have the territory staked. Once he establishes his territory and names it, he can talk about it. That is why Beebe needs to affirm that Modernism is "independent" and "autonomous."

Apart from establishing the *integritas* of Modernism, Beebe needs to point out what constitutes this movement, what are the separable, identifiable features of which it is made up. Stephen explains to the bemused Lynch that "the synthesis of immediate perception is followed by the analysis of apprehension." Beebe cannot proceed from one step to the next as Stephen does, for his internal analysis of Modernism is a necessary part of the first step—i.e., the demonstration of Modernism as an autotelic object. Nevertheless, he evinces the complexity of Modernism, its internal phases, its basic characteristics. He lists the four main characteristics as formalism, irony, the use of myth as an ordering device, and reflexivism.[15] In spite of this complexity, however, and in spite of the many elements both formal and thematic which constitute Modernism, "the over-all design seems clear."[16] In other words, Beebe apprehends the internal structure, as it were, of Modernism; or as Stephen puts it:

You apprehend it as complex, multiple, divisible, separable, made up of its
parts, the result of its parts and their sum, harmonious. That is *consonantia*.
(*P*, 212)

The next and final stage of apprehension is *claritas* which Stephen, after straightening out what he takes to be a slip into inexactitude on Aquinas's part, equates with *quidditas*. "The radiance of which he [i.e., Aquinas]
speaks," says Stephen, still addressing Lynch, "is the scholastic *quidditas*,
the *whatness* of a thing" (*P*, 213). Maurice Beebe follows this pattern to the
end. He, too, is in search of "whatness"; in his case, it is the whatness of
Modernism. He reiterates the question asked by Harry Levin twelve
years earlier: "What Was Modernism?" He raises the question once again,
not simply because it has yet to be answered conclusively, nor because it
is widely asked, but especially because of his conviction that it is only now
that we are in a position to tackle it. Beebe considers his vantage point of
historical distance from Modernism a great and indispensable asset. It
appears that he wants to look at this phenomenon *sub specie aeternitatis*; that
is, to look *back* and see it as a whole. In this respect, as well, he reveals
himself to be steeled in the school of Stephen Dedalus, for like the young
artist he wants to view the world (in this case the world of literature)
from the standpoint of the godhead. Indeed, his very images are spatial as
he is concerned with the "over-all design" and the autonomy of Modernism rather than with its unfolding and the ways in which it is variously
interpreted, reinterpreted, defined and redefined. It is as if he wants to fly
above history and obtain a bird's-eye view of it. What Maurice Beebe is
after, and what he erroneously thinks he could perceive and present, is a
definitive image of Modernism which is solid and immutable. That is why
he feels "more relief than grief" at the announcement of the death of
Modernism. Dead things are static, their development has been arrested
(and, it will be recalled, "arrest" is crucial to Stephen's theory), and they
cannot suddenly, or even gradually, become something other than what
they have been; they stand eternally in the perfect tense because they are
consummated, completed—or so, at least, we are led to think. Modernism
has not been dead for long and so "only recently has it become possible to
define Modernism with some degree of confidence that we shall not have
to keep adjusting our definition in order to accommodate new visions and
values."[17]

The idea of having a crystallized and hardened definition of Modernism sounds attractive. (While we're at it, why not formulate similar definitions for all literary periods and movements?) It would certainly have
its advantages. Once the critic knows that the text he is handling is Mod-

ernist, once he knows where it fits, he is left with the relatively simple task of tracing and demonstrating the characteristics of that movement or period in the text. Or, if he approaches matters from the opposite direction, the literary scholar may spend his time isolating the salient features of a text and then, after matching those features to the characteristics of the various periods or movements to which his text could possibly belong, he should find it reasonably easy to determine in which niche or category to place it. It does not take long, however, to realize that this approach is quite unacceptable since it is, on the one hand, conducive to boredom (What would thousands of litterateurs do if there were no adjustments to be made to our definitions?), and, on the other, it will transform literary historians and critics into a special breed of coroners and into an uninspiring group of cemetery watchmen. There will have to be autopsies to determine not only when and of what each movement died, but also the nature and the characteristics of every new corpse. Unfortunately, Sartre's portrayal of critics behaving in precisely such a way, although satirical and hyperbolic, is not entirely fictional.

> It must be borne in mind that most critics are men who have not had much luck and who, just about the time they were growing desperate, found a quiet little job as cemetery watchmen. God knows whether cemeteries are peaceful; none of them are more cheerful than a library. The dead are there; the only thing they have done is write. They have long since been washed clean of the sin of living, and besides, their lives are known only through other books which other dead men have written about them. . . . The trouble makers have disappeared; all that remains are the little coffins that are stacked on shelves along the walls like urns in a columbarium. . . .
> It is a holiday for him [i.e., the critic] when contemporary authors do him the favor of dying. Their books, too raw, too living, too urgent, pass on to the other shore; they become less and less affecting and more and more beautiful. After a short stay in Purgatory they go on to people the intelligible heaven with new values. . . . As for the writers who persist in living, he asks them only not to move about too much, and to make an effort to resemble from now on the dead men they will be.[18]

Sartre's description of the critic anxiously awaiting the death of the author ought not to be dismissed as a vicious indulgence in caricature. A brief survey of a sample of literary studies, particularly studies of the past sixty years or so, would quickly reveal that numerous critics assume a distanced position in regard to the works they examine. The same is often true of literary historians. The western metaphysical tradition, oriented as it is towards objectivity, requires of the speculative as well as the analytic thinker that he view the world and its phenomena from a privileged metaphysical perspective. Hence the repeated efforts to understand and explain literary texts as well as literary movements *sub specie aeternitatis*, that is from the end. Thus, one views a text or movement as a whole, as a *totum simul*. To do this, of course, the text and the tradition must first be seen as having been completed, in other words, as having died. For if a movement or tradition or text is still in the process of becoming, if it is still changing, then, quite clearly, it cannot be grasped wholly and definitively. The Imagists' compulsion to seize the whole text simultaneously as a single and autonomous Image is still with us—Modernism, it seems, is far from dead—and manifests itself not only in the treatment of texts but also in the study of literary history. Maurice Beebe's treatment of Modernism is not different in this regard from his treatment of individual texts such as *A Portrait* or *Ulysses*. Nor is his method unique to himself.

In the course of discussing *Ulysses* as a central Modernist text (a discussion which, by way of illustrating the major tenets of Modernism at work in *Ulysses*, offers *Ulysses* as the perfect epitome of Modernism itself, so that this one text becomes virtually a symbol which stands for the whole of Modernism, of which it is itself a central constitutive part), Beebe remarks in passing how "We shall be hearing much this year about the fifty-year anniversaries of the *Waste Land* and *Ulysses*."[19] His prediction came true. Critics could hardly be expected to resist the temptation to look back over a fifty-year span. In 1972 several books on Joyce were published, and four of them focused on *Ulysses*.[20] Furthermore, at least three journals marked the occasion with special issues.[21] Maurice Beebe's essay, "*Ulysses* and the Age of Modernism," appeared in the special issue of the *James Joyce Quarterly*. The *Quarterly* essays were later published in book form as *ULYSSES: Fifty Years*. The first essay in that collection is by A. Walton Litz.[22] Litz, like Beebe, sees *Ulysses* as a central Modernist text, and to prove his point he tries to demonstrate that it occupies a very crucial place in the critical thinking as well as the creative endeavors of the two other giants of Modernism, Eliot and Pound.[23] The similarity of Litz's and Beebe's approaches is equally evident in the former's essay on T. S. Eliot which appeared in a volume also occasioned by a fiftieth anniversary. In his essay "*The Waste Land* Fifty Years After," Walton Litz states: "Few works have remained *avant-garde* for long. But now that 'modernism' has passed into the realm of literary history, *The Waste Land* must pass with it."[24] (One is reminded of Samuel Johnson's rash dictum: "Nothing odd will do long. *Tristram Shandy* did not last.")[25] *The Waste Land*, like *Ulysses*, is offered as a paradigmatic example of Modernism at its peak. But both texts can be set up as paradigms only because they, like the movement of which they are a part and which they represent, are perceived to be dead.

The essays by Walton Litz and Maurice Beebe are only two instances from among many others which serve to illustrate how a teleologically oriented criticism finds it necessary to pronounce the death of a text and of a literary-historical phase in order to be able to deal with the text comfortably. This kind of criticism derives part of its justification from some of the most prominent writers of the Modern period. T. S. Eliot's "Tradition and the Individual Talent," for example, is frequently invoked since in that very influential essay Eliot wrote of the "feeling that the whole of the literature of Europe from Homer and within it the literature of [one's] own country has a simultaneous existence and composes a simultaneous order."[26] Undeniably, "simultaneous order" and "simultaneous existence" are possible only from a teleological standpoint and, therefore, Eliot appears to be calling for a view of the tradition from a position beyond time and history. Moreover, the call for a "simultaneous order" amounts to nothing less than a desire to (in Derridean language) transcend difference in favor of identity. But one must not forget, as is too easily forgotten, that in the same essay Eliot also explains how every genuine new work of art brings with it a revision of the tradition that preceded it. Eliot implies that the past is never closed off and is not impervious to change. "Tradition and the Individual Talent," as Richard Poirier rightly insists, "by virtue of its assertions about the proper shape of literary history, is in fact remarkable not for the orders it proposes but for those it disowns: any notions of the past or of literature as a fixed thing, any notion that an achieved order is ever more than provisional."[27] Eliot can, of course, be coerced to fit neatly into the total design constructed by orthodox historians of Modernism. He can be made to serve two functions: first, his works may be interpreted in such a manner as to yield those characteristics which are considered to be the trademarks of a Modernist text, and second, his criticism may be construed to legitimize precisely *that* interpretation of his text and the texts of others. The use of Eliot's essay "*Ulysses*, Order and Myth," for instance, has for a long time conditioned much of the thinking lavished on both *Ulysses* and *The Waste Land*. One misreading perpetrates another; or rather, one misreading is the necessary buttress of another misreading.

II. James Joyce on Death and the Dead

Joyce had much to say about the role played by the past in an individual's life. It is hard to imagine how any careful reader of Joyce could possibly entertain the idea that what is past and gone is fixed. There is no such reassurance to be found in Joyce's writings. On the contrary, in "The Dead" he illustrates how the present can alter the past and also how the past can burst into the present and shatter it. This is what Gabriel Conroy is made to confront in the novella, and this is what we discover through our reading of it. The inhabitants of Dublin are dead because they are imprisoned and shackled by a fixed and monolithic past. They are paralyzed by their own allegiance to and preservation of a dead tradition. But when the past escapes the deadness imposed upon it, when it manifests itself as something new and unknown, when it ceases to be the familiar object of a dull memory, then the past has the power to jolt the Dubliner into recognizing for the first time what he previously thought he knew so well. This experience is disturbing and painful, like a birth, for it deprives one of mastery over a world rendered comfortable by habit. It is like a birth because it opens one's eyes to the world as if for the first time, and this newly experienced world is vast, unruly, cold. One's emergence into this world is marked by a loss of the at-homeness of the previous womb-like (or tomb-like) existence—a loss which is accompanied by an awakening to one's dreadful status as an exile.

In "The Dead" the various characters exhibit two ways of looking at the past. Most of them are capable only of recollection—a dead past evoked by dead men. Gabriel and possibly Gretta, however, experience something different in the latter part of the story. They do not recollect the past, they repeat it; and this repetition, unlike the recollections in which they themselves and others indulge earlier in the story, causes pain. The distinction suggested by Joyce in "The Dead" between a past evoked by a complacent memory and a past that breaks through the complacency to sunder the habitual is a crucial element not only of the final story but of *Dubliners* as a whole. It is, therefore, important to dwell for a moment on the difference between mnemonic recollection and repetition.

A fine and extremely lucid discussion of memory is offered by Samuel Beckett in his essay on Proust. Beckett distinguishes between "voluntary memory" and "involuntary memory." "Voluntary memory" is the province of the creature of habit, the man who proudly possesses a good memory and exercises strong control over it.

> The man with a good memory does not remember anything because he does not forget anything. His memory is uniform, a creature of routine, at once a condition and function of his impeccable habit, an instrument of reference instead of an instrument of discovery. The paean of his memory: "I remember as well as I remember yesterday . . ." is also its epitaph, and gives the precise expression of its value. He cannot *remember* yesterday any more than he can remember to-morrow. He can contemplate yesterday

hung out to dry with the wettest August Bank holiday on record a little further down the clothes line. Because his memory is a clothes-line and the images of his past dirty linen redeemed and the infallibly complacent servants of his reminiscental need.[28]

This kind of memory, an omnivorous burial ground for the past, is, according to Beckett, not memory at all.

The memory that is not memory, but the application of a concordance to the Old Testament of the individual, he [i.e. Proust] calls "voluntary memory." This is the uniform memory of intelligence; and it can be relied on to reproduce for our gratified inspection those impressions of the past that were consciously and intelligently formed. It has no interest in the mysterious element of inattention that colours our most commonplace experiences. It presents the past in monochrome. The images it chooses are as arbitrary as those chosen by imagination, and are equally remote from reality. Its action has been compared by Proust to that of turning the leaves of an album of photographs. The material that it furnishes contains nothing of the past, merely a blurred and uniform projection once removed of our anxiety and opportunism—that is to say nothing. There is no great difference, says Proust, between the memory of a dream and the memory of reality. . . . It insists on that most necessary, wholesome and monotonous plagiarism—the plagiarism of oneself. This thoroughgoing democrat makes no distinction between the "Pensées" of Pascal and a soap advertisement. In fact, if Habit is the Goddess of Dulness, voluntary memory is Shadwell and of Irish extraction.[29]

"Voluntary memory" is a protective screen that keeps reality at bay. It functions both as a fixing agent to secure the pastness of the past and as a safe haven for escape. Through its agency one can postpone almost indefinitely the unpleasantness of facing the real world and defer for as long as possible the necessity to act.

Ample illustration of "voluntary memory" and its intimate relation to paralysis is found in Joyce's *Dubliners*. From the very first story, "The Sisters," the connection is firmly established. Father Flynn's death arouses in the young boy a deeply unsettling awareness of mystery and uncanniness. He is face to face with death which is really nothing. Death is not an object the boy can examine; there is no key that opens death to the understanding of the intellect. Alone in bed, the boy, unsettled by the vague innuendoes Cotter had uttered and by the strangeness of the priest's behavior and death, seeks refuge in the "infallibly complacent servants of his reminiscental needs." "In the dark of my room I imagined that I saw again the heavy grey face of the paralytic. I drew the blankets

over my head and tried to think of Christmas. But the grey face still
followed me" (D, 11). The boy's attempted escape into pleasant memory
does not quite succeed. He is not yet a seasoned creature of habit. His
elders are more successful because they have learned how to resort to
mnemonic dullness in order to ward off the dreadful circumstances of the
present. The deceased priest's two sisters, Nannie and Eliza, sit with a
glass of sherry in their parlor and engage the boy's aunt in vacuous conversation. The talk, naturally, centers around Father Flynn, but it
amounts to little more than the rehashing of the past couched in trite
phrases. All the familiar cliches associated with such occasions are employed. Although the atmosphere is melancholic and gloomy, even mor-
bid, it is marked by the absence of any real sense of loss. Some of the
recounted memories evoke a few tears, but there is no hint of anguish.
The story ends with a recollection of the incident that might have led to
Father Flynn's mental imbalance and of how his queerness became evident. While all this is a source of mystery to the uncomprehending young
boy, it is little more than gossip to the adults. Their sense of mystery,
unlike the boy's, has long been paralyzed and, therefore, they cannot
respond to death with the quickness of the living but with the imper-
viousness of the dead. It is as if nothing has changed for them. What they
talk about, and the way they talk about it, could just as easily have been
derived from a bad dream as from the memory of reality.

The stories in *Dubliners* contain numerous variations on this theme. In
"The Dead" one finds many examples of the action of memory which
Proust compared to leafing through a photograph album. Such invoca-
tions of the past are a source of amusement; they supply the materials for
nostalgic indulgence, and they have the effect of suffusing the reminiscing with a feeling of well-being. The gathering at the Misses Morkan
provides an ideal setting for voyages down memory lane. It is the
Christmas season and cold outside. Within the cosy confines of the Morkan house, a pervasive sense of festivity dominates the atmosphere. The
biting cold and the worries of ordinary existence are left behind at the
door with the galoshes. At certain moments during the party minor incidents threaten to disrupt the general bonheur, or to mar the enjoyment
of some individual. Gabriel, for instance, is upset first by the maid's response to his well-meant words and later by Miss Ivors. These incidents
are smoothed over so that the harmony and warmth of the evening are
preserved. At one point Freddy Malins strikes a jarring note with an ag-
gressive retort. There is a moment of silence, but before any ill-feeling
can take hold, Mary Jane initiates a discussion on opera. Almost instantly
attention is directed to the past. Mr. Browne recalls the great singers of
an era he believes is gone for good. "Why did they never play the good old

operas now, he asked, *Dinorah, Lucrezia Borgia*? Because they could not get voices to sing them: that was why" (*D*, 199). Bartell D'Arcy suggests there are equally good contemporary singers, such as Caruso. Mr. Browne is reluctant to accept that possibility; he is too enamored of his image of a golden age. It is an image fixed solidly in his mind and he will not allow the subsequent emergence of new singers to disrupt his well-established pantheon. The golden age came to an end sometime in the past; it existed once and for all and is now a closed book. Kate Morkan shares Mr. Browne's feeling. She remembers a tenor named Parkinson whom Mr. D'Arcy and Mr. Browne are not old enough to have heard sing. For Kate Morkan "there was only one tenor," and that was Parkinson. The dozens of tenors who appeared on the scene after him obviously mean little to Miss Morkan. So even if Caruso was, indeed, by all accounts the greatest tenor of all times, Miss Morkan would not even notice. She knows that there can never be any other tenor of Parkinson's stature. She clings to her past which, of course, gives her security. Change will not touch her. Great tenors will come and go while her image of Parkinson's unique greatness remains solid, permanent and inviolate.

Throughout the evening Gabriel Conroy returns to the past a number of times. He talks, in his speech, of a generation now supplanted by a young new breed which is forgetful of the old virtues. He bemoans the loss of a more spacious age and of all the great individuals who passed away with it, and he exhorts his hearers not to forget them. A little later, while waiting for a cab, Gabriel amuses his aunts, Mary Jane, and Mr. Browne with a humorous account of his grandfather's absurd outing with Johnny the horse. Later still, on his way to the hotel with Gretta and in the company of Mr. D'Arcy, Gabriel fans his desire for Gretta by culling from his memory various images which when put together form a picture of a younger Gretta and a younger passion. Gabriel's use of the past conveniently obscures the realities of the present. His wife "had no longer any grace of attitude." But in his present state of happiness he desires her. "Moments of their secret life together burst like stars upon his memory" (*D*, 213). This is "voluntary memory" which, as Beckett explains, "can be relied upon to reproduce for our gratified inspection those impressions of the past that were consciously and intelligibly formed." And "the images it chooses are as arbitrary as those of imagination, and are equally remote from reality." Gabriel relies on his memory precisely because it is removed from reality. He recollects selectively; he is interested only in restoring those fleeting moments of pleasure from former days. "He longed to recall to her those moments, to make her forget the years of their dull existence together and remember only their moments of ecstasy" (*D*, 213–214). By enmeshing himself in the images of memory, Gabriel strives to arrest time at some point in the past and he blinds himself to the real Gretta who is with him here and now. Gabriel, that is, tries to stave off change by casting a glance backwards rather than on his actual present and future.

"Voluntary memory," or recollection, is the grasp man has over what he knows. He is loath to relinquish this grasp simply because the unknown makes him apprehensive. Through the action of recollection man creates for himself an image of the world in which he is at home. Even when the image conjured up by "voluntary memory" is not an entirely pleasant one, it remains preferable to the uncertainty that would prevail in its absence. An excellent example of this is presented by Joyce in the story of "Eveline." The youthful Irishwoman is a prisoner of an unkind past and an unpromising present. Her chance to break loose comes in the form of Frank who wants her to join him and live with him in Buenos Aires. Eveline, fully aware that what is being offered her is a chance for freedom, and strongly attracted by the prospect of escaping her miserable circumstances, wavers at the last moment and finally misses her chance. Her fear of entering an unfamiliar world is stronger than her wish to escape her sufferings in a world to which she is accustomed. When actually presented with the possibility of an attractive but uncertain (because unknown) future, Eveline starts revising her negative assessment of her situation. "It was hard work—a hard life—but now that she was about to leave she did not find it a wholly undesirable life" (D, 38). Eveline is turned to stone by her meditation on the past and by the evocation of her mother's ghost.

In this short story, Joyce devotes five of six pages to his main character's recollections. The time has come for her to leave her family and her country, to truncate her connections with the past. She is about to escape with her lover, Frank. "He would give her life, perhaps love, too. But she wanted to live. . . . He would save her" (D, 40). Yet, in the end, the chains of her past hold her back; she does not break through the gate of a dead past into the future but instead holds on fiercely to the barrier. Eveline, unable to forget and rendered immobile by the mnemonic ghosts she evokes, joins the company of the dead. In the final moments, when "all the seas of the world tumbled about her heart" (D, 41), and when she is on the verge of stepping into that world to seize it and fashion her life out of it, in those final moments when she needs to act determinedly in order to declare her commitment to life, she opts to look back and allows her will to be sapped of all power by insubstantial ghosts: the strains of an Italian song, her dead mother, and God. "Down far in the avenue she could hear a street organ playing. She knew the air. Strange that it should come that very night to remind her of the promise to her mother, the promise to

keep the home together as long as she could. She remembered the last
night of her mother's illness; she was again in the close dark room . . ."
And, "she prayed to God to direct her, to show her what was her duty"
(*D*, 40–41). Eveline does not even bring herself positively to reject the
concrete, turbulent vital world that beckons her; she simply fails to embrace it or plunge into it. "He was shouted at to go on but he still called to
her. She set her white face to him, like a helpless animal. Her eyes gave
him no sign of love or farewell or recognition" (*D*, 41). Eveline's past and
her home are her universe and she dares not disturb that universe by
embarking on a journey into an unknown future in a unfamiliar Buenos
Aires. She clings to the security of what she "knows": a fabricated past
which is rendered more real than her present urges. Eveline, in the dor-
mancy of her will to freedom, becomes an empty husk (a gnomon), a
paralytic, a victim of anemia induced by an excess of memory.[30]

There are rare occasions, however, when the barricades of habit and
"voluntary memory" do not suffice and the mysterious, the unknown,
the uncanny break through one's defenses. Conrad's Lord Jim and Axel
Heyst, for example, experience the cataclysmic intrusions of what Beckett, following Proust, calls "involuntary memory." Stored in the depths of
one's "involuntary memory" are all those elements of reality which one
has sought to avoid or avert one's attention from. It is a repository of the
surprising, unmastered, unsettling encounters to which one's eyes are
barred and against which one's intellect is normally anaesthetized—
encounters and experiences which cannot be made to fit into one's carefully constructed, static image of the world and which, therefore,
threaten to disrupt the fabric of one's sight-screen.

> . . . in that "gouffre interdit à nos sondes," is stored the essence of our-
> selves, the best of our many selves and their concretions that simplists call
> the world, the best because accumulated slyly and painfully and patiently
> under the nose of our vulgarity, the fine essence of a smothered divinity
> whose whispered "disfazione" is drowned in the healthy bawling of an all-
> embracing appetite, the pearl that may gave the lie to our carapace of paste
> and pewter. May—when we escape into the spacious annexe of mental
> alienation, in sleep or the rare dispensation of waking madness.[31]

And this how Beckett describes "involuntary memory":

> Involuntary memory is explosive, "an immediate, total and delicious defla-
> gration." It restores, not merely the past object, but the Lazarus that it
> charmed or tortured, not merely Lazarus and the object, but more because
> less, more because it abstracts the useful, the opportune, the accidental,
> because in its flame it has consumed Habit and all its works, and in all its

brightness revealed what the mock reality of experience never can and never will reveal—the real. But involuntary memory is an unruly magician and will not be opportuned. It chooses its own time and place for the performance of its miracle.[32]

The radical difference between the results of "involuntary" and "voluntary" memory is that the former reveals or discloses while the latter conceals or veils. More accurately, "involuntary memory" discovers that which "voluntary memory" covers. Gabriel Conroy experiences this discovery at the Gresham Hotel, to which he returns following his aunts' party. He enters the hotel room looking forward to spending the night alone with his wife. Aflame with desire, Gabriel can look at Gretta only as the object towards which his lust is directed. Meanwhile, Gretta is disturbed by the memory of Michael Furey which was instigated by the song "The Lass of Aughrim" at the party. Her mind not at rest, she cannot direct her attention to Gabriel as he expects her to. Gabriel does not realize at this point that Gretta could be preoccupied with her own thoughts. All he can think about are his own desires and how he can satisfy them. Gretta's abstractedness, her remoteness does not fit into his designs and he is angry. The wave of anger is dissipated by a kiss. Gabriel feels he is once more in command of the situation. He even thinks he knows what Gretta is thinking. "I think I know what is the matter" (D, 218). If he knows, then he can master her; but he does not know. So his anger returns and this time he attempts to regain control by means of irony. This too fails, and Gabriel is defeated; his defenses collapse as his memories can no longer keep out the reality of Gretta's otherness, of his own great limitations. The past, no longer held in check by memory, unleashes in Gabriel's mind a number of unpleasant recognitions.

> Gabriel felt humiliated by the failure of his irony and by the evocation of this figure from the dead, a boy in the gasworks. While he had been full of memories of their secret life together, full of tenderness and joy and desire, she had been comparing him with another. A shameful consciousness of his own person assailed him. He saw himself as a ludicrous figure, acting as a pennyboy for his aunts, a nervous well-meaning sentimentalist orating to vulgarians and idealising his own clownish lusts, the pitiable fatuous fellow he had caught a glimpse of in the mirror. Instinctively he turned his back more to the light lest she might see the shame that burned upon his forehead (D, 219–220).

Gabriel knows that his surety is being challenged by something uncanny, something he cannot grasp—in fact, by nothing. "A vague terror seized Gabriel . . . as, at that hour when he had hoped to triumph, some impalpable and vindictive being was coming against him in its vague world." For a while he manages to stem the tide by employing the traditional weapon, "an effort of reason" (*D*, 220). This allows Gretta to finish recounting her story. But hers is not really a story; she does much more than simply narrate a sequence of events. In a strange way she seems to be experiencing the events of her youth as if for the first time. This is, perhaps, a genuine repetition as opposed to a tranquil recollection of the past. Unlike the women in "The Sisters," Gretta does not resort to a rehash of past events. Her memory is far from soothed by this sudden emergence of Michael Furey. Gretta's painful sobs and her isolation (for her grief is her own and Gabriel, although right beside her, cannot really share it) stand in sharp contrast to the tranquil melancholy of Father Flynn's sisters. Gretta suffers alone, and so does Gabriel. Once his wife falls asleep, Gabriel looks with new eyes at himself and the world that surrounds him. He looks at reality, not at his images of it. What he sees is a world grounded in temporality, a world which unlike the fixed pictures of memory is constantly changing and heading towards death. Only the dead are immune from change—and even they are not entirely fixed, either, for the living are constantly changing their views and interpretations of the past. Gabriel also realizes how very ordinary he is, "how poor a part he, her husband, had played in her life" (*D*, 222).

What Gabriel experiences in this scene is a loss of control. The paralyzed world of habit to which he is accustomed collapses as realities he has long been blind to arise like Lazarus from the dead. Gabriel suffers a defeat or a fall, but he also obtains, for a brief moment, a new vision. His deepest emotions come to the fore as his lust gives way to love. From the time he had left the party he had looked at Gretta as the object of his desires and he had been blind and indifferent to her feelings. Now, however, he exhibits a genuine sense of care for her. His egocentrism surrenders to generosity and sympathy. "Generous tears filled Gabriel's eyes. He had never felt like that himself towards any woman but he knew that such a feeling must be love" (*D*, 223). In other words, his own capacity for love, or lack of it, does not become a yardstick by which to judge others. He is willing to admit that others have loved and love more fully than he can. The dead have given Gabriel a glimpse of life, real life; they have escaped from the dead past to which they are assigned by "voluntary memory," or recollection, and have shaken the paralyzed Gabriel. They have made him discover anew, in an authentic way, what he thought he knew and understood but did not *really* know. One can also put it another way and state that Gabriel discovers the past and finds that it is far from dead or static. Furthermore, his discovery of the past changes his present and makes him turn his face, even though only for a moment, to the future.

III. On Fixing the Past, Mapping Labyrinths, and Erecting Structures

Why is it so important for critics like Maurice Beebe to fix the past? Is it not because they want to grasp it? Is theirs not an attempt to halt the incessantly shifting sands of history, to dam the flow of time? If a phase of literary history can be isolated and frozen, it will be possible to examine it with certitude. Patterns may be detected and mapped. What is being sought is a stable and coherent form, but such forms can be perceived only if the object stands still and if the observer attains the proper distance from it to see it as a whole. Arrest (i.e., stasis) and aesthetic distance are two essential characteristics attributed to Modernism, but those very critics who determine that the notions of arrest and aesthetic distance are central tenets of Modernism are themselves proceeding from the assumption that arrest and aesthetic distance are also necessary features of the critical act. This is a *circulus vitiosus*. The tradition is never questioned. Indeed, those very critics who assert that Modernism is dead are, in fact, attesting to its longevity. While these commentators and explicators show that Modernism has a beginning, a middle and an end, they are still participating in its plot and perpetuating its duration. In this manner, the Modernist tradition, once detected, is blindly adhered to, its grip reinforced. It is as if Modernism has become a habit from which those who re-member it cannot shake themselves loose. What the critic tries to illuminate becomes the source of his blindness. T. S. Eliot anticipated this pitfall and actually warned against it. "Yet if the only form of tradition, of handing down, consisted in following the ways of the immediate generation before us in a blind or timid adherence to its successes, 'tradition' would be discouraged. . . . Tradition is a matter of much wider significance. It cannot be inherited, and if you want it you must obtain it with great labour."[33]

Tradition can, as Beckett says of "voluntary memory," become "an instrument of reference instead of an instrument of discovery." This happens when one allows tradition to guide one's own response to it. Discovery is not possible so long as tradition retains mastery over us. Heidegger makes the point forcefully in *Being and Time*, where he argues that tradition, when received uncritically, not only blinds us to the sources of our own presuppositions but also "makes us suppose that the necessity of going back to these sources is something which we need not even understand."[34]

Joyce's texts have become among the most inaccessible texts of the past century. The massive amount of critical writing on Joyce has been more successful in obscuring his work, in covering it than in disclosing it and appropriating it for our time. This concealment has come about because several of the "categories and concepts handed down to us" as self-evident have been drawn from Joyce's texts, and since they have for so long been deemed self-evident, these categories and concepts have become virtually inaccessible. They supply a center around which a coherent image of Modernism and a consistent interpretation of Joyce's work can be constructed. In other words, concepts derived from Joyce's texts have become the ground on which Joyce's work is seen to be founded. To question these concepts, therefore, is to place the whole structure at risk, to threaten it with collapse. In addition, since Joyce's works have been placed at the very center of Modernism, they are "monuments" crucial to the "ideal order." If an interpretation of the Joycean texts were to show them to be different from what they have been generally taken to be— if, in other words, Joyce's texts come to be seen in a new way—then the very structure called Modernism would lose its center. Any radically new departure, any authentic new "beginning" in Joycean criticism is ipso facto a threat to the established ideal order and is, consequently, a matter of great concern to the creators and curators of that order and its monuments. They have an interest in seeing that Joyce remain a dead monument in the pantheon of the past. Joyce *redivivus* would wreak havoc; he would plunge us all back into the labyrinth.

The labyrinth is what the Joyce establishment wants to avoid at all costs. A way out of the labyrinth is what many critics believe they have found in Joyce, or to be more exact in Joyce's *A Portrait of the Artist as a Young Man*. Stephen's aesthetic theory offers a justification for upholding the autonomy of the work of art, the requirement of aesthetic distance, and the demand for stasis. The notion of aesthetic distance is of supreme importance to the New Critical concept of irony—the concept on which the traditional version of Modernism is based. From the fictional Stephen Dedalus, then, is derived the critical discourse which the critics themselves employ in their explications of that same fiction. And, needless to say, Stephen's pronouncements on aesthetics are placed at the center of the texts in which they are found. The "disinterested" critics are serving an obvious self-interest when they appropriate Stephen Dedalus's aesthetic theory and invest it with an authority which is not furnished by the text itself. That Joyce's *kunstlerroman* was not immediately recognized as a serious critique of the aesthetic theories flourishing at the turn of the century can be due only to the desire of the earliest as well as many of the subsequent readers to find in a *A Portrait* a text which could not only be coerced into a general pattern of Modernist sensibility but could also be construed to support those ideas and preconceptions which they brought to bear upon it. When an influential critic, such as W. K. Wimsatt, finds in Stephen's and in Joyce's (for he identifies the novelist with his artistic creation) exposition of the aesthetics of stasis an improvement upon the Thomistic doctrine of *apprehensio* and the Kantian notion of "disinterest,"[35] the identity of orthodox Modernist aesthetics and Stephen Dedalus's becomes complete. It becomes virtually impossible for the proponent of the former to perform a critical destruction of the latter. For as often as they read *A Portrait*, critics of the same persuasion as Wimsatt will find a confirmation of the aesthetic theory upon which their critical approach is based. Their critical forays can lead only to a reaffirmation of their theoretical views.

A major stumbling block which has prevented *A Portrait* from being seen as something other than a confirmation of New Critical doctrine has been the association of Stephen Dedalus and James Joyce. There have been, of course, some excellent critics who have directed their attention to this issue, but they, too, have more often than not read *A Portrait* from the traditional teleological vantage point and judged the work successful because of its harmonious form. Even Hugh Kenner, whose marvelous essay "The *Portrait* in Perspective" proved extremely influential in dissociating Joyce from Stephen, regards *A Portrait* as "conceived in an extratemporal mode." While critical of Stephen, Kenner still shares many of the young man's opinions on aesthetics. Kenner is aware that for Joyce "a work of art always has ontological . . . content," but the only ontology he discovers in *A Portrait* is the "treatment of particular manifestations as the signatures of metaphysical reality."[36] This is another way of describing the epiphanic mode, and it betrays a strong streak, ever present in thought labeled "Modernist," of neo-Platonic doctrine which, as E. H. Gombrich explains, "turns on the advice that the true artist should not copy nature—he must ennoble, 'idealise' it by representing not crude reality but the Platonic idea behind it."[37] It is no accident that Kenner compares *A Portrait*, which he calls "a Poem," to a "Chinese ideogram" in which "the whole has a total intelligibility based on the interaction of these parts juxtaposed by association." It follows, quite consistently, that Joyce's task as an artist is "the raising of particulars to intelligibility."[38] Lurking behind Kenner's statements are echoes of Stephen's ideas on stasis, *integritas, consonantia* and *quidditas*. Seen in this light, the separation of Joyce from Stephen, though important, remains rather tame, for it fails to discover the seriousness with which the foundations of Stephen's aesthetics, and by extension traditional Modernist thought generally, are shaken by *A Portrait*.

Many years after the appearance of Kenner's influential essay, numerous Joyce critics are still echoing Stephen's discourse in their own approaches to Joyce's texts. Numerous others are still engaged in demonstrating for the umpteenth time how tightly woven the symbolic structure of *A Portrait* really is. And, in the view of a majority of Joyce critics, what is found in *A Portrait* is further developed and refined in *Ulysses* and *Finnegans Wake*, [39] making Joyce's *bildungsroman* a most convenient starting point for an examination of Joyce's entire opus since it contains the seeds of what in later works attains greatness and perfection. [40] *A Portrait* becomes, then, like the beginning of an Aristotelian drama heading inevitably and necessarily towards its *telos*. One example of a detailed examination of the symbolic structure in *A Portrait* is Bernard Benstock's "A Light from Some Other World: Symbolic Structure in *A Portrait of the Artist*." Benstock, adhering to the view that *A Portrait* is a Modernist work, asserts at the outset that when Joyce cast *Stephen Hero* aside and embarked on the project which is now *A Portrait*, "The nineteenth century was scrapped and the twentieth century ushered in." What marks this break with tradition and the ushering in of a new era is, in Benstock's view, Joyce's decision "to replace the narrative and descriptive functions of the auctorial voice" with "a complicated set of 'symbols and portents' as the structural device of his novel." [41] This is another way of showing how *A Portrait* resembles a Chinese ideogram.

Benstock never gives the narrative quality of the novel a chance to reveal itself. He looks at the book only from the end; his is a teleological viewpoint with a vengeance. Joyce's novel, for Benstock, does not really unfold. He looks at it at once, as a whole, stretched out before him. (Like a modern Tamburlaine surveying a map of his conquests, perhaps?) As he traces a particular level of symbolism or a set of juxtapositions he moves with ease from one passage to another, or from one word to its echo in another part of the text. By the time Benstock's explication is over, one does not think of *A Portrait* as a novel but as a very complex diagram or structure or geometric design. Thus, for example, when he traces the recurrence of dark eyes in the text, Benstock carries his readers in one brief paragraph from page 22 to page 35, to 39, to 194, to 245, to 197, to 229, to 108, back to 12 and forward again to page 48 and page 108 of the Viking Press edition. Perhaps the rapidity of his movement aims at capturing the impression of simultaneity—to grasp the structure as a whole and at once. The criss-crossing goes on at a furious pace for about twenty-five pages. By that point the reader is bound to be dizzy. However, the reader who remains lucid till the end will doubt his clear vision, for Benstock turns out to be an unreliable cartographer—or, maybe, at this juncture he has gotten himself dizzy. He devotes the two final paragraphs to what he considers the "most tantalizing symbolic cluster in *A Portrait of the Artist*." This cluster consists of the "assemblage of cows and bulls," and here, of course, we have a bridge connecting us to Stephen in *Ulysses*—"the bullockbefriending bard."[42]

Benstock starts to trace this pattern by referring to *Diseases of the Ox*, the book Cranley pretends to be reading at the library. This is how Benstock proceeds:

> . . . It is Cranley who admits having eaten "cowdung" (205,206); and to Cranly the aesthetician argues about the kinesis of "hacking in fury at a block of wood" to make "an image of a cow" (214). Is it accidental that when Stephen and Cranly are walking outward from Dublin Cranly seized his arm and "steered" him back? (247). Lynch figures in a minor version: to Stephen's definitions of *integritas* and *consonantia* he exclaims, "Bull's eye!" and "Bull's eye again!" (212) and leads Stephen in pursuit of the "heifer" (248). Perhaps it is as "disciples" that Cranly and Lynch are present in the pattern, since the Christ myth informs an important part of the cattle associations.[43]

The only problem with this neatly outlined pattern is that it fictionalizes fiction; Benstock imagines the patterns he needs to make his point. Cranly never admits to having eaten cowdung, and Lynch is the only audience Stephen has when he talks of hacking at a block of wood. Lynch does not figure in a minor version at all; he is the only person to whom Stephen divulges his aesthetic theory and he proves himself less gullible than the throngs of critics who deduce paradigms out of Stephen's elaborate speculations. There would be nothing wrong with Benstock's coercive tactics if he were prepared to admit that the structures are not Joyce's constructs but the reader's—the reader who does not discuss the process of discovery that comes with reading the novel, but simply the pleasure of mastery over what has been read.

The criticism leveled by Paul Bovè against Jonathan Culler can be justly applied to Bernard Benstock, Maurice Beebe, and a host of others. These critics have remained unaware "of the dangerous equivalence which exists between Western technological imperialism and a Kantian habit of mind which approaches the world and texts with preconceptions, with expectations, with questions which it will force nature or the text to answer."[44] Bovè reinforces his point by quoting a brief passage from Kant's "Preface" to the second edition of *The Critique of Pure Reason*.

> Reason, holding in one hand its principles, according to which alone con-
> cordant appearances can be admitted as equivalent to laws, and in the other
> hand the experiment which it has devised in conformity with these princi-
> ples, must approach nature in order to be taught by it. It must not, how-
> ever, do so in the character of a pupil who listens to everything that the
> teacher chooses to say, but of an appointed judge who *compels* the witness to
> answer questions which he himself formulated.[45]

Whenever this attitude prevails in literary criticism one finds the critic
violently extracting from the text whatever he has predetermined to
"find" in it.

The originality of *A Portrait of the Artist as a Young Man* and the force with
which Joyce broke loose of novelistic and aesthetic traditions he inherited
cannot strike the reader who is not prepared to place his long-held notions and interpretative position in a situation of risk. One has to venture
out of the security offered by ossified convictions and examine those preconceptions derived from the same tradition the study of which they
guide. As Derrida puts it, this "is a question of putting expressly and
systematically the problem of the status of discourse which borrows
from a heritage the resources necessary for the deconstruction of that
heritage itself."[46] The Joyce-industry has only on the rarest occasions
shown any inclination to address itself to this problem. Although new
findings in Joycean scholarship and criticism are seldom not greeted en-
thusiastically, radical departures are regarded with suspicion. It cannot
be accidental that while the volume of print lavished on Joycean topics is
virtually incalculable, the impact which Joyce scholarship has had on the
wider concerns of literary and critical theory in general has been unimpressive. Even innovative approaches in Joyce criticism frequently go no
further than the application of ideas borrowed from other than the usual
sources; rarely are these "new" sources or ideas questioned before or
during the course of their application. The sense of crisis which has per-
vaded criticism for the past decade has not made a tremendous impact on
the incessantly growing body of Joyce studies. There can be little question but that Joyce is dead and is being kept dead even while his corpus is
still supplying enough fodder for countless academics.

Some promising departures from the mainstream of Joyce criticism
have, of course, been made. A healthy breath of fresh air arrived in 1968
with the appearance of *L'Exil de James Joyce, ou l'art du remplacement*, by Hélène
Cixous.[47] The book was translated into English as *The Exile of James Joyce*.[48]
Both versions received very poor reviews in the quasi-official organ of
the Joyce industry, the *James Joyce Quarterly*, a fact that hardly need sur-

prise anyone. One cannot escape noticing the prejudices shared by the two reviewers. Francois Van Laere, in his pathetically misogynist review (so abominably translated that one wonders why no competent Joycean could be found to render a few pages of French into decent English— unless Van Laere himself wrote in abominable French), misses the "minimum of academic ceremonial which is normally provided in an index."[49] Charles Rossman starts his review by pointing out a spelling error in the English version: Richard Ellmann is listed as "Ellman, R." This error he regards "as emblematic of the book as a whole."[50] The literary cartographer is at a loss when the familiar points of reference are not available or are unclear. Rossman is displeased by the diffuseness of the book, and he bemoans the fact that Cixous never comes to a definite conclusion about *the meaning* of, say, *Ulysses.* It seems that Rossman hankers after the old dispensation. Van Laere certainly does. He cannot accept the validity of Cixous's approach because she is not objective, "rather she voluptuously interrogates herself about what she thinks of him [i.e., James Joyce.] And why?"[51] Why not? Van Laere's nostalgia for the conventional and the entrenched is unmistakable. Unhappy with Cixous's discussion of Joyce's gastronomic references, Van Laere compares her treatment unfavorably to Benstock's. "Thanks to the reading established by Bernard Benstock (cf. *James Joyce Quarterly*, Spring, 1965), we see the gastronomical allusions fall neatly into a *system* in *Finnegans Wake*, that Joycean work in which the culinary references are doubtless revealed as the most numerous and the most crucial. Crucial not because of their possible biographical origin, with which we moreover have nothing to do, but because of their special, structural, functional value as a partial encyclopedic system, grouped with other systems in the heart of a vast system of systems, it too encyclopedic, which constitutes the work in its totality."[52] Van Laere's rage for order is not soothed by Cixous; hence, his displeasure. Van Laere's statement reads like a parody of much Joyce criticism— a criticism concerned, almost obsessively, with pinning Joyce down, with mapping his labyrinths.

Much less disturbing to the Joyce establishment has been Robert Scholes's effort to bring his interest in structuralism to bear upon his writing on Joyce. In his opinion, "the most important thing we have learned in the past fifty years is a way of thinking called 'structuralism,' which . . . has profoundly altered our ontology and our epistemology." Scholes attributes the inability of many critics to understand Joyce fully to their unwillingness to give up their traditional approaches in favor of more recent ideas. Indeed, according to Scholes, "the reluctance of many critics to accept the later Joyce (and by this I mean the last chapters of

Ulysses as well as *Finnegans Wake*) is an aspect of this larger reluctance to accept the structuralist revolution."[53] Scholes's work, however, while definitely interesting, remains unexciting for he devotes his energies largely to describing and applying structuralist theory rather than to its critical analysis and development. Structuralism, then, provides Scholes with a stable set of ideas and procedures around which and by means of which he is able to construct new readings of Joyce's texts. Furthermore, the results obtained by Scholes's innovative approach do not differ markedly from the conclusions generally proffered by the more traditional formalist explicators.

Another critic who, through "a structuralist analysis," proposes a break away from the conservative line of Joycean scholarship is Margot Norris. She makes use of a whole array of nontraditional approaches in order to revive the radical thinking of the earliest *Finnegans Wake* critics. What the writers of *Our Exagmination round His Factification for Incamination of Work in Progress* lacked, according to Norris, "were scholarly pegs on which to hand their theories."[54] Norris finds the appropriate "pegs" in the writings of Freud, Lacan, Heidegger, Barthes, Levi-Strauss, and others. She also makes use of some ideas derived from Jacques Derrida's "Structure, Sign and Play in the Discourse of the Human Sciences," but, rather oddly, never mentions his essay "La Pharmacie de Platon," in spite of Derrida's tantalizing note: "L'ensemble de cet essai n'étant lui-même rien d'autre, comme on l'aura vite compris, qu'une lecture de *Finnegans Wake*."[55] Margot Norris's application of recent critical theory to the study of *Finnegans Wake* remains ultimately unsatisfactory because it is superficial and in some instances simplistic. Moreoever, her use of ideas derived from critical theory as merely a set of "pegs" is reductive and achieves little more than replacing one omnivorous old critical machine with a newer and more fashionable (but no less ravenous) one. It is as if Joyce's texts were an inert but chaotic mass waiting to be controlled and ordered first by one set of critical devices and subsequently by another—in either case proving the viability of the mechanical operation tested on it.

As far back as 1962, Robert M. Adams made some very keen comments on the Joycean critics' incessant search for all-embracing structures and patterns.

> Now of course nobody can tell with complete assurance that these [Joycean] researches will not one day yield the complete coherent pattern of symbolic relationships which their creators tacitly or explicitly envisage. (A few of the more visionary have announced it as a fact—every element in Joyce's entire canon is a part of a single controlled composition: but most seem to hold it out as a hope or an ideal for criticism to work toward.) But by

this time, I think we are in a position to say that the pattern very probably won't work out. . . . . At the moment we are under no immediate big-pervasive-pattern presumption—but it seems like a terribly apt time to start looking for alternatives.[56]

A few genuine "alternatives" have been offered recently, but the bulk of Joycean scholarship and criticism is still trying to persuade itself that there is a magnificent structure to be found at the center of Joyce's corpus or that there exists somewhere in the welter of critical theory a magic key which can unlock the mystery of Joyce's texts and reveal their meaning.[57]

Toward Beginning Yet Again

Anyone attempting an authentically new approach to Joyce must possess negative capability in order to be able to steer clear of the irritable (or should one say hysterical?) reaching "after fact or reason," such as is exhibited in the tireless quest for systems within systems. Ideally, the task of liberating the reader of Joyce's work from the boundaries within which traditional literary interpretation and, more specifically, New Criticism have confined him should involve a detailed critical study of the history of Western metaphysics and aesthetics (the latter has rarely not been a branch of the former), a careful examination of the novelistic tradition, and a close consideration of the massive body of criticism which now surrounds and obscures the texts. Such a mammoth task would be a breakthrough for the readers of Joyce, for all those interested in the study of the novel, and, most important, for anyone engaged in an exploration of Modernism—it would, indeed, be a necessary and desirable move in the direction of rewriting literary history. The first obligatory step, however, for anyone embarking on such an ambitious new beginning must be to take action against those institutions of knowledge which have for so long exercised such a powerful and self-perpetuating hold over scholarship. "Among these institutions," as Edward Said has pointed out, "is specialization, an ideological professionalism, and a hierarchical system of values that places the reinforcement of traditional explanations at the top (by granting rewards and prestige) and keeps beginning speculations that deal heedlessly with the artificial barriers between 'original' and 'critical' works at the very bottom."[58]

3

The Demystification of Irony

In 1917 an Italian critic, Diego Angeli, published a review-essay on *A Portrait of the Artist as a Young Man* in *Il Marzocco,* a highly regarded and influential literary journal published in Florence. He entitled the review-essay, "Un romanzo di Gesuiti"—loosely, "A Jesuit Novel." James Joyce liked the review so much that he translated it into English and arranged for it to be published in the *Egoist.*[1] In his essay, Diego Angeli goes beyond praising Joyce and his novel, calling him "truly a master" and "a new writer in the glorious company of English Literature"; he censures the many Anglo-American critics who reacted unfavorably to *A Portrait* and who did not recognize in Joyce's work "the first streaks of the dawn of a new art visible on the horizon." According to Diego Angeli, the English writers were living in "splendid isolation" from the exciting literary movements and innovations sweeping the European scene and they were, therefore, unable to appreciate Joyce's importance and the value of his contribution to the development of the novel. Furthermore, Joyce's indebtedness to the Catholic tradition set him apart from his Protestant critics.

> When one has read the book to the end one understands why most English and American critics have raised an outcry against both form and content, understanding, for the most part, neither one nor the other. Accustomed as they are to the usual novels, enclosed in a set framework, they found themselves in this case out of their depth and hence their talk of immorality, impiety, naturalism and exaggeration. They have not grasped the subtlety of the psychological analysis nor the synthetic value of certain details and certain arrests of movement. Possibly their own Protestant upbringing renders the moral development of the central character incomprehensible to them.

Diego Angeli's attack on the conservatism and narrow traditionalism which blinded numerous critics to the merits of *A Portrait of the Artist as a Young Man* is, to a very large extent, justifiable. At the same time, though, he is too sweeping in his denigratory characterization of the Anglo-American literary scene. For although many English and American litterateurs were still blissfully ignorant and arrogantly contemptuous of what was going on in continental Europe, there were, nonetheless, several others who were avidly keeping abreast of new ideas in European philosophy, literature and criticism and were starting to disseminate those ideas and to incorporate them into their own work. The writers who contributed to the *Egoist*, for instance, were leading their readers away from conventional expectations. It was in the *Egoist* that *A Portrait of the Artist* first appeared in serialized form. The reaction against positivism which was rampant in France was gaining ground in England and manifested itself in the influence exercised by the Imagist and Symbolist movements. Henri Bergson's works were receiving significant attention, too. His famous *Essai sur les donées immédiates de la conscience,* first published in 1889, appeared in England in 1910 when F. L. Pogson translated it as *Time and Free Will.* By that time a few learned journals had already published some articles dealing either directly or tangentially with Bergson's ideas. T. E. Hulme's essay "The New Philosophy" appeared in 1909, in the July 1 and 29 issues of *New Age.* In 1913, Hulme published his translation of Bergson's *Introduction to Metaphysics.* Hulme also imported the ideas of Wilhelm Worringer on abstraction in art, while Ezra Pound seemed to be in touch with everyone and everything that was going on in Europe.

What Diego Angeli could not have known at the time he wrote his essay on *A Portrait of the Artist* is that in his scattered, somewhat fragmentary and generally unsystematic writings T. E. Hulme had already articulated, although in a sketchy form, those ideas and major concerns that were to become the foundations of a rather heterogeneous critical movement—the New Criticism—which eventually achieved dominance over the literary scene for half a century and supplied a "set framework" for the appreciation, interpretation and critical appropriation of many twentieth-century literary works, including *A Portrait.* Nor could Diego Angeli have foreseen how the New Critics while acclaiming *A Portrait* also deprived it of its disturbing qualities and prevented many of its readers from discerning within it a severe critique of the basic tenets of the New Critical version of Modernism—most notably a critique of aesthetic irony. However, before illustrating how *A Portrait of the Artist* constitutes a challenge to the foundations of New Critical theory and practice, it is necessary to dwell at some length on the central importance of the concept of irony. The discussion on irony will also shed some light on the entanglement of religion and aesthetics which ensues from the New Critical insistence on the transcendence of art and the supremacy of irony. It will then be possible to return to James Joyce and show how, through his portrayal of Stephen Dedalus, he lays bare the insufficiencies of aesthetic irony as a response to the loss of order and demystifies the privileged stance normally assumed by the ironist. In the end one should be able to see that *A Portrait of the Artist as a Young Man,* far from being an affirmation of the other-worldliness of art, is, in fact, a celebration of man-in-the-world.

I. Irony, the New Criticism and Modernism

During the first half of our century the leading practitioners of Anglo-American literary criticism, the so-called New Critics, expended considerable energy in defining the boundaries of their discipline. They sought, first of all, to establish the dogma that the literary work of art is an autonomous object which bears no necessary relation to and indeed transcends the contradictory world of history and material concerns. This dogma, in turn, allowed the New Critics to separate the work of the literary critic from that of the historian, the sociologist, the anthropologist, etc., and to institute (even institutionalize) literary criticism as a distinct academic discipline with a territory which was properly and exclusively their own. So keen were these critics on establishing exclusive rights for the study of literature that they often tried to divorce their discipline even from those modes of inquiry which for long had been intimately associated with literary textual analysis, namely theology and philosophy. This separation made it possible for the literary critic to assert a privileged relationship to the literary text which was itself believed to be a privileged form of discourse. The study of literature qua literature fell under the domain of literary criticism which alone could bring to its task of explication and evaluation the tools appropriate to it. In the prefatory remarks to a collection of his essays, Allen Tate makes this point very directly: "Lessing says that poetry is not painting or sculpture; I am saying in this book, with very little systematic argument that it is neither religion nor social engineering."[2]

Yet, while Tate, Cleanth Brooks, I. A. Richards, Robert Penn Warren and others argued in their theoretical formulations for the autonomy of literature and literary criticism from religion, their writing is replete with religious vocabulary and is based on assumptions derived from what Heidegger calls the ontotheological tradition—that is to say, the Western metaphysical tradition which privileges the transcendent at the expense of the historical, essence over existence, the atemporal other-worldliness of Being over the temporality of being-in-the-world.

In order to open the way for an understanding of the confusion that arises in New Critical discourse from the declarations of autonomy on the one hand and the dependence on the vocabulary and presuppositions of traditional philosophy and theology on the other, one must start with a consideration of irony, for it is around the concept of irony that all New Critical theory and practice revolve. Irony is both the fundamental category of New Critical thought and the locus at which aesthetic and religious discourse intersect, become knotted and confused. Indeed, one may argue that, in a sense, the New Critical concept of irony depends to a very large extent on the confusion between aesthetics and religion, a confusion which stems from the unquestioned, hence uncritical, acceptance of the transcendent ideal of Western metaphysics.

The New Critical alliance with traditional metaphysics and religious thought was self-conscious, even if uncritical. Thus, for example, when Cleanth Brooks sets out to reconcile the theoretical positions of I. A. Richards and William M. Urban—two proponents of the New Criticism who appeared to hold divergent views—he does so by arguing that they shared a similar "conception of metaphysics."[3] And W. K. Wimsatt, in his essay "Horses of Wrath: Recent Critical Lessons," gives explicit articulation to the New Critical connections with religion and metaphysics, especially in his conclusion, in which he asserts:

> the religious doctrines have a backing of depth and substantial mystery— whereas the naturalistic are in the end phenomenological, sensate, and flat. So the religious mind would seem, in the end, to be more hospitable to the tensional and metaphysical view of poetry than the naturalistic mind is able to be. And this is borne out in recent history. The metaphysical criticism which was "new" in the 1940s (working by the norms of wit, irony, metaphor, drama, tension) has had some of its strongest champions among poets and critics of the Anglican school and has enjoyed for the most part at least a friendly reception in Roman Catholic schools and journals.[4]

The norms of the New Criticism mentioned by Wimsatt in this passage—wit, irony, metaphor, drama, tension, and, one should add, paradox and ambiguity—could all be subsumed under the general heading of irony, in the sense of the word as it is used by New Critics generally. Irony is much more than a norm; it constitutes the very core of New Critical thought and, as Paul Bovè has shown, it occupies "a position so dominant in modern literary study that to question it is to question the best practical criticism and much of the best critical theorizing of the century."[5] One could go even further and suggest that to question irony (as it is understood and employed by the New Critics) is to question the long alliance between literary criticism and metaphysics and to cast doubt on some of the fundamental aspects of the metaphysical tradition itself. For to question irony is to challenge the validity and desirability of a stance which abandons the temporal world of difference in favor of a transcendent world of identity; it is to take issue with the denigration of the "phenomenological, sensate, and flat" order of nature; it is to undermine the image of the artist or critic standing outside history and above contradiction (i.e., above "all complexities of mire and blood") in a state of eudemonic contemplation—a posture normally associated with the gods looking down disdainfully on the world from their privileged perches atop Mount Olympus. In other words, to question the New Critics' ironic stance is to threaten the authority of their purportedly disinterested language and to subvert the basis of their claims to objectivity.

For a long time, the normative importance of irony and the whole critical system built around it were rarely questioned and therefore the New Criticism remained virtually unchallenged in the American academy until well into the 1960s. Gradually, however, it started to lose some of its preeminence under the pressure of new movements which emerged for the most part in continental Europe and especially in France and Germany. The boundaries so carefully erected by I. A. Richards, John Crowe Ransom, Allen Tate, W. K. Wimsatt, Cleanth Brooks, and others have been transgressed by foreign critical theories, methods and approaches that cannot be ignored or dismissed. The adherents of the New Criticism have been forced to confront a variety of critical schools of thought which, while they differ significantly one from the other, pose a direct challenge to at least two central long-standing dogmas of Anglo-American criticism: the radical separation of literary criticism from other spheres of inquiry and the privileged status of literary and critical discourse. Paul de Man describes the situation succinctly. "The trend in Continental criticism, whether it derives its language from sociology, psychoanalysis, ethnology, linguistics, or even from certain forms of philosophy, can be quickly summarized: it represents a methodologically motivated attack on the notion that a literary or poetic consciousness is in any way a privileged consciousness, whose use of language can pretend to escape, to some degree, from the duplicity, the confusion, the untruth that we take for granted in the everyday use of language."[6]

Almost two decades have passed since Paul de Man announced the crisis in criticism, and now the various trends in continental criticism of which he spoke command the attention of many literary critics and theoreticians. It would be a serious mistake, though, to consign the New Criticism, now grown old, to the ash heap of spent movements. For one thing, many problems raised by the New Critics are far from resolved. Furthermore, it cannot be said with any certainty that some of the basic assumptions of the New Criticism do not still inform certain theories or schools of criticism which label themselves postmodern.

There are other compelling reasons for returning once again to a consideration of the central tenets of the New Criticism, in particular the concept of irony. First of all, as Paul Bovè observes, "because irony has become habitual . . . among practical and evaluative critics both as a kind of structure necessary to all poems and as a criterion for judging 'good' poetry, it is crucial to reduce irony, to lay bare its unexamined assumptions, and to make clear to those who employ it and defend it as necessary to literary discourse exactly what is at stake in the 'game' they have chosen to play."[7] Secondly, although the New Criticism with its primary focus on irony does not enjoy the authority it once did, the version of Modernism which it bequeathed us still has wide currency. Texts such as E. M. Forster's *A Passage to India*, Virginia Woolf's *To the Lighthouse*, and above all Joyce's *A Portrait* and *Ulysses* are still widely considered as exemplary products of the ironic imagination advocated by the New Critics. Unless the New Critical concept of irony is seriously questioned, the whole canon of Modernism will remain, even in a postmodern age, ossified in a monumental tradition handed over as self-evident and received uncritically. As long as the New Critical concept of irony remains the normative category in the interpretation of Modernist texts, those same texts will serve only to confirm the version of Modernism formulated by the New Critics. And the texts which make up the Modernist canon will remain caught up in a vicious circle of interpretation.

In order to break the vicious circle of interpretation and make Modernist classics such as *A Portrait* available to a postmodern audience—in other words to read the Modernist canonical texts anew and in a manner which does more than merely illustrate, confirm and legitimate the prevailing account of Modernism—one must first de-authorize the privileged status of New Critical theory. This is best done through a hermeneutic approach which calls for both a destruction (in the Heideggerian sense) of all privileged discourse and an interpretation of texts that opens up what has been forgotten or concealed by habit.

In his essay on "The Language of Faith" Paul Ricoeur writes eloquently about these two inseparable aspects of hermeneutics:

> . . . there is a profound unity between *destroying* and *interpreting*. I think that any modern hermeneutics is a hermeneutics with a double edge and a double function. It is an effort to struggle against idols, and, consequently, it is destructive. It is a critique of ideologies in the sense of Marx; it is a critique of all flights and evasions into other worlds in the sense of Nietzsche; a struggle against childhood fables and against securing illusions in the sense of psychoanalysis. In this sense, any hermeneutics must be disalienating, aimed at disalienation, at demystification. . . .
>
> But we understand better that this task pertains also to the act of listening, which is finally the positive aspect of hermeneutics. What we wish to

hear through this destruction a more original and primal word [I would rather say a "forgotten" and "concealed" word], that is, to let speak a language which though addressed to us we no longer hear. . . . It is this access to interpretation which is the driving force of hermeneutics.[8]

The demystification of irony was carried out hermeneutically a long time ago by Soren Kierkegaard who revealed not only the alienating power of irony but also the spuriousness of the alliance between aesthetic irony and Christian belief. It is no accident, of course, that Kierkegaard's views never received much attention from among the New Critics even though he wrote extensively on issues which concerned them deeply. Kierkegaard's distinctions between ironic and religious discourse help immensely to clarify the confusion inherent in New Critical thought, and his destruction of irony opens the way for an interpretation of a text such as *A Portrait of the Artist* that demystifies those very same New Critical categories, norms, and procedures which have been used to master and appropriate it.

Before turning to Kierkegaard's destruction of irony it is important to consider, albeit briefly, the historical conditions out of which emerged the fundamental ideas embraced by the New Criticism. It is not possible, of course, to trace in detail the countless factors involved in the rise of the New Criticism; but it remains essential to observe that it, too, has a genealogy, that it does not have its origin in a prelapsarian metaphysical realm of absolute truth. As Foucault, following Nietzsche, has shown, the authority of a field of knowledge is demystified by the genealogist who "refuses to extend his faith in metaphysics . . . listens to history . . . [and] finds that there is 'something altogether different' behind things: not a timeless and essential secret, but the secret that they have no essence or that their essence was fabricated in a piecemeal fashion from alien forms. Examining the history of reason he learns that it was born in an altogether 'reasonable' fashion—from chance; devotion to truth and the precision of scientific methods arose from the passion of scholars, their reciprocal hatred, their fanatical and unending discussions, and their spirit of competition—the personal conflicts that slowly forged the weapons of reason."[9]

The dogma of ironic disinterestedness arose out of the New Critics' great interest in countering what they perceived as a major threat to their authoritative guardianship of "higher" values. The threat came from the rise of positivism and naturalism, generally regarded as symptomatic of the modern "glorification of the scientific vision at the expense of the aesthetic."[10] The New Critics believed, not without justification, that if the methods and procedures of science were to become normative for all forms of inquiry, including literary criticism, their own claims to a special kind of knowledge could be swept aside. Hence, they argued repeatedly that their concern with qualitative knowledge was a necessary counter to the reductionist scientific concern with quantitative knowledge. In other words, they presented themselves as the preservers of those spiritual (i.e., non-material) values which the modern age was in imminent danger of losing. They saw in the "loss of tradition," in the "loss of a fixed convention," and in the "loss of belief" the incontrovertible signs of the "loss of spiritual order and of integrity in the modern consciousness."[11]

It is customary to start the story of the disintegration of the unity of Western thought with a reference to Nietzsche's announcement of the death of God. It is also customary to add that the death of God implies the death of Man. There is no need on this occasion to traverse familiar ground and enumerate the circumstances and the various implications of these obituary notices. All that needs to be stated for the moment is that with his announcement Nietzsche pointed out the disappearance of the center which held the Western cosmos together.

Nietzsche's pronouncements were not, of course, the first occasion on which the centeredness of the universe appeared to be precarious. Earlier in the nineteenth century various intellectual forces converged which rendered the traditional understanding of God very suspect. The most successful response to that crisis was put forth by the religious humanists who replaced the orthodox conception of God with an idealized version of Man. Yet, even this new theory of Man as God, best formulated perhaps by Feuerbach in The *Essence of Christianity*, remained fundamentally faithful to the metaphysical tradition; it still satisfied the desire for a stable center. The religious humanism of the nineteenth century demonstrated, in fact, the tenacity with which Western man holds to the idea of the centeredness of the universe. Every time the center is threatened by obsolescence it is replaced by a different and in some cases more complex and refined version. Over and over again, a new vantage point is devised from which to obtain a coherent vision of an orderly cosmos.

With the advent of Nietzsche, however, what has been threatened is not just the center but the very concept of centeredness itself, that is the authoritativeness of any metaphysical vantage point, *any* fixed point of reference from which a description of an ordered universe may be obtained. For this reason, the problems besetting the twentieth century are unique, even though, all too often, these problems have been handled by means which are very much in keeping with the mainstream of the Western ontotheological tradition. And this is where one locates a peculiar aspect of the New Criticism: it emerges at a time when the Western metaphysical tradition which culminated in Hegel's work has reached a dead end; it is confronted with the dreadful reality of the death of God which means the death of metaphysics, and yet it remains uncritically wedded to that same metaphysical tradition. At a time when the centrality of *logos* and the governing power of *telos* have been severely undermined, the New Criticism gives priority to a literary theory which is logocentric and metaphysical. Furthermore, it does this by relying heavily on concepts derived from a theology the validity of which is no longer self-evident.

The religious vocabulary of the New Criticism can be found in its earliest texts, that is in the writings of T. E. Hulme. The New Criticism may not have actually started with Hulme, but he has been recognized by many New Critics as their progenitor. Upon reading *Speculations*, T. S. Eliot declared Hulme "the forerunner of a new attitude of mind, which should be the twentieth-century mind, if the twentieth century is to have a mind of its own."[12] Robert Stallman, in his survey of the development of New Critical theory remarks that Hulme is important "not because he was an original thinker, but because of his influence upon those who have dominated and largely directed the course of contemporary criticism."[13] Cleanth Brooks likewise considers Hulme "something of a prototype."[14]

At the very heart of Hulme's thought lies what he calls the "religious attitude," an attitude based on the dogma of Original Sin, a vivid awareness of the fallenness of the world. "What is important," Hulme insists, "is what nobody seems to realize—the dogmas like that of Original Sin, which are the closest expression of the categories of the religious attitude. That man is in no sense perfect, but a wretched creature, who can yet apprehend perfection."[15] He vigorously rejects all humanistic views and in the essay on "Humanism" he again makes reference to "the religious attitude; where things are separated which ought to be separated, and Perfection is not illegitimately introduced on the plane of human things" (*S*, 34). It need hardly be said that Hulme concentrates his energies on attacking humanism which, in his view, has dominated Western thought since the Renaissance, but is also manifest in Greek thought. He preaches the death of man as the focal point of the universe and he propounds a view of the world without center. He does this by means of a religious discourse largely derived from medieval theology. He uses religious ideas to lambaste humanism and romanticism, and in the process he dehumanizes religion, too. He betrays no interest in the redemptive doctrine which is as central to Christian thought as Original Sin, and he never discusses the mystery of the Incarnation. The Incarnation would have presented a very serious problem to Hulme had he chosen to take it into account since it would have had to be reconciled with his insistence that the transcendent realm of God and the spirit should be kept totally separate from the realm of man and nature. Hulme's point of departure is that there exists an *"absolute discontinuity* between vital and religious things" (*S*, 11).

Hulme obviously does not believe that an order of reality lies behind the confusion of appearances; he does not subscribe to the view that "the world is other than what it seems to be" (*S*, 80). Perfection, for Hulme, is not discoverable in the fallen world of matter. But he also maintains that there is a sphere above that of worldly existence: that is, the sphere of the Absolute, of Perfection which is separated by an unbridgeable chasm from the fallen world of man. It is the function of art to point man toward that realm and by so doing highlight the detestable corruptibility of the vital world. Hence, Hulme's advocacy of abstract art, his preference for the geometric and hard line as opposed to the naturally vital and flowing one. "The geometrical line is something abstractly distinct from the messiness, the confusion, and the accidental details of existing things" (*S*, 87). Abstract art by shunning the natural enables man to transcend the temporal and contemplate the eternal. "A perfect cube looks stable in comparison with the flux of appearance, but one might be pardoned if one felt no particular interest in the eternity of the cube; but if you can put man into some geometric shape which lifts him out of the transcience of the organic, then the matter is different." This, according to Hulme, is what Byzantine artists and Wyndham Lewis and Jacob Epstein managed to do; and Hulme approves of their work because it "turns the organic into something not organic, it tries to translate the changing and limited, into something unlimited and necessary" (*S*, 106–107).

Hulme's theories are the result of his negative response to the humanism and positivism of his time. He clearly regarded both movements as unsatisfactory answers to the problems of the age. One can fully sympathize with Hulme and those of his contemporaries who refused to accept the easy solutions offered by the pseudoprophetic voices of the time. Tennyson's paths to faith were quite unconvincing, the humanistic impulse to edify mankind through literature was too pietistic, the gospel of "fellow-feeling" which permeates so many nineteenth-century novels proved too susceptible to sentimentalism, and positivism received enough serious blows, particularly from Bergson, to lose its preeminence. It was no longer possible to uphold the view of an integrated universe. Hulme, therefore, argued for the acceptance of a world that did not make sense. But he did not stop there. He posited a universe that made sense if only it were seen to be made up of separate spheres.

Hulme revolted against his age by becoming a reactionary, for he offered as a solution something he had recovered from the past. From medieval thought he borrowed an uncompromising contempt for the world. Then, since he wished to find a safe niche for art, he divorced good art from the world. In order to manage this he had to argue for the autonomy of the work of art. But how can a work of art produced out of the materials of a corrupt world be free from corruption? Is not the language of poetry also the language of everyday commerce and scientific investigation? No; the artist transforms his materials and he derives his forms from the realm of abstraction, not the fallen vital world of nature. The discourse of poetry is different from the discourse of science and the language of ordinary mortal communication and has as little connection as possible with it. For some time the French symbolists had already been forging "pure poetry"—i.e., poetry the language of which has no reference to the world outside the poem. The separation of one discourse from another was hardly a novel ideal.

It has been recognized for many centuries that a fragmented world gives rise to and calls for a proliferation of modes of discourse. Nevertheless, it is interesting to notice that whereas originally the recognition of the validity of autonomous modes of discourse made possible the emergence of a separate scientific discourse in a milieu dominated by the mythico-symbolic language of theology, in the Modernist period we find the same notion of autonomy employed to make possible the establishment of a poetic discourse separate from the scientific language which dominated the scene. Nor was the new language of literature especially original or autonomous; it relied too heavily on an inherited theology which had lost its validity and even most of its relevance. Hulme's enterprise, then, was more than anything else an exercise in re-collection; he gathered pieces from a past on which he consistently cast a nostalgic glance. And it was not just from Christian theology that he borrowed. He also found relevant and useful ideas in the Greek tradition. His idea of the work of art as an object pointing towards perfection and standing above the world of change owes much to the Greeks; for, although Hulme denies that the world is harmonious, that it is a cosmos in the full sense of the word, his concept of the work of art suggests a heterocosmos with much the same properties as Plato's cosmos. (Hulme's followers were to articulate the idea of the poem as heterocosmos much more fully.) Hulme also equated his notion of "detached interest" with Plato's "aesthetic contemplation" (S, 136). Obviously, by dipping so freely into the past in order to construct his own theory, Hulme sometimes contradicts himself. Thus, for example, he criticizes the romantic attitude because it "seems to crystalize in verse round metaphors of flight" (S, 120). He remains blind to the fact that his own repeated emphasis on abstraction is also a form of flight. Hulme's theory of art is as much a part of the aesthetic tradition of "hovering" as the romantics'.

Notwithstanding the contradictions within Hulme's theories, the most serious deficiency of his thought lies elsewhere. Hulme was a reactionary; he looked back while pretending to be facing forward. He not only concocted a theory out of the bits and pieces of tradition that suited him in order to confront a problem brought about by the bankruptcy of that tradition; he not only further devalued religion while ostensibly preaching the revival of the "religious attitude," but more seriously he totally ignored the most important crisis of his time. Hulme's reactionary stance is best manifested by the way he resorted to the western metaphysical tradition at a time when that tradition had been declared irrevocably dead. Just when the center was gone and a cosmos was no longer possible, Hulme pointed the way to an alternative—the work of art as a heterocosmos, and thus diverted attention from the dreadful confrontation with nothingness. Even as it was being understood that Nietzsche's announcement of the death of God meant the absence of an Absolute, Hulme was sermonizing on the supremacy of the Absolute.

The death of God did not simply create a void; rather, it removed the screen which concealed the abyss, and in so doing it caused the collapse of order and of the very possibility of order. Early twentieth-century poetry frequently expresses both the new sense of absence and its ramifications. The minor poet G. A. Green in an unexceptional poem "A Mood" laments the loss of the source of Universal love.

> The strength of immortal Love;
> The comfort of millions that weep;
> Prayer, and the Cross we adored—
> All is lost! there is no one above;
> We are like the beasts that creep;
> They have taken away our Lord.[16]

For Rupert Brooke the absence of God means almost the opposite. Now that there is no God, there is nothing to rail and rant against.

> Because God put his adamantine fate
> Between my sullen heart and its desire,
> I swore that I would burst the Iron Gate,
> Rise up, and curse Him on His throne of fire.
> Earth shuddered at my crown of blasphemy,

But Love was as a flame about my feet;
Proud up the Golden Stair I strode; and beat
Thrice on the Gate, and entered with a cry—

All the great courts were quiet in the sun,
And full of vacant echoes: moss had grown
Over the glossy pavements, and begun
To creep within the dusty council-halls.
An idle wind blew round an empty throne
And stirred the heavy curtains on the walls.[17]

I chose to quote Brooke's poem and a part of Greene's not because they
are notable poetic achievements but because they express most overtly
the quandary of the twentieth century. There are, of course, famous
poets' marvelous poems which reveal the same anxiety, but those poems
come to us through so many New Critical readings that we are more
likely to remember how they are shaped than what they are about.

Twentieth-century literature situated as it is in a time of crisis cannot
be separated from that crisis. The death of God and its corollary, the end
of metaphysics, pose problems of the most radical nature, problems
which are at once philosophical and religious. Because they are not even
addressed, these problems cannot be solved by the theories of T. E.
Hulme. One would have thought, therefore, that whatever influence
Hulme exercised would be short-lived. Yet, such has not been the case.
His idea that poetry, like religion, belonged to a different sphere from
that of man's worldly concerns[18] and his insistence on abstract form
helped generate a critical attitude which by means of aesthetic irony affirms the autonomy of the literary work with such adamancy that it rejects, at least in theory, the pertinence of such questions as may be labeled
theological or philosophical in the pursuit of criticism. The New Critics
do not part ways with Hulme when he expounds his views on the "religious attitude." To the New Critics, Hulme's religious position constitutes the proper response to Arnoldian humanism. It is also the foundation of one of the most crucial Modernist dogmas—the dogma of
aesthetic distance. The Hulmean "religious attitude," first of all, frees the
critic from the fragmentary world; it enables him to regard even those
poems which are the products of that shattered world as completely removed from it. In other words, it renders the critic safe from any danger
that the dread of a decentered world may intrude upon him through the
work of art and disturb his contemplative tranquility. The most a work of
art can do is induce the critic to express Epicurean disdain for that world.

Secondly, by way of its association with abstraction as opposed to empathy, the Hulmean "religious attitude" is an ironic attitude of stasis which forbids any involvement with actuality. This means that even if the literary work emanates from the writer's religious concerns and struggles, the critic remains aloof from such concerns—and this aloofness would be perfectly consistent with Hulme's notion of the "religious attitude."

The distinction between the poem as a work of art and the poem as a record of the artist's experience, a statement of his concerns, and the product of his intentionality—and therefore anchored quite firmly in the world of temporal concerns—leads the New Critic into some very sticky problems. Strict adherence to the dogmas of autonomy and aesthetic disinterest can exact a very heavy price.

One example will suffice to point out the horror to which ironic detachment leads. In 1949 the Fellows in American Letters of the Library of Congress awarded the first Bollingen Prize in Poetry to Ezra Pound for his *Pisan Cantos*. (The *Cantos* had appeared in 1948, the same year as William Carlos Williams' second volume of *Paterson*.) The Fellows were among the most renowned writers and critics of their day: Conrad Aiken, W. H. Auden, Louise Bogan, Katherine Garrison Chapin, T. S. Eliot, Paul Green, Robert Lowell, Katherine Anne Porter, Karl Shapiro, Allen Tate, Willard Thorpe, and Robert Penn Warren. (Karl Shapiro publicly dissociated himself from the decision.) Anticipating the controversy that would greet the announcement of the award to a collection of poems that contained passing but unmistakable racial slurs and antisemitic utterances, the Fellows explained in their public statement that for them to "permit other considerations than that of poetic achievement to sway the decision would destroy the significance of the award and would in principle deny the validity of that objective perception of value on which civilized society must rest."[19] Archibald MacLeish, defending the decision, refers to Whitehead's opinion that while the philosophic contribution of the ancient poets "is now nearly worthless . . . their detached insights are priceless." MacLeish then expresses his belief that Pound's "poem, with all its evil and its ignorance about it, accomplishes in some manner what a poem should accomplish. I think it accomplishes this because its poet, for all the childishness of his opinions, is loyal in the end not to his opinions but his art."[20] It is much too late now to join the Pound controversy; I present these scattered quotations to give a context to the casual use of phrases such as "objective perception," "detached insights," "loyal to art." It is also interesting to note how MacLeish is uninterested in the childishness of Pound's opinions. One assumes that he would be equally uninterested in the poet's opinions if they were serious. The aesthetic response to a poem must have no commerce with the world of social and political reality, nor must it concern itself with the questions of philosophy and theology. What better example could be found to illustrate Cleanth Brooks's theory in action? For it was Brooks who in *The Well Wrought Urn* advocated a system of criticism built around the idea that "We can judge the work, not by the truth and falsity, as such, of the idea which it incorporates, but rather by its character as drama—by its coherence, sensitivity, depth, richness, and toughmindedness."[21]

When the New Critic declares the autonomy of poetry, he builds for poetry an isolated niche away from religion and everything else. Or, as R. W. Stallman puts it in his concluding remarks to a compendium of essays by the major exponents of the New Criticism:

> The question of the specific merit of a poetic statement as truth or false-hood does not arise when the beliefs of the poet are ordered into an intrinsic whole. . . . One irrelevance is the truth or falsity of the belief expressed in the poem *as* poem. It was a mistake of the early Richards to think that what, in the way of acceptance, is demanded of a poem is the poet's own beliefs. . . .
> Belief, as applied to the arts, is a sociological category. To assign objective status to the content of a poem apart from its form is to reduce the poem's meaning to its original state, and this is to locate it in the historical process. . . . A work of art is autonomous. It is a construct having a life of its own, and it is limited by its technique and intention. The New Critics isolate the meaning of a poem only in terms of form.[22]

The question of belief is, therefore, an irrelevance to the poem itself and to the critic *as* critic. Yet many, not to say most, New Critics profess belief in that very same religion, Christianity, which so frequently appears to invade the territory of poetry. So they possess two minds, as it were. When they approach the literary work, the religious system they believe in becomes like myth, a source of "great radical metaphors"; they enter the realm of what Cleanth Brooks calls the "as-if" or as A. C. Bradley put it in "Poetry for Poetry's Sake," they "suspend belief." But can the truly religious person really "suspend belief"? This is a path fraught with danger, for once one enters the realm of the "as-if," which is also the realm of irony, it is probable that the "as-if" will take over. The only relationship the religious man may have with the "as-if," if he does not want to cast his religiousness aside, is a relationship of irony. That is, the truly religious man must adopt the stance of the ironist towards irony itself: Kierkegaard calls this mastered irony. Because the New Criticism succumbs to irony rather than mastering it, a confusion arises in its ranks. How is it possible for a Christian thinker to stop being a Christian while dealing with a literary text? Does one ignore the Christianness of those Christian elements one encounters in the texts? Do such elements become merely formal attributes?

The autonomy of literature, springing as it does from a rejection of a fragmented world and as a reaction against the materialistic foundations of positivism, finds itself espousing a cause normally associated with religion. At the same time autonomous literature also declares its independence from religion. And here is where the confusion abides, for the aesthetic sphere does not free itself of the discourse of religion. Furthermore, the language of the ironist/aesthete, because the aesthete is not infrequently a Christian, finds its way into religion. What starts as the establishment of autonomous spheres ends up in the confusion of one sphere with another, so that eventually it becomes nearly impossible to discover the true meaning of religion. Imperceptibly, religious discourse has been gradually devoured by the implacable machine of literary critical discourse. Any analysis of the relationship between religion and literature as art eventually comes round to asking this question: how does one separate religion and aesthetics? Unless one can distinguish the one from the other, one cannot come to any conclusion regarding the relationship between them, if such a relationship is at all possible. In order to draw the necessary distinctions, one needs to destroy (in Heidegger's sense) the Western metaphysical tradition; for it is by virtue of their shared allegiance to metaphysics that the spheres of religion and literature got themselves enmeshed in each other. Such a destruction can be found in the work of Kierkegaard who not only engaged in a detailed analysis of irony but also addressed himself to the problems posed by the vagueness that has come to obscure the real boundaries that separate authentic religion from aestheticism.

One may start by asking two questions of Kierkegaard. What does the poet seek in his poetic activity? The poet, says Kierkegaard, "seeks away from [his] suffering and finds ease in poetic production, in the poetic anticipation of a more perfect, i.e., happier, order of things." By contrast the genuinely religious man seeks "to comprehend the suffering and to remain in it, so that reflection is directed *upon* the suffering and not away from it."[23] And what is gained by poetry in its pursuit of a more nearly perfect order of things? By means of irony poetry abandons the limitations of human finitude; it hovers in a dream world of infinite possibility, and thus it gains a "victory over the world." But this is a strange sort of victory.

> It is through a negation of the imperfect actuality that poetry opens up a higher actuality, expands and transfigures the imperfect into the perfect,

and thereby softens and mitigates that deep pain which would darken and obscure all things. To this extent poetry is a reconciliation, though not the true reconciliation; it does not reconcile me with the actuality in which I live, for no transubstantiation of the given actuality occurs. Instead, it reconciles me with the given actuality by giving me another actuality, a higher and more perfect. . . . The poetical may well be a sort of victory over actuality but the process whereby it is rendered infinite is more like an abandonment of, than a continuation in, actuality.[24]

It is precisely because poetry rejects the "imperfect actuality" that it has been mistakenly seen as an ally of religion; for religion is often associated with a rejection of the existing world and with the search after the perfection found only in a transcendent realm. But Kierkegaard does not accept this characterization of the religious attitude. He makes it clear that a discourse is not necessarily religious even though it is heard in church and deals with faith, God, or Christ; indeed, "an aesthetic view of life, even if interlaced with both the name of God and of Christ, remains an aesthetic view of life" (*CUP*, 391n). Nor is the introduction of Christianity into a discourse necessarily a religious act, because it "may involve merely an aesthetic relationship" (*CUP*, 391n). What truly separates the aesthetic man from the religious man is that the former is (by virtue of his irony) detached, views existence from a distance, employs the foreshortened perspective, and seeks the joys of contemplation. Art and poetry, according to Kierkegaard, "are not essentially related to an existing individual; for their contemplative enjoyment, the joy over what is beautiful, is disinterested, and the spectator of the work of art is contemplatively outside himself *qua* existing individual" (*CUP*, 177n). The disinterested stance of the ironist is also static and averse to change. Its knowledge is one of *theoria* as opposed to *gnosis. Theoria* leaves the observer and the observed unchanged; in *gnosis* there is a constant opening to change because *gnosis* implies an incessant interchange.

The religious man is not averse to change even though it offers him no remission from suffering; unlike the ironic aesthete he does not search for an "explanation and glorification of life" (*CUP*, 390). The ironist/poet looks for the happy ending, the order imposed by *telos.* By contrast, the religious man "operates conversely by means of the lack of any ending, that there is no result, precisely because suffering essentially belongs to the religious life" (*CUP*, 396). The poet regards suffering as merely accidental to existence and therefore he tries to explain it away through the enchanting fictions of the ironic imagination. The poet, of course, like every other human being exists in a suffering reality, but in his aesthetic activity he escapes from suffering. The religious man attempts to penetrate suffering ever more deeply; for him there is no other reality. That is why the religious man avoids the foreshortened perspective adopted by the poet whose irony is steeped in the metaphysical tradition. "As soon therefore as the religious orator makes use of the foreshortened perspective, whether he concentrates all the suffering in a single moment or paints a cheerful picture of better times in prospect, he goes back to the aesthetic realm, and his interpretation of suffering becomes a fictitious religious movement" (*CUP*, 399). Kierkegaard offers a brief but very illuminating example of such a movement. ". . . there is a backsliding in the religious discourse when a man says for example: 'After my many errors I finally learned to keep close to God, and since that time He has not left me in the lurch; my business flourishes, my projects have success, I am now happily married, and my children are well and strong, etc.' The religious man has here again fallen back into the aesthetic dialectic" (*CUP*, 399n).

The sketchy vignette reminds one of the broad outlines of many a *bildungsroman*. One remembers such novels as *Waverley, Great Expectations,* and *Adam Bede.* In each case the protagonist errs and suffers for his errors, but as he gradually learns to follow the path of righteousness he regains his happiness and well-being. The tremendous suffering undergone by each character yields a happy ending. It is the "to live happily ever after" conclusion of a "once upon a time" tale. By providing happy endings of this nature a novelist illustrates Kierkegaard's observation that "the religious discourse is severe, the aesthetic lenient" (*CUP*, 400n). One must hasten to add that a happy ending in the conventional sense is not necessary to prove the argument; an unhappy ending may be equally lenient. Kierkegaard shows this by using *Romeo and Juliet* as his example. The fact that "poesy has the courage to slay Juliet" does not prove him wrong, "for to permit Juliet to die is the tender sympathy of the aesthetic, but to proclaim new suffering, and hence to let fall a new blow, is the severe sympathy of the religious" (*CUP*, 400n). The same remark can be applied to another play which is not only closer to our time but also epitomizes the symbolic imagination so highly admired by the New Critics. In Villiers de L'Isle Adam's *Axel* the hero and heroine conclude the play with a suicide which transports them from the world of suffering into a state of permanence and ideal love. It is ironic that Axel and Sara attain ecstasy by subjecting themselves to the passage through the most dreaded moment of all—death. By dying they gain the immutability of the two lovers portrayed on Keats's Grecian urn. They become a "cold pastoral"; they voluntarily submit to an apotheosis into beautiful but dead aesthetic objects. "It will be easily seen," even if Edmund Wilson had not pointed it out, "that this super dreamer of Villiers's is the type of all the heroes of the Symbolists."[25] Pater's Marius, Laforgue's Lohengrin, Huysmans's Des Esseintes, Yeats's Michael Robartes, Joyce's Stephen Dedalus, and a host of other figures all share the fundamental characteristics of Axel. They all "would rather drop out of the common life than have to struggle to make themselves a place in it—they forego their mistresses, preferring their dreams."[26] These aesthetes prefer escape from the world to the pain and suffering concomitant with grappling with reality. Thus, for instance, Stephen Dedalus transforms his lust into a villanelle. He escapes and avoids the potential embarrassment of human sexual encounter by wallowing self-indulgently in the unreal beauty of words. He totally abandons the tangible universe in order to derive his pleasure safely from the solitary savoring of his own verbal contrivances.

> A soft liquid joy flowed through the words where the soft long vowels hurtled noiselessly and fell away, lapping and flowing back and ever shaking the white bells of their waves in mute chime and mute peal and soft low swooning cry; and he felt that the augury he had sought in the wheeling darting bird and in the pale space of sky above him had come forth from his heart like a bird from a turret quietly and softly. (*P*, 226)

It is immediately evident that Stephen inhabits the world of a very private dream. He has his own mythology. He stakes for himself a domain virtually inaccessible to anybody else. Ensconced in this remote aesthetic niche Stephen Dedalus forgets, just as, Kierkegaard maintains, Friedrich Schlegel forgot, "that to live is something different from to dream."[27]

The flight of the ironist is more than a simple escape. It is, as has been reiterated, an affirmation of the metaphysical. But what other refuge does man have in a world of suffering? Clearly, because the metaphysical is no longer possible, Western man is at a loss; he can turn his attention only to himself and to the immediate world around him. Yet there is one consolation left to metaphysically deprived post-Nietzschean man. Paul Ricoeur explains that "Man is consoled when in language he lets things be, or be shown." The vocabulary here is Heideggerian, but as Ricoeur goes on to say, "Kierkegaard calls this consolation 'repetition.'" Repetition in the Kierkegaardian sense is directly opposed to the ironist's flight from reality. It means "dwelling," or, better still, repetition is the "tension [that] is maintained between [man's] concern for the heavens, for the divine, and the rooting of his existence on earth."[28] This tension is what makes man an *inter esse*, a being anchored in the world but also aware of the heavens above him. *Inter esse* cannot be detached, objective, removed, contemplative; it is, in fact, a negation of the disinterestedness of metaphysics.

II. *A Portrait* as a Critique of Aesthetic Irony

When Stephen Dedalus, in *A Portrait of the Artist as a Young Man*, and Lily Briscoe, in *To the Lighthouse*, look down at the world from the heights of their aesthetic ecstasies, they do not see the chaotic and formless mess of temporality: their vision is clear; it has form. The bits and pieces which make up the phenomenal world are not, for Dedalus and Briscoe, fragments strewn haphazardly around, nor the individual links of an extensive chain, but rather the constituent parts of a harmonious mosaic. The two fledgling aesthetes take the apparently unrelated details of experience and transform them into a complete and self-contained whole. Their ironic imagination, it seems, enables them to rise above the flux of temporal existence and above the instability and contradictoriness of actuality and to produce a stable image in which time is arrested. They provide excellent examples of what has been called "the spatialization of time" which is frequently taken to be a fundamental characteristic of Modernist literature.

The desire to rise above the flux of temporality, the impulse to reach for stability and immutability, explains, according to Wilhelm Worringer (from whom T. E. Hulme derived many seminal ideas on art), the move towards abstraction in art. In Worringer's version of the history of art, primitive man sought refuge from his worldly terror in the unworldly abstraction of art.

> Tormented by the entangled inter-relationship and flux of the phenomena of the outer world, such peoples were dominated by an immense need for tranquility. The happiness they sought from art did not consist in the possibility of projecting themselves into the things of the outer world, of enjoying themselves in them but in the possibility of taking the individual thing of the external world out of its arbitrariness and seeming fortuitousness, of eternalizing it by approximation to abstract forms and, in this manner, of finding a point of tranquility and a refuge from appearances. Their most powerful urge was, so to speak, to wrest the object of the external world out of its natural context, out of the unending flux of being, to purify it of all its dependence upon life, i.e., of everything about it that was arbitrary, to render it necessary and irrefragable, to approximate it to its *absolute* value.[29]

Worringer's description of the urge to abstraction does not stop with primitive art. He identifies other periods during which man expressed his fear or dislike of the "unending flux of being" through abstract art—among them the age of Byzantium.

Primitive art and, even more so, Byzantine art were championed by many influential critics of the early twentieth century. Roger Fry, Clive

Bell and T. E. Hulme preferred Primitive and Byzantine art to the "descriptive" or "empathic" art of the High Renaissance. Clive Bell, for instance, declared that "the Pre-Raffaelites were men of taste" because in spite of their amateurishness they "felt the commonness of the High Renaissance and the distinction of what they called Primitive Art, by which they meant the art of the fifteenth and fourteenth centuries."[30] The careful avoidance of three-dimensionality in pre-Renaissance art was especially admired because it produced an abstract effect and emphasized pure form.

T. E. Hulme's professed preference for Byzantine art stems from his desire to move as far from the existential experiential world as possible, an impulse shared by the persona of Yeats's much celebrated Byzantium poems—two texts which enjoy a very secure place in the traditional Modernist canon. In those two poems there is a self-conscious and willful retreat from everything that bears an immediate relation to actuality. Byzantium, a realm totally antithetical to nature, is characterized by the absolute absence of life and vitality and, above all, change. It is a metallic world in which the aesthete finds refuge from temporality through a complete severance from the sensual.

> Once out of nature I shall never take
> My bodily form from any natural thing,
> But such a form as Grecian goldsmiths make
> Of hammered gold and gold enamelling
> To keep a drowsy Emperor awake.[31]

The assumed form is bird-like and the reader may be tempted to find in it a connection with the natural world: the golden bird is an idealized imitation of real flesh and blood birds. But one is quickly reminded in "Byzantium" that this "Miracle, bird or golden handiwork" is "More miracle than bird or handiwork." This is a spiritual, intangible form—it is, indeed, pure form, so pure as to be contemptuous of "Common bird or petal." It is a spatial form inhabiting a timeless empyrean.

The persona in Yeats's poems understands that perfection and mutability are mutually exclusive; he opts for the perfection of Byzantium and abandons his attachment to the vital world of the body. T. E. Hulme's criticism is imbued with the same desire for perfection. He, therefore, celebrates those artistic manifestations which are least related to the material world of change and contradiction.

> Renaissance art we may call a "vital" art in that it depends on pleasure in the reproduction of human and natural form. Byzantine art is the exact contrary of this. There is nothing vital in it; the emotion you get from it is not a

pleasure in the reproduction of natural or human life. The disgust with the trivial and accidental characteristics of living shapes, the searching after an austerity, a *perfection* and rigidity which vital things can never have, lead here to the use of forms which can almost be called geometrical. Man is subordinate to certain absolute values: there is no delight in human form, leading to its *natural* reproduction; it is always distorted to fit into the more abstract forms which convey an intense religious emotion.

These two arts thus correspond exactly to the thought of their respective periods. Byzantine art to the ideology which looks on man and all existing things as imperfect and sinful in comparison with certain abstract values and *perfections*. The other art corresponds to the humanist ideology, which looks on man and life as good, and which is thus in a relation of harmony with existence. (*S*, 53–54)

This brief passage brings to the fore some of the most basic elements in Hulme's aesthetics. First of all, central to his argument is the inseparability of abstraction and perfection, and hence the preference for rigid geometric forms, that is, those forms least suggestive of the corporeal and the material, and closest to the ethereal. The unworldliness of Hulme's ideal, the positing of perfection above the realm of being-in-the-world, lead him to endorse an art which does not appeal to the senses but inspires, instead, a spiritual or religious experience. The inevitable corollary to the prominence given to the spiritual realm, as opposed to the physical world, is *contemptu mundi*. Briefly, Hulme favors an art in which form is prior to content.

This is the kind of work of art Lily Briscoe produces. The action which brings *To The Lighthouse* to a close is the drawing of a line in the center of the canvas, a line which completes the painting; it is a line which, by giving the painting a center, gives it a coherent, autonomous form. Lily Briscoe's work of art is not representational and it exists independently of the historical circumstances surrounding its composition. Furthermore, Briscoe's canvas does not need a viewer; it has an independent existence, which is why Lily Briscoe is not disturbed by the likelihood that it might end up in an attic, never to be seen by anyone. And, finally, the completion of the painting is simultaneous with Lily Briscoe's epiphanic vision, an intense religious experience which, it must be added, is purely personal and which she has no urge to share or communicate. Lily Briscoe comes readily to mind simply because her medium is painting, and so her work invites an immediate comparison with Hulme's reflections on the subject. Nevertheless, Stephen Dedalus's pronouncements on aesthetics and his own perception of the world from the privileged vantage point of an artist are remembered just as readily. Stephen's aesthetic discourse is steeped in religious vocabulary. His disdain for the concrete world and even for the human form, both of which Hulme finds "imperfect and sinful," finds expression at each stage of his development.

While ordaining himself a priest of art on the beach, Stephen looks down on his peers, naked and at play in the water. The banter does not cheer Stephen who stands solitary and aloof; their sight fills him with disgust.

> He recognised their speech collectively before he distinguished their faces. The mere sight of that medley of wet nakedness chilled him to the bone. Their bodies, corpsewhite or suffused with a pallid golden light or rawly tanned by the suns, gleamed with the wet of the sea. Their divingstone, poised on its rude supports and rocking under their plunges, and the roughhewn stones of the sloping breakwater over which they scrambled in their horseplay, gleamed with cold wet lustre. The towels with which they smacked their bodies were heavy with cold seawater: and drenched with cold brine was their matted hair.
>
> He stood still in deference to their calls and parried their banter with easy words. How characterless they looked: Shuley without his deep unbuttoned collar, Ennis without his scarlet belt with the snaky clasp, and Connolly without his Norfolk coat with the flapless sidepockets! It was a pain to see them and a swordlike pain to see the signs of adolescence that made repellent their pitiable nakedness. Perhaps they had taken refuge in number and noise from the secret dread in their souls. But he, apart from them and in silence, remembered in what dread he stood of the mystery of his own body. (P. 168)

The source of Stephen's dread is an awareness of mortality. He is struck by the defenselessness and vulnerability of humanity manifest in its nakedness. The unclothed bodies of Stephen's friends lack dignity; they are even pitiable. The human body, which inspired many artists of the High Renaissance, such as Michelangelo, to produce statues of monumental dignity, is here seen by Stephen as King Lear saw it in the person of Edgar during a raging storm on the heath. "Thou art the thing itself; unaccommodated man is no more but such a poor, bare, forked animal as thou art." Only the outward trappings stand between man and the horrendous vision of his mortality—a thin defensive sheath against the invasion of dread. Stephen is repelled by the "corpsewhite" bodies of his friends. Stripped of their sartorial quirks, Shuley, Ennis and Connolly are indistinguishable: they are all mortal. Stephen speculates, probably correctly though certainly condescendingly, that his peers escape their dread of mortality by immersing themselves in the crowd, by losing their individuality in the common mass. "Perhaps they had taken refuge in numbers and noise from the secret dread of their souls." Stephen will not follow their course and for a fleeting moment he "remembered in what dread he stood of the mystery of his own body."

Stephen, though, does not proceed to confront his dread. Like the adolescents on the beach he escapes from it, although he chooses a different route. Instead of submerging himself in number and noise he soars above the world of common men, the fallen temporal world cursed by mortality. Invoking the fabulous artificer, he takes leave of the world and his physical body; rid of his "body of death," he soars above the waters, sunward. He transforms his dread into "an ecstasy of fear" (*P*, 169). This point must be emphasized, because it constitutes the very kernel of Stephen's aestheticism. Stephen's flight is not merely *toward* Beauty (or a Dantesque god of pure radiance); it is, primarily, a flight away from dread. To put it in other terms, Stephen's aestheticism is a refuge from nothingness. The nothingness Stephen flees is twofold. On the one hand, there is the nothingness which threatens him the moment he becomes one out of many. If, like his peers, Stephen were to take "refuge in numbers," he would lose his individuality, his uniqueness; he would become a number, a nothing. By standing alone, however, by refusing to fall into what Heidegger calls "the 'they' [das Man] and the 'world' of its concern,"[32] he has to confront dread. This he is not prepared to do, either, and so he resorts to his imagination and delivers himself to it. Through the imagination he expects to shed his temporality. The unrealistic nature of his expectation does not occur to him, in spite of the abundant ironies of the situation in which he entertains it. He wades through the shallow waters, his shoes slung nonchalantly over his shoulders, his toes feeling the seaweed, but he feels disembodied and, like Icarus, heading skywards above the waters and the members of the fallen human race who are caught in those same flowing waters. The whole of humanity is caught in the tides of time, with the exception of Stephen. He remains totally blind to the fact that Icarus fell into the waters, and that he, too, is bound to undergo a similar fall. Stephen is as human as those around him; what makes him different is the illusory feeling of disembodiment.

At the very center of Stephen's aesthetic vision lies the ideal of stasis, the antithesis of temporality. When he elaborates on his idea of stasis, Stephen reveals the distrust he shares with Hulme of anything suggestive of the body and its appetites. He excludes desire and loathing from the sphere of aesthetic pleasure. He betrays a preference for the abstract and the geometric, to the total exclusion of the physical and the vital. Lynch tries to bring him down to earth.

—You say that art must not excite desire and loathing, said Lynch, I told you that one day I wrote my name in pencil on the backside of the Venus of Praxiteles in the Museum. Was that not desire? (P, 205)

Stephen initially brushes off this objection; he regards Lynch's actions as unrepresentative of normal human behavior. Lynch neither accepts nor refutes this—he laughs gleefully in remembrance of his outrageous pranks. Stephen then reminds Lynch of the truism that "we are all animals."

—As for that, Stephen said in polite parenthesis, we are all animals. I also am an animal.
—You are, said Lynch.
—But we are just now in a mental world, Stephen continued. The desire and loathing excited by improper esthetic means are really unesthetic emotions not only because they are kinetic in character but also because they are not more than physical. Our flesh shrinks from what it dreads and responds to the stimulus of what it desires by a purely reflex action of the nervous system. Our eyelid closes before we are aware that the fly is about to enter our eye.
—Not always, said Lynch critically. (P, 206)

Lynch's erotic attraction to the statue was, to Stephen's mind, "simply a reflex action of the nerves" (P, 206).

Throughout the discussion on aesthetics Lynch remains unimpressed; while availing himself of Stephen's cigarettes and passing comments intended to retrieve Stephen's mind from its dizzy heights, he presses his companion into making statements totally devoid of any relation to actual experience. Stephen dismisses Lynch's physical desires too easily as animalistic and purely mechanical, and he equates aesthetic pleasure with stasis. He also suggests a close connection between beauty and truth (both produce mental stasis) and reveals his concept of truth to be geometric. "You would not write your name in pencil across the hypotenuse of a rightangled triangle." To which Lynch retorts, "No . . . give me the hypotenuse of the Venus of Praxiteles" (P, 208). Notwithstanding many such comments, Lynch fails to open Stephen's eyes to the tangible world of existential experience. Even when a noisy cart drowns Stephen's voice, the young aesthete remains unperturbed and responds to Lynch's string of oaths with a further elaboration of his hypothesis. In many respects Lynch is the voice of common sense; he stands in an immediate relationship to the world around him. He has his bodily appetites and he is not ashamed of them; he has earthiness and vitality, qualities he finds dismally lacking in Stephen's theories. Although his remarks fail to pull Stephen down from his perch and anchor him to the solid earth, they undercut Stephen seriously. The aspiring artist, on the other hand, is so intent on finding a way out of his messy world that he ignores all those pointers which warn him of the futility of his endeavor. He wades through the water thinking of Daedalus without once recalling the plunge Icarus took into the sea. He is rudely interrupted by a rattling dray but goes on talking about the abstract qualities of beauty. He discusses the Venus of Praxiteles and man's admiration of female beauty without seriously considering the importance of physical sexual tendencies. In all this Stephen stands in striking contrast to the very human Lynch. Contemptuous of humanity, Stephen reaches after a dehumanized other-worldly ideal, and in the process shows himself impervious to, as his mother puts it, "what the heart is and what it feels" (*P*, 252). When he resolves to "go to encounter for the millionth time the reality of experience" (*P*,253), one is bound to remember that "in vague sacrificial or sacramental acts alone his will seemed to go forth to encounter reality" (*P*, 159). He intends to forge works of art out of the gross earth, to be, like God the creator, refined out of existence; but, one suspects, with Lynch, that in the process he will also refine reality out of existence, that he will completely dehumanize his temporal experience by spatializing it, that in creating a conscience for his race he will anaesthetize his own.

Seen in this light, Stephen's aesthetic theory is hardly acceptable. It is inspired by an overwhelming desire to escape not just the confines of an impoverished, unsettled family and a priest-ridden city, but also the more fundamental and dreadful realities of mortality, mutability and imperfection. After his security and surety are shattered one Christmas day during his boyhood, Stephen moves steadily toward refining an aesthetic posture through which he can recover the fairy tale world of his infancy. Stephen wishes to stop time so that he may reenter the "once upon a time" prelapsarian world he lost when contradictory reality intruded so abruptly and so early into his life. In order to recapture that timeless world, however, Stephen has to alienate himself from society, espouse a dehumanized and dehumanizing aesthetic theory, reaffirm that contempt for the world which induced him, in the first place, to take refuge in art, and develop an inverted humility that is best described as pride. One certainly sympathizes with Stephen as, undoubtedly, thousands upon thousands of readers have done. His is not an easy struggle and, even worse, it is bound to end in failure, for man cannot erase his fallen nature. Or, at least, one hopes that Stephen's angelic flight will be cut short because in order to sustain it Stephen must become hardened in his haughtiness, confirmed in his cold remoteness, and ossified in his dehumanized aesthetics. If his mother's prayer is not fulfilled and Stephen does not suffer a fall into humanity, then the sun instead of mellowing his heart will melt his wings and plunge him, like Icarus, into the abyss.

In *A Portrait of the Artist As a Young Man* Joyce describes, through the eyes of Stephen, the desire for order and stability. Stephen encounters the unpleasantness of life rather early and quite naturally he tries to escape it. As Stephen looks for ways out of his predicament the reader empathizes with him and, perhaps, starts to share his expectations. There are aspects of reality portrayed in the novel, however, which Stephen ignores, but which strike the reader rather forcefully. Thus, for instance, one cannot help noticing the incongruities and ironies inherent in the scene on the beach. Similarly, Lynch's observations, so deftly handled by Stephen, raise serious questions not tackled by Stephen. But most important of all is the movement of the novel, a movement which checks the reader's expectations at every turn. Over and over again, Stephen undergoes some unpleasant experience only to emerge from it with a sense of self-satisfaction and peaceful tranquillity. He invariably finds this peace by way of a lonely retreat into a mysterious region, far from the physical world of rough and tumble experience. At the end of each chapter Stephen has what might be called a spiritual or a religious experience, but one which is more accurately described as an aesthetic experience— what makes it appear religious is its transcendent and unworldly quality. Yet whenever Stephen attains this state of stasis, the reader is conscious of a more real world being left behind and is led to conclude with Kierkegaard that the "existing poet who suffers in his existence does not really comprehend his suffering, he does not penetrate more and more deeply into it, but in his suffering he seeks away from the suffering and finds ease in poetic production, in the poetic anticipation of a more perfect, i.e., a happier, order of things" (*CUP*, 397). It is of such a poet that Joyce presents a portrait in his novel. The reader is made to see the limitations of the aesthetic life as well as its seductiveness, for it is certainly an attractive course that Stephen adopts. It enables him, for a while at least, to master a world replete with suffering. Thanks to his aestheticism Stephen temporarily removes the sting from life, as is evident repeatedly throughout the novel.

In the first chapter, after the unjust pandybatting, Stephen is acclaimed the hero of the school by his fellow students. Stephen is thrilled, but he reaches the highest point of joy only when the clamor is over, he is alone, and everything and everyone recedes into a remote background.

> The cheers died away in the soft grey air. He was alone. He was happy and free: but he would not be anyway proud with Father Dolan. He would be very quiet and obedient: and he wished he could do something kind for him to show him that he was not proud.
>
> The air was soft and grey and mild and the evening was coming. There was the smell of evening in the air, the smell of the fields of the country where they digged up turnips to peel them and eat them when they went out for a walk to Major Barton's, the smell there was in the little wood beyond the pavilion where the gallnuts were.
>
> The fellows were practising long shies and bowling lobs and slow twisters. In the soft grey silence he could hear the bump of the balls: and from here and from there through the quiet air the sound of the cricket bats: pick, pack, pock, puck: like drops of water in a fountain falling softly in the brimming bowl. (P. 59)

The vaguely religious nature of this experience, which seems to transform the playgrounds into an idyllic garden, is faintly suggested by the "brimming bowl" with its connotation of a chalice, and by the resolutions of obedience and humility. In fact, the "brimming bowl" of the fountain becomes "*The chalice flowing to the brim*" (P, 223) in the villanelle. The scene conveys an air of unreality; all the concrete details are blurred. But Stephen's sense of being "alone . . . happy and free" stands out vividly, and it becomes even more pronounced as he grows in his detachment. His ecstatic epiphany on the beach, which marks his apotheosis as an artist, culminates in a celebration of his freedom and solitude, although at this point obedience is replaced by willfulness.

> He was alone. He was unheeded, happy and near to the wild heart of life. He was alone and young and wilful and wild-hearted, alone amid a waste of wild air and brackish waters and the seaharvest of shells and tangle and veiled grey sunlight and gayclad lightclad figures of children and girls and voices childish and girlish in the air. (P, 171)

A similar sense of other-worldliness pervades Stephen's sexual experience at the conclusion of the second chapter. Dislocated by the incessant wanderings of his family and dismayed by the sordidness which surrounds him, Stephen first turns to the illusory world of romance. Like a latter day Don Quixote he immerses himself in the unreal world of *The Count of Monte Cristo*. He then seeks relief through the satisfaction of his lustful longings. His precocious sexual experience, however, in spite of the sensual abandon from which it springs, has a nonphysical quality. The description of his encounter with the prostitute ends on a peculiarly asensual note. The body fades slowly into the background and his "soul" plays a larger role than his senses. His eyes are closed, his hearing and his smell are dimmed, and his quasi-mystical sensation is more mental than physical.

> With a sudden movement she bowed his head and joined her lips to his and he read the meaning of her movements in her frank uplifted eyes. It was too much for him. He closed his eyes, surrendering himself to her, body and mind, conscious of nothing in the world but the dark pressure of her softly parting lips. They pressed upon his brain as upon his lips as though they were the vehicle of a vague speech; and between them he felt an unknown and timid pressure, darker than the swoon of sin, softer than sound or odour. (P, 101)

Stephen's subsequent remorse and fearful guilt lead him into an intensely pietistic phase. The terror so carefully and calculatedly produced by the preacher during the retreat induces a spiritual purification that strengthens Stephen's distaste for the physical side of his nature. At the end of the third chapter, when he receives communion, Stephen enjoys a great sense of freedom: he is free from his body, now cleansed and far removed from the bestial level he had fallen into; he is freed from temporality as he receives the body of Christ and feels infused with a sense of the eternal.

> He knelt before the altar with his classmates, holding the altar cloth with them over a living rail of hands. His hands were trembling, and his soul trembled as he heard the priest pass with the ciborium from communicant to communicant.
> —Corpus Domini nostri.
> Could it be? He knelt there sinless and timid: and he would hold upon his tongue the host and God would enter his purified body.
> —In vitam eternam. Amen.
> Another life! A life of grace and virtue and happiness! It was true. It was not a dream from which he would wake. The past was past.
> —Corpus Domini nostri.
> The ciborium had come to him. (P, 146)

At the end of the book Stephen stands at a different altar and before a different god. Yet what he prays for is not so different: he still wants to be rid of his earthliness, to soar freely away from the desires and loathings of his body, to transcend temporality and enjoy the stasis of aesthetic contemplation.

These passages indicate an overall pattern in *A Portrait*; but this pattern is largely Stephen's. It is through him that Joyce narrates the story; for the most part the reader sees only what Stephen deems sufficiently important to merit his attention. In keeping with his desire to create an order out of the chaos of experience, Stephen's imagination selects those incidents and perceptions which when molded together form a coherent whole. Since Stephen's overriding perception of himself is that of one born to serve the ends of art, he looks upon his life as a series of experiences held together by a center, that center being Stephen's own ability to rise aesthetically above the unpleasantness of reality and to dwell in a region reserved for the sensitive artist. In spite of this selectivity, however, the reader can detect contradictions unheeded by Stephen. A closer look at two of the passages just quoted will suffice to illustrate this point. Stephen's experiences at the communion railing and on the beach are in many respects analogous. In both instances he feels liberated and is elated by a renewed sense of life. Yet, these sensations are the result of a withdrawal from life. In the third chapter Stephen's withdrawal takes the form of a disgust for his body and all its normal appetitive inclinations. When he is purged, through confession, of all the sins which defile him, he believes that he enjoys a freedom so unreal as to be dreamlike. And, indeed, it is a dream; for no man, not even the holiest, can live as if he has no body. Stephen learns that soon enough, but before too long he resorts to an angelic disembodiment once again—this time under the guise of the artistic priesthood. When he imaginatively takes leave of his earthbound friends and leaves the flow of existence behind him, he once again hails life. It is obvious that Stephen fails to understand the meaning of life. He seems to think of life as something ethereal and trancelike. He persistently tries to disengage himself from existence and at the same time insists on calling his angelic state of detachment "life". What the reader sees, and Stephen does not see, is that the order Stephen imposes on his world is forged; it is an order obtained by sleight of irony. Thus, wherever the sordid world presents itself in all its unpleasantness and disorder, Stephen seems capable of either transcending it or finding in it a clue to his artistic destiny. To the reader, however, the presentation of Stephen's milieu in the utmost naturalistic detail serves another purpose. It highlights the distinction between life and art and Stephen's confusion of the two.

After each of the concluding scenes described above, the reader is let down, or better, he is brought down to earth. One would like to see Stephen rise above his seedy circumstances, but soon one realizes that seedy circumstances are the stuff of which life is made. No sooner does the first chapter wind up in an aura of subdued tranquillity than the second chapter opens with the foul smell of Uncle Charles's tobacco. The idyllic scenes of the previous chapter are gone as the playgrounds of Clongowes are replaced by the backgarden with its un-Edenic reeking outhouse. In similar fashion, the lyrical language which concludes the second chapter gives way to the harsh vulgarities of Dublin's red-light district; the low whisper of the tides grates against the dregs of watery tea and the revolting greasiness of fried bread. For Stephen these incongruities are merely grist to the artist's mill; out of them he concocts a unified whole. The fried bread and the unpleasant memories of Clongowes are welded together. "The yellow dripping had been scooped out like a boghole and the pool under it brought back to his memory the dark turf coloured water of the bath of Clongowes" (*P*, 174). What the reader sees as a disjointed and dislocated life, Stephen perceives as a mosaic of interrelated incidents. The reader can find no center to hold together the troubled strife-ridden Ireland and the disintegrating fabric of the Dedalus household. Stephen places himself at the center and with his imagination holds all the pieces in order. While his father and great uncle discuss the confused state of Irish politics, Stephen dreams of his Messianic calling. "The hour when he too would take part in the life of that world seemed drawing near and in secret he began to make ready for the great part which he felt awaited him the nature of which he only dimly apprehended" (*P*, 62). As the novel progresses his vision becomes clearer and more defined, but his link with actuality becomes increasingly tenuous. Stephen's engagement in life diminishes in direct proportion to his growth as an aesthete, so that by the end he is so aloof that life can hardly touch him. This is inevitable, for if he wants to make order out of chaos he has to abandon the confusion, and by doing so he also gets away from the concomitant pain and discomfort. In Sartre's *Nausea*, Roquentin reflects on how man "tries to live his own life as if he were telling a story," and he realizes that "you have to choose: live or tell."[33] Stephen chooses to tell, and therefore he falsifies life, not merely because he changes matter into words, but because he wants to make out of temporal existence a fixed, immutable aesthetic object.

Stephen releases himself from involvement and participation in the world around him by transforming life into an aesthetic experience. He objectifies life, crystallizes change in a fixed moment of apprehension; in other words he spatializes time by giving it form. This has been recognized by Joycean critics from the start. What has not been generally recognized is that *A Portrait* is also an analysis and a critique of the ironic imagination which enables the aesthete to assume a posture of detachment. Stephen's aesthetic theory has proved so appealing that many readers have accepted it and regard the novel as a perfect exposition and a perfect example of that theory. Hence, the vicious circle of interpretation in which Joycean criticism has been, for the most part, entrapped. But this vicious circle did not originate with *A Portrait*.

The substitution of one *Weltanschauung* for another can be seen at work in the critical as well as the creative writings of the turn of the century. Numerous essays on *A Portrait* offer ample illustration of this movement. Quite interestingly, Stephen Dedalus himself is fully aware of the two alternatives and he provides a brief outline of the positivist approach before he expounds discursively on his preference for an unworldly aesthetic theory based on irony. In response to Lynch's blunt question, "What is beauty?", Stephen proposes to approach the question by using female beauty as an example. Different people admire different types of female beauty. This, according to Stephen, "seems to be a maze out of which we cannot escape." The complexity of the labyrinth, however, does not daunt him any more than it did Daedalus. He sees "two ways out," the first of which is a mechanistic explanation of beauty and physical attraction.

> One is this hypothesis: that every physical quality admired by men in women is in direct connection with the manifold functions of women for the propagation of the species. It may be so. The world, it seems, is drearier than even you, Lynch, imagined. For my part I dislike that way out. It leads to eugenics rather than to esthetic. It leads you out of the maze into a new gaudy lectureroom where MacCann, with one hand on *The Origin of Species* and the other hand on the new testament, tells you that you admired the flanks of Venus because you felt she would bear you burly offspring and admire her great breasts because you felt that she would give good milk to her children and yours. (*P*, 208–209)

Stephen presents his version of scientific determinism in a very unappealing manner. Clearly, his sympathies lie elsewhere. He finds the emphasis on the mechanical distasteful and, therefore, he contrasts "eugenics" unfavourably with "esthetic," inferring that the latter transcends the drab materialism of the former. He does not, however, object to MacCann's de-sexing or de-eroticising of the male attraction to the female body; after all, Stephen's own poetic efforts stem from a delight in words and not from sexual attraction. Furthermore, Stephen's whole theory, based on stasis, entails the banishment of desire and loathing from the pursuit of beauty. What Stephen finds lacking in the first hypothesis is that element of other-worldly radiance, that spiritual sensation which he associates with the apprehension of beauty. There is, in this respect, a strange incongruity in MacCann's association of Darwin's work and the New Testament. Darwin's work, the textbook of materialistic determinism, was seen to embody, quintessentially, the scientific intellectualism against which the aesthetic movement revolted at the turn of the century. Stephen cannot be expected to look kindly on the accommodation of such views within a religious system. He is too fond of the mystery of things to embrace a religion or the teachings of religious educators which diluted that mystery and interpreted it in mundane terms. There is hidden here a clue for the understanding of Stephen's rejection of his country's religion in favor of an aesthetic theory couched in the language of that same religion. Stephen, it seems, rebels against the naturalization of the supernatural. His aesthetic theory preserves the element of the supernatural in an aesthetic, pseudoreligious, not to say mystical, context.

After the raucous interruption by the dray, Stephen proceeds to the second hypothesis, the one he favors.

> —This hypothesis, Stephen repeated, is the other way out: that, though the same object may not seem beautiful to all people, all people who admire a beautiful object find in it certain relations which satisfy and coincide with the stages themselves of all esthetic apprehension. These relations of the sensible, visible to you through one form and to me through another, must be therefore the necessary qualities of beauty. Now, we can return to our old friend saint Thomas for another pennyworth of wisdom. (*P*, 209)

A series of digressions prevents Stephen from pursuing his explanation for a while. At the first opportunity, however, he picks up the thread of his argument and returns to Thomistic wisdom.

> —To finish what I was saying about beauty, said Stephen, the most satisfying relations of the sensible must therefore correspond to the necessary phases of artistic apprehension. Find these and you find the qualities of universal beauty. Aquinas says: *ad pulcritudinem tria requiruntur, integritas, consonantia, claritas. I translate it so: Three things are needed for beauty, wholeness, harmony, and radiance.* (*P*, 211–212)

Stephen's aesthetic theory, based on *integritas, consonantia,* and *claritas,* excludes the functionalism as well as the materialism of the first hypothesis. Universal beauty, in Stephen's mind, is not tied to physical laws and is divorced from any kind of social framework or cultural context. The aesthetic image, or the work of art, is autonomous; it has a purely internal harmony and is the sole source of its own radiance. Since it has no reference outside itself, it does not lend itself to a practical purpose, such as eugenics, for example. The work of art does not form part of a larger design, nor does it depend upon anything external to it; it is autotelic. For these reasons the apprehension of the aesthetic image produces

an utterly spiritual state which bears no relation to the purposeful and
the didactic. Yet, Stephen's theory has one thing in common with the
positivistic hypothesis he dismisses so sarcastically by caricaturing Mac-
Cann. What the two have in common is the establishment of a wholeness, a universal. MacCann explains man's attractions to female beauty
in terms of a universal biological law, a law that gives coherence to human
behavior. For MacCann, order is to be found in the natural law which
governs the whole of creation. Stephen finds order and coherence in the
aesthetic image. Both views are, in the widest sense, metaphysical. In
addition to order, however, Stephen also finds radiance, an element absent from the dreary laws of the positivists. Stephen's experience of the
physical world reveals chaos to him, not universal laws. He cannot, therefore, find in the material world the order he craves. Indeed, it is the disintegration of the material world around him that sets him on the quest for
beauty. The laws of science did not hold, for Stephen and many of his contemporaries, the answers they were looking for. They, therefore, turned
their sights elsewhere—but they still looked for order, which is what
science purported, futilely, to offer them. They found this order in a
transcendental art which relied on the abstract and the geometric to dis-
sociate itself from the phenomenal world of scientific concern. Stephen
Dedalus would, no doubt, have preferred the Venus of Praxiteles to be
geometric, or else more abstract and less suggestive of the carnal. For, as
Wilhelm Worringer pertinently observes,

> all transcendental art sets out with the aim of de-organicising the organic,
> i.e., of translating the mutable and conditional into values of unconditional
> necessity. But such a necessity man is able to feel only in the great world
> beyond the living, in the world of the inorganic. This led him to rigid lines,
> to inert crystalline form. He translated everything into the language of
> these imperishable values. For these abstract forms, liberated from finite-
> ness, are the only ones, and the highest, in which man can find rest from the
> confusion of the world picture.[34]

Worringer also points out that in the course of the evolution of art in
the Western world, "Science emerged, and transcendental art lost
ground."[35] He wrote this in an appendix to *Abstraktion und Einfuhlung* which
was first published in 1908, but was completed two years earlier. The
appended essay, "Transcendence and Immanence in Art," was included in
the third edition of the work which appeared in 1910. His statement,
then, is a fair description of the situation in the earliest years of this
century. But already, by then, scientific positivism was losing ground
while the transcendental element in art was being re-emphasized; and

Worringer himself exercised a significant influence in bringing this change about. Stephen Dedalus resembles many early twentieth-century artists and critics who were attempting to recover the pre-scientific and pre-naturalistic approach to art. Their art is similar, if not identical, to what Worringer calls "non-Classical, i.e., transcendental art." His description of the impulse behind this art, which he associates with the "ancient aristocracy of the Orient," is easily applicable to the *fin-de-siècle* aesthetes.

> Inextricably drawn into the vicissitudes of ephemeral appearances, the soul knows here only *one* possibility of happiness, that of creating a world beyond appearance, an absolute, in which it may rest from the agony of the relative. Only when the deceptions of appearance and the efflorescent caprice of the organic have been silenced, does redemption wait.[36]

The fragmentary world of appearances is the fallen world. The act of redemption consists of putting the pieces together again; the fragments must somehow be forged into an integral whole. Worringer suggests that this can be done only by transcending matter and reaching the purer level of the spirit—the level of angels. The religious vocabulary he uses is not incidental; he conceives of the transcendental impulse—the urge to abstraction—as a religious drive, or else an impulse analogous to the religious. Redemption has inescapable religious connotations and in transcendental art the redemptive act is the achievement of wholeness. Within this frame of reference, the artist who attains wholeness, harmony, and radiance is a redeemer, as well as a redeemed man. Stephen Dedalus considers it his messianic calling to liberate man's spirit from the shackling chaos of actuality and to give shape (i.e., form) to that chaos.

Stephen, in the tradition of neo-Platonism, associates the disunity of the material world with the corruptibility of matter, especially as manifested most intensely in mortality. Man's fall is a fall into matter from the unity of the spirit. Redemption takes the form of a liberation from the fallen material world, a defiance of death. In the resurrection from the dead, therefore, lies the supreme proclamation of redemption. Christ redeemed fallen man by way of a self-sacrificial act, but his death would have had no meaning had it not been for his resurrection. In the words of St. Paul, "If this [resurrection] were not true, what do people hope to gain by being baptised for the dead?" (*I Cor.* 15:29). Stephen's self-consecration to the priesthood of art at the Bull is marked by a metaphoric parallelism to Christ's resurrection. "His soul had risen from the grave of boyhood, spurning her graveclothes" (*P*, 170). Through his ironic imagination he rises above the world of mortality; his soul is freed from mutability. He will also free the rest of creation through his art as he proposes to take gross matter and from it "would create proudly out of the freedom and power of his soul, as the great artificer whose name he bore, a living thing, new and soaring and beautiful, impalpable, imperishable" (*P*, 170). Notwithstanding the direct reference to Daedalus, the model Stephen has in mind is primarily Christ. In fact, his notion of the soul's infusing creation with a spiritual, imperishable life is derived directly from St. Paul's discussion of the significance of Christ's resurrection.

> It is the same with the resurrection of the dead: the thing that is sown is perishable but what is raised is glorious; the thing that is sown is weak but what is raised is powerful; when it is sown it embodies the soul, when it is raised it embodies the spirit.
>
> If the soul has its own embodiment, so does the spirit have its own embodiment. The first *man*, Adam, as scripture says, *became a living soul*; but the last Adam has become a life-giving spirit. That is, first the one with the soul, not the spirit, and after that, the one with the spirit. The first man, being from the earth, is earthly by nature; the second man is from heaven. As this earthly man was, so are we on earth; and as the heavenly man is, so are we in heaven. And we, who have been modelled on the earthly man, will be modelled on the heavenly man.
>
> Or else, brothers, put it this way: flesh and blood cannot inherit the kingdom of God: and the perishable cannot inherit what lasts forever. I will tell you something that has been secret: that we are not all going to die, but we shall all be changed. This will be instantaneous, in the twinkling of an eye, when the last trumpet sounds. It will sound and the dead will be raised, imperishable, and we shall be changed as well, because our present perishable nature must put on imperishability and this mortal nature must put on immortality. (*I Cor.* 15:42–53)

The scriptural passage is quoted at length to illustrate how closely Stephen identifies himself with Christ. He is the second Adam, a "life-giving spirit," raised above the rest and transformed. He does not wait for the trumpets of the last judgement when the saints are raised and transformed instantaneously, "in the twinkling of an eye," just as Stephen is "purified in a breath" (*P*, 169). Meanwhile, his earthly acquaintances retain their mortality, but Stephen is "modelled on the heavenly man," Daedalus. He was weak like them, but now that he is raised he has become powerful. Whereas they dive from "their divingstone, poised on its rude supports and rocking under their plunges" (*P*, 168) into the sea of life, Stephen rises from "the stoneblock for he could no longer quench the flame in his blood" (*P*, 170). Shuley, Ennis, and Connolly," corpsewhite or suffused with a pallid golden light" (*P*, 168), are wet and cold; Stephen, "his cheeks aflame and his throat throbbing with song" (*P*, 170), is "radiant and commingled with the element of the spirit" (*P*, 169).

A comparison of Stephen with Christ may be carried even further. There are very conspicuous differences between the two, though, and these differences have a direct bearing on any consideration of Stephen's aesthetic theory, for they reveal its serious shortcomings. First of all, the sacrificial element of the redemptive act is blatantly absent. It is true that Stephen is hailed as "Bous Stephaneforos" (*P*, 168). He is the garlanded poet being led to the sacrifice like a bull; but no real sacrifice takes place. Stephen as the sacrificial bull is not any more real than the fairy tale moocow that met baby tuckoo or the cow Daedalus made for Queen Pasiphae. Everything occurs on a purely symbolic level supported by allusions to the mythical Daedalus and a figurative association with Christ. This has the effect, on the one hand, of elevating Stephen to the universalized level of myth, and on the other hand, of annulling the historical reality of Christ by putting him on a par with a mythical figure. The fundamental importance of Christ's actual suffering and death disappears in this context. Stephen connects his sudden apotheosis with Christ's resurrection. Yet Christ did not gain redemption by means of his resurrection, but by his incarnation, suffering and death. Christ became incarnate; he went through the process of human life, and he physically died *before* he earned his resurrection. Stephen's transformation consists of an imaginary disembodiment—an antithesis to the incarnation. He wishes to get rid of his human situation; he seeks redemption without physical death. He does not want to live in history and go through the normal travails of life, for it is precisely the pain involved in the process of running the course of life that drives him to employ irony in the service of a transcendental aestheticism.

It might be adduced in Stephen's favor that he undergoes the pain of severing his ties with family and country in order to pursue his calling. But Stephen takes this drastic step only because he wants to be rid of everything that ties him to the actual world of duty, responsibility, and obligation. His abandonment of all that is close to him is governed by an overwhelming desire for detachment from a life of existential involvement. In addition, Stephen assumes the priesthood but shuns baptism. It is the sacrament of baptism that Christ made available by his death. Fallen man is submerged into the water just as Christ submerged himself into the darkness of death. Stephen, however, avoids the water; he is terrified by the very thought of immersion into it. He wants to hover above it, not be drowned in it. Although there can be no sharing of eternity without death, Stephen seeks a "real" eternity without a "real" death. Since he opts for angelism he cannot be a Christic figure. While he seems familiar with St. Paul's discussion of the resurrection, he is either ignorant of the Pauline teaching on angels or deliberately forgets it.

> Since all the children share the same blood and flesh, he too shared equally in it . . . For it was not the angels that he took to himself; he took to himself descent from Abraham. It was essential that he should in this way become completely like his brothers so that he could be a compassionate and trustworthy high priest of God's religion, able to atone for human sins. That is, because he has himself been through temptation he is able to help others who are tempted. (*Heb.* 2:14–18)

One thing, above all else, Stephen adamantly refuses to do is "become completely like his brothers." The idea of being a member of a larger family repels Stephen. When made aware of a vocation of becoming a Jesuit, Stephen is at first thrilled by the singular privilege such a calling, if accepted, would bestow upon him. Soon he realizes, however, that he must decline because "of the pride of his spirit which had always made him conceive of himself as being apart in every order" (*P*, 161). His true calling, he reflects, is to be different and unique, an individual set apart from the rest. "His destiny was to be elusive of social or religious orders. . . . He was destined to learn his own wisdom apart from others or to learn the wisdom of others himself wandering among the snares of the world" (*P*, 162). Stephen cultivates his aloneness from his youngest days, and he never wavers from it. Nevertheless, he deceives himself when he equates his aloofness with a romantic vision of himself "wandering among the snares of the world." What the world has to offer is poverty, disorder, and vulgarity, which Stephen tries to ward off by standing apart. In fact, the irrepressible disorder of his family prevents him from developing a sense of brotherhood even with his blood relatives. "He felt that he was hardly of the one blood with them but stood to them rather in the mystical kinship of fosterage, fosterchild and fosterbrother" (*P*, 98). The phrase "mystical kinship" has a hollow ring. If it carries the suggestion that he felt a spiritual rather than a physical bond to his family, it is false. During his intensely pious stage, when Stephen believes he is most religious, he is incapable of becoming "completely like his brothers." "To merge his life in the common tide of other lives was harder for him than any fasting or prayer, and it was his constant failure to do this to his satisfaction which caused in his soul at least a sensation of spiritual dryness together with a growth of doubts and scruples" (*P*, 151–152).

The prolongation of spiritual drought intensifies Stephen's doubts; he becomes increasingly unsure of his elevated sense of grace. "The clear certitude of his own immunity grew dim and to it succeeded a vague fear that his soul had really fallen unawares" (*P*, 153). Stephen turns to religion to find a haven from the pains of existence, but his spiritual life presents him with two problems he desperately wants to avoid. First, he is expected to gain brotherly love, and second, he is beset by doubt. It may be that the second is the result of his failure to accomplish the first requirement, though not necessarily so. The Christian ascetic testifies to the strength of his faith, not in the radiant light of mystical union, but in the dreadful darkness of spiritual aridity. In any case, Stephen does not get from religion what he most desires; therefore, it is quite natural that when summoned by the spiritual director at Belvedere, during the time he is beset by doubts and scruples, he does not see in the priestly calling the fulfillment of his ambitions. Soon afterward, however, he finds the priesthood that appeals to him in an absolute and unequivocal manner. The artistic calling endows him with uniqueness and wipes out his harrowing doubts and scruples. Stephen's aesthetic vision purifies him in a way that the spiritual progress of the genuine ascetic cannot. In ascetic literature the purgative stage of the soul on its way to God is described as a period of darkness, or as St. John of the Cross calls it, "*una noche oscura.*" Stephen, by contrast, is purged by light, his doubts removed in a flash. In an instant he is "delivered of incertitude and made radiant" (*P*, 169). But this is a cold radiance; it has none of the warmth of love, which Stephen seems incapable of harboring. The closest Stephen comes to an immediate and vivid awareness of love is during his ascetic period. But even then he conceives the supreme virtue in cold and abstract geometric terms. "The world for all its solid substance and complexity no longer existed for his soul save as a theorem of divine power and universality" (*P*, 150). It is important to note how Stephen resorts to a spatial image which engages his sight and has little, if any, effect on his feelings. As in the aesthetic theory, Stephen is heavily dependent on sight as opposed to the other senses. The various senses, especially smell, are associated with the mundane, the earthliness Stephen wants to rise above. As his soul gets nearer beauty or God, the senses are discarded, except for sight which is privileged because it provides the window through which the radiance penetrates, and also because it is the sense by which the spatial image is apprehended and contemplated. Sight belongs more to the soul than to the body. "Gradually, as his soul was enriched with spiritual knowledge, he saw the whole world forming one vast symmetrical expression of God's power and love" (*P*, 149).

Stephen's use of religious terminology in his formulation of the aesthetic theory highlights the discrepancies between religion and aesthetics. One sees that by setting up his theory Stephen is escaping those elements of religion with which he cannot cope. Central to the aesthetic theory is the solitariness of the artist whose detachment from human involvements is supposedly complete. It is a theory that enables Stephen to justify his pride and make a virtue of his unwillingness or inability to love. William York Tindall put it very succinctly. "The trouble with Stephen is pride."[37] Far from transubstantiating a religious attitude into a spiritual aesthetic theory, Stephen merely manipulates religious vocabulary to fit that theory which suits him best. This constitutes, at best, a brilliant sleight of mind which might dazzle one, as a magician does, into not perceiving the forgery that is being perpetrated. It is a remarkable feat on Joyce's part that he faithfully portrays Stephen's intellectual tour de force without any obtrusive authorial comment, while at the same time he subtly enables his reader to see through Stephen's shamming. The connection between religion and aesthetics does not hold, and since Stephen's aesthetic theory relies so heavily on its religious content, it, too, fails to convince. Robert J. Andreach, upon examining Stephen's spiritual development in the light of the Christian mystical tradition, finds that Stephen's spiritual life is regressive. "Since the orthodox spiritual life is reversed and inverted, since Stephen suffers from the cause of a blighted spiritual life, and, what is most important, since he does not create art after the composition of the juvenile villanelle, the conclusion must be that his spiritual development is all wrong."[38]

Religion and aesthetics are two inseparable elements in *A Portrait*, just as they are in Stephen's theorizing. This is necessarily so because the novel is in a sense written by Stephen Dedalus. Joyce's original intention to append to the novel the signature "Stephanus Daedalus pinxit"[39] was entirely appropriate. Stephen sees a close relationship between religion and aesthetics because, to his way of thinking, both point towards transcendence and stem from the same metaphysical ideal. But there is a strong element in the Christian religion which is nonmetaphysical; it is that element which is so strongly emphasized in Ignatian spirituality. Christ's humanity, most particularly his incarnation in historical time, renders suspect the appropriateness of Stephen's association of religion with an aesthetic posture of exalted indifference and disdain for common humanity.

The discrepancy between a religion founded on the recognition that temporality is the necessary context of man's redemption and an aesthetic religion which in extolling perfection denigrates the imperfection of the incarnate world marks a breach in Stephen's position, and as such it offers a point of departure for a critique of Stephen's metaphysical aesthetic irony and its traditional foundations. This discrepancy has been noticed by some critics, but its full implications have not been thoroughly traced. William York Tindall, for instance, finds it "apparent that, proclaiming static art, free from morality, Stephen's theory displays his aloof inhumanity," whereas Joyce, "plainly moral and humane in purpose and substance," produced work which "must be distinguished sharply from the theory of his inconsistent aesthete." Yet, Tindall also maintains that "Joyce's morality is general and, like his irony, distancing."[40] This confuses the issue since ironic distance is the reason for Stephen's aloof inhumanity. If Joyce, like his fictional creature, stands above or hovers over the world of immediate actuality, then he, too, inhabits a realm detached from the world of temporality in which humankind is caught up. Tindall compounds the problem when he illustrates Joyce's distancing technique by quoting a passage which typifies Stephen's penchant for abandoning the concrete in favor of an unreal and intangible vision. In this passage Stephen transforms into a poem his experience with E. C. on the tram.

> During this process all those elements which he deemed common and insignificant fell out of the scene. There remained no trace of the tram itself nor of the trammen nor of the horses: nor did he and she appear vividly. The verses told only of the night and the balmy breeze and the maiden lustre of the moon. (*P*, 70)

Here, as on many other occasions, Stephen takes an incident that occurred at a very specific place and time and transforms it into a romantic dream which lacks context and is set in an atemporal "once upon a time" world. It is Stephen's mode of claiming victory over the world of existential experience through aesthetic irony. He transubstantiates that world into words because he can love words in a way he can never love the world and its human inhabitants.

This method of Stephen's, rather than resembling Joyce's, stands in sharp contrast to it. The minute detail which evokes a vivid sense of actuality for the reader of *A Portrait* disappears the moment Stephen transforms his experiences into poetry or poetic visions. This is an unavoidable consequence of Stephen's aesthetic inclination. He does not want to dwell in the world of the particular; he generalizes in order to find the universal. The world of the particular changes and is, therefore, uncomfortable, whereas universal principles are eternal and absolute. Stephen's pursuit of the universal is so singleminded that he spares no interest or care for the particular. He changes details or leaves them out capriciously; he also distorts facts arbitrarily. The "common and the insignificant" trammen drop out of sight in his poetic production because they are of no use to him. E. C. ceases to be a real person as Stephen fictionalizes her and the real experience he has shared with her. On the tram he knows that he "could hold her and kiss her." But, in fact, "he did neither"

(*P*, 70). His poem, however, tells a different story. "Some undefined sorrow was hidden in the hearts of the protagonists as they stood in silence beneath the leafless trees and when the moment of farewell had come the kiss, which has been withheld by one, was given by both" (*P*, 70–71). This amounts to what Kierkegaard calls "the special pursuit of irony: to cancel all actuality and set in its place an actuality that is no actuality."[41] The reader is made aware of Stephen's ironic distancing by the discordance between the actuality surrounding Stephen and his obliviousness to it. Just before he writes the poem "To E-C-" Stephen recalls the time "in Bray the morning after the discussion at the Christmas dinnertable, trying to write a poem about Parnell on the back of one of his father's second moiety notices" (*P*, 70). Stephen removes himself from the political confusion of Ireland, the painful divisions it causes within his family, and his father's financial problems even when they are closest to him, and he indulges in a purely imaginative exercise. The effect of this ironic posture is best described by Kierkegaard: "When the imagination is allowed to rule in this way it prostrates and anaesthetises the soul, robs it of all moral tension, and makes life a dream."[42]

The ironic imagination also deprives the soul of its capacity for love. The distancing required by irony and the human involvement necessitated by love are two antithetical movements. Stephen can never love E. C.; he can only observe her detachedly. When he was with her on the tram, "he stood listlessly in his place, seemingly a tranquil watcher of the scene before him" (*P*, 69). The composition of the poem is merely the formalization of his detachment. One cannot help noticing the total absence of love in Stephen, and the close connection between his coldness and his unswervingly ironic stance. A remarkable incongruity thrusts itself upon the reader's attention when Stephen opens and concludes his writings with religious mottos. "From force of habit he had written at the top of the first page the initial letters of the jesuit motto: A. M. D. G." (*P*, 70). And when he concludes the poem, "the letters L. D. S. were written at the foot of the page" (*P*, 71). The letters he inscribes are inappropriate not because they bracket a poem celebrating profane love, but because they belong to a religion which regards love as the supreme virtue, while Stephen's aesthetic impulse is utterly devoid of love. For Stephen the external trappings of religion have lost all reference to the genuine tenets of faith. His use of religious terms should not be mistaken for a sign of any real connection between his thinking and religion. Stephen's poetry is characterized by aloofness, self-satisfaction, and pride, whereas the phrases *Ad Maiorem Dei gloriam* and *Laus Deo Semper* are humble expressions of praise to and adoration of God. Stephen cannot praise God while he is usurping God's prerogative; rather, he employs irony to divest himself of his humanity and assume godhood.

It makes no sense to say that Joyce, unlike Stephen, is humane but that he is also, like Stephen, ironic. Yet, there is a sense in which Joyce is ironic, as Tindall makes evident in his discussion on art and forgery. "As forger, then, one thing to himself, another to Joyce, Stephen is ambiguous at best. Deceiving himself maybe and the simpler reader, he does not deceive ironic Joyce—or envious Gogarty for that matter."[43] The apparent contradictions inherent in Tindall's exposition can be resolved only by differentiating between Stephen's irony and Joyce's. This can be done with the help of Kierkegaard's notion of "mastered irony." Stephen's irony is unmastered. It abandons the limitations of human finitude and hovers in a dream world of infinite possibility. For Stephen, "poetry is victory over the world," not because his irony enables him to bring about a reconciliation of the world and the imagination, but rather because it leads him to "an abandonment of . . . actuality."[44] The careful reader of *A Portrait* knows that "no transubstantiation of the given actuality occurs" when Stephen transforms his experiences into poetry. What really occurs is a substitution. Joyce is not fooled, either; through *A Portrait* he brings the reader to an awareness of the human situation in actuality. Joyce is conscious of the fact, made explicit by Heidegger, that "Possibility, as an *existentiale*, does not signify a free-floating potentiality-for-Being in the sense of the 'liberty of indifference' (*libertas indifferentia*)."[45] It is Stephen, not Joyce, who by means of irony appropriates the "liberty of indifference" and entertains aesthetic visions of infinite possibility.

Joyce's is a mastered irony. He pulls his reader back from Stephen's "aesthetic stupor"[46] and brings actuality forcefully forward to undercut his protagonist's angelic flights. He emphasizes, albeit indirectly, that which Stephen is all too willing to let recede into vague oblivion. In this respect, Joyce's mastered irony distinguishes itself from Stephen's irony. This is how Kierkegaard describes mastered irony:

> Irony as a mastered moment exhibits itself in its truth precisely by the fact that it teaches us to actualize actuality, by the fact that it places due emphasis upon actuality. This cannot mean that it wishes quite St. Simonistically to idolize actuality, nor does it deny that there is, or at least that there ought to be, in every human being a longing for a higher and more perfect. But this longing must not hollow out actuality; on the contrary, the content of life must become a true and meaningful moment in the higher actuality whose fullness the soul desires. Actuality in this way acquires its validity—not as a purgatory, for the soul is not to be purified in such a way that it flees blank, bare, and stark naked out of life—but as a history wherein con-

sciousness successively outlives itself, though in such a way that happiness consists not in forgetting all this but becomes present in it. Accordingly, when romanticism longs for a higher, this may well be true; but as man shall not put asunder what God has joined together, so neither shall man join together what God has put asunder, for such a sickly longing is simply an attempt to have the perfect before its time. . . .

. . . When irony has been mastered it no longer believes, as do certain clever people in daily life, that something must always be concealed behind the phenomenon.[47]

Joyce moves away from unmastered irony in a novel written from the point of view of a fledgling aesthete whose overriding goal is to coerce life and experience into a harmonious radiant form and to retreat by way of the ironic imagination into a solitary world of perfect beauty. In this regard, *A Portrait* shares a basic similarity with Kierkegaard's pseudonymous works. Joyce reveals some of the same things Kierkegaard reveals in his writings, namely that an aesthetic view of the world takes no account of the temporal dimension of man, and that even though aestheticism may be couched in the vocabulary of Christianity it is in fact irreligious. Irony and Christian belief must not be confused. If at times they do not appear to be far apart it is only because irony "even fancied becoming a Christian."[48] Irony, if not mastered, cannot be Christian because it dispenses with history which is the sole vehicle of redemption, and also because the "ironist is reserved and stands aloof; he lets mankind pass before him, as did Adam the animals, and finds no companionship for himself."[49] Human love, or charity, is a virtue the ironic poet cannot afford to nourish. The moment he engages himself in history, the aesthete quits the elevated seat from which he watches history. The moment he loves, the aesthete loses the ability to watch the spectacle of human love. One cannot be a spectator and a participant at once.

Stephen's "image of irony is," William F. Lynch correctly observes, "deep in the mood of the modern intelligence, again preventing it from a real affection for the more miserable parts of itself and the world." William Lynch, however, is shocked to find this image of irony espoused by Joyce who, he asserts, "could perhaps say it more easily in a theory like the following [he quotes, "The Artist like the God of Creation . . ."] from *A Portrait of the Artist as a Young Man* than when writing the great soliloquy of Molly Bloom."[50] Although conscious of the dehumanizing effect of irony, he simplistically attributes Stephen's aesthetic theory to Joyce and fails to notice that *A Portrait*, properly read, is as great a reservoir of human interest and care as Molly Bloom's soliloquy in *Ulysses*. The same mistake was committed by an early reviewer of *A Portrait*. In an unsigned review which appeared in *New Age* (12 July 1917), Joyce is reprimanded for his lack of charity, and he is invited "to read that famous thirteenth chapter of Corinthians and apply to himself the teaching."[51] It may well be that Joyce had that very chapter in mind when writing *A Portrait*.

> If I have all the eloquence of men or of angels, but spoke without love, I am simply a gong booming or a cymbal clashing. . . . If I give away all that I possess, piece by piece, and if I even let them take my body and burn it, but am without love, it will do me no good whatever.
>
> Love is always patient and kind; it is never jealous; love is never boastful or conceited; it is never rude or selfish; it does not take offence, and it is not resentful. (*I Cor.* 13:1–5)

Stephen Dedalus aspires to the eloquence of angels, gives up all his material possessions and personal attachments, but he has no love. He is unkind, conceited, and selfish. Joyce is not uncharitable; rather he reveals in his novel the lovelessness that accompanies the aesthetic search for perfection, a search so intense as to be impatient with and unkind to imperfect humanity. Contrary to what the reviewer in *New Age* asserts, it is not Joyce who "fears to suffer," but Stephen, whose flight from suffering amounts to a flight from love. In his pursuit of aesthetic perfection he disdains the miserable lot of imperfect men-in-the-world.

The same reviewer also objects to the fact that "Stephen Dedalus never becomes a living soul," and "his mind has no apparent relation to his experience." He regards these shortcomings as the inevitable results of "a composition that does not hang together, a creation into which the creator has forgotten to breathe the breath of life." There is a remarkable mixture of blindness and insight in these comments. The reviewer is to a large extent correct in his assessment of Stephen, but blatantly wrong in blaming Joyce for Stephen's faults. In so doing he misses the central feature of the novel: the critique of aesthetic irony and the angelic imagination. Stephen is lifeless because he refuses to live; he remains adamantly a detached dramaturge, an aesthete, an iconographer. If Stephen could help it, this composition would "hang together," for a work of art, according to his aesthetic principles, has to form a coherent whole. Life is messy and fragmentary, and Stephen's is no exception. But from his aesthetic vantage point he strives to organize his life as an orderly process unfolding towards a telos. Because he sees his own life in this fashion, Stephen's existence becomes a work of art and ceases to be a "life", that is, a history. By making a work of art out of his life Stephen might perceive his Being, but he loses sight of his be-ing as process. The *New Age* reviewer wittily remarks that "Samuel hewed Agag to pieces, but the pieces were not Agag; and the fragments here offered of Stephen Dedalus are no substitute for 'a portrait of the artist as a young man.' " It is true that the sequences in *A Portrait* never form a complete portrait, a framed icon. The only icons reside in Stephen's mind. He forces masses of experiences into framed pictures which have the clarity and self-contained unity of symbols and archetypes. Juxtaposed to these frozen images is the disintegrative and formless vital actuality that constantly threatens to disrupt Stephen's aesthetic order and that repeatedly retrieves the reader from the lifeless static patterns of Stephen's imagination. Joyce hews Stephen to pieces as Samuel did Agag. Only God can put Agag together again. Stephen who assumes the role of God tries to put the fragments of his life together, but if he ever succeeds he will still fail to breathe life into it.

A Portrait of the Artist as a Young Man when read temporally, rather than from the end, offers itself as an excellent starting point for a destruction of aesthetic irony. The *New Age* reviewer, however, starts with the assumption that the novel can be a valid work only if it is seen to have a well-wrought form when viewed as a simultaneous whole. His eyes remain closed to the possibility of an antiform, and he is therefore not ready to conceive of a novel which calls into question the very basic notions of aesthetic *integritas* and *consonantia*. Since he is predisposed to look only for form and evaluate the novel with the yardstick of traditional formal paradigms, he is caught in a vicious circle of interpretation. Although very conscious of the absence of human warmth and sensitive to Stephen's remoteness from reality, he remains unaware that these deficiencies are the necessary corollaries of the aesthetics of ironic form. One cannot have a live portrait. A portrait does not partake of the everyday live world; it is a dead, although sometimes a beautiful object. The moment Stephen transforms life into art he gives it a stable form, but he also deprives it of movement and change, since he crystallizes and freezes it into a static object. Not only is art incapable of imparting the breath of life, but it is successful, for Stephen, only when it removes the breath out of life. Nowhere is this made more obvious than in Joyce's *A Portrait*. The force of this incompatibility, however, cannot emerge if the reader persists in looking for a familiar formal structure. The search for form can easily become an obsession so that the success of such a search remains the only criterion employed in evaluating the novel. Such is the case, for example, with Edward Garnett, one of the very earliest readers of *A Portrait*. In his reader's report for the publishers, Duckworth and Company, Garnett deemed *A Portrait* "ably written," but also judged it "too discursive, formless, unrestrained, and ugly things, ugly words, are too prominent." He argued that "the types and characters are well drawn," but the novel too "unconventional." His main objection, though, centered on the novel's lack of form. According to him, it could be salvaged only "if it is pulled into shape and made more definite." And "unless the author will use restraint he will not gain readers." Quite predictably, he found the ending objectionable because it does not bring everything together; rather "at the end of the book there is a complete falling to bits." He suggested that to improve the manuscript "time and trouble [should be] spent on it, to make it a more finished piece of work, to shape it more carefully as the product of the craftsmanship of an artist."[52]

Garnett seems to have believed, like Aristotle, in the primacy of plot. According to this view, the plot holds all the various elements of a novel or a play together, and Aristotle regarded it as the very soul of tragedy. The plot gathers all the details and gives each one a relation to the rest so as to produce a coherent whole. Thus, every single detail gains significance by virtue of its relation to the whole and only in relation to the whole. The plot guides everything towards the governing purpose or *telos*, which is also the meaning of the play or novel. By means of the plot, the artist gives meaning to the particulars, harmonizing them into a large and unified picture. Without a plot the artist cannot represent the universal, because every single element remains isolated and contingent. In the absence of plot there can be no *telos* and, more importantly perhaps, there can be no significant form. The various elements within a work of art move towards a *telos*. The movement ceases and the stasis of completion is attained when the *telos*, that is, the goal of the entire process, is realized. At that point, *ousia*, the essence of a thing, and *eidos*, its form, may be discerned. For, in Aristotle's view, *ousia* and *eidos* are the goals of the process of change, a process which not only ends in a still point, but derives its meaning from that point.[53] It is the task of the artist to disclose the *eidos* by representing reality not in the way it manifests itself in history or nature, but ideally. The poet does away with the isolated particulars and incidental details which make nature appear so formless, and he impresses matter with *eidos*. This act Aristotle calls *poiesis*.[54] In the context of these poetics, which also supply the foundations for Stephen's aesthetic theory, the work of the artist is, therefore, distinguished by form, since it is form that holds the work together and infuses it with meaning—hence, Garnett's identification of form with artistic merit.

It appears probable that both Garnett and the *New Age* reviewer looked for a specific formal structure in *A Portrait*. Their expectations might have led them to search for a causal chain of development in the novel. They did not find any such structural underpinning, and so they concluded that the novel lacked form. This is not to suggest that Joyce's novel is a "well-made piece" in the traditional sense and that these two critics were not sufficiently sophisticated to notice it. One merely suspects that these two readers were doubly conservative and approached Joyce's work with a very traditional frame of reference. This suspicion is generated by the fact that several other early reviewers were impressed by the coherent, though unconventional, shape of *A Portrait*. These reviewers, aware that the traditional positivistic novel was on the wane, regarded Joyce's novel as representative of the new kind of literature which was making strong headway on the European continent. John Macy, reviewing both *Dubliners* and *A Portrait* for *Dial*, placed Joyce among the new generation of English and Irish novelists, who "under the influence of French literature, freed themselves from the cowardice of Victorian fiction and assumed that everything under the sun is proper subject-matter for art." Although Macy is here referring to a shedding of restrictive decorum and prudishness, he is also conscious of a more important trend, namely the privileged position accorded to the novelist. "If the young hero is abnormal and precocious, that is because he is no ordinary boy but an artist, gifted with thoughts and phrases above our common abilities." The artist does not speak the language of ordinary men, and he is not constrained by the inherited tradition. In Joyce, as in the great artists, "the effect of complete possession of the traditional resources of language is combined with an effect of complete indifference to traditional methods of fiction."[55]

John Macy praised Joyce for his ability to include in his work subject matter and details not normally found in a novel, and for his success in making out of this material a work of art. Nobody would argue with the first point, but many found in Joyce's all-inclusiveness the very core of his weakness and failure as an artist. In *Freeman's Journal* Joyce was unfavorably compared to the great masters, who "have not been blind to the aspects of life that Mr. Joyce exploits, but they see them in their proper perspective and do not dwell on them to the exclusion of everything else. They know the value of proportion and the importance of sanity and clear judgment and realize that to see life steadily one must see it whole." Joyce's failure, in the opinion of this reviewer, "is due in a measure to a false theory of aesthetics, but it stems even more from temperamental defects." Joyce's faulty aesthetics and defective temperament reveal themselves in the fact that "despite his repulsion his pen, instead of pointing to the stars overhead, is degraded into a muck-rake."[56] These observations were echoed by J. C. Squire in a much more sympathetic review for the *New Statesman*. He praised Joyce for his honesty, his portrayal of characters, and his remarkable prose; but he also found the unsavory details excessive and unnecessarily shocking. His conclusion: "What Mr. Joyce will do with his power in the future it is impossible to conjecture. I conceive that he does not know himself: that, indeed, the discovery of a form is the greatest problem in front of him. It is doubtful that he will make a novelist."[57]

It is ironic that these critics share the main concerns of Stephen Dedalus. Like the young aspiring artist they are repelled by the unpleasant aspects of the physical world; they look for form and proportion and are suspicious of the heavy reliance on detail. One characteristic of Stephen's aesthetic efforts is the manner in which he disposes of those very details that initially inspire him. The various women he encounters or knows, for instance, all lose their individuality and become symbols or archetypes, or else are merged into a single figure which bears no relation to actuality. Stephen attaches the same importance to form as the reviewer for *Freeman's Journal*. The reviewer probably sympathized with Stephen's aesthetic theory but, quite rightly, he did not attribute that theory to Joyce. At the same time, those elements in the novel which displeased him failed to jar him into the realization that Stephen's escape from the sordidness of reality and his obsessive search for radiant form result in a dehumanization far more disturbing than the disquieting descriptions of nasty smells and unorthodox situations. Like Stephen, he looked to art for a release from everyday life and therefore objected to a novel "which is more reminiscent of the pangs of dyspepsia than of the joy of art."[58] This reviewer, like others, was caught in a vicious circle of interpretation. He noticed the absence of traditional form in the novel, and he was struck by the intrusion of actuality into an artistic realm he normally associated with transcendent pleasure ("pointing to the stars overhead"), but he remained totally blind to the shortcomings of aesthetic irony and the attribution of primacy to form. He approached the novel with a set of expectations which he was not ready to abandon. He could resort only to condemning the novel, which if left uncensured would have challenged the basis of his views on both art and life. The reviewer would have broken out of his vicious circle if he had examined his presuppositions and the tradition from which they were derived. In short, he could have used his prejudices as a source of insight.

There is, at least, one virtue to many of the condemnatory reviews of Joyce's *bildungsroman*: the indignant critics made no attempt to coerce the novel to fit into their set of expectations or their normative canon. A coercion of this nature may be seen at work in the laudatory essays of many other interpreters. For the most part, the early reviewers of *A Portrait* who pronounced the novel successful attributed its success to the formal properties of which its denouncers found no trace. Admittedly, these approving critics looked for a formal structure entirely different from the positivistic plot or the causally sequential unfolding that their deprecatory counterparts demanded. Their concept of form was decidedly iconic, a concept which is not only very similar, if not identical, to Stephen Dedalus's, but is also the cornerstone of the standard description of the Modernist imagination. The iconic form of the work of art, however, is not revealed by *A Portrait*, although Stephen expounds it within the novel itself. The novel was found to conform to this aesthetic paradigm only because those elements of the novel which campaign against it and undercut its formulation were ignored. It seems as if, for these critics, the constant sense of movement and the overriding impression of not-at-homeness, which render Stephen's aesthetic theory so hollow in its escapist acclamation of life and so dehumanized, not to say callous, in its arrogant indifference to the plight of others, were not overwhelmingly present in Joyce's novel. The critics set out expecting a novel written in the new epiphanic or iconic mode, and that is precisely what they found for they were not ready to revise their "fore-project." They saw in Stephen a kindred imagination, or an imagination with which they were familiar and could appropriate. Even if they realized that Joyce and Stephen were different, they did not explore that difference—at least not to the extent of finding hidden in the novel a critique of Stephen and his aesthetics. They somehow made *A Portrait* "work out" in accordance with their aesthetic norms and they applauded it, without realizing that they should have been applauding themselves for the brilliant way in which they forced the novel to fit their preconceptions. Their brilliance had one flaw, however. The interpretations they produced were based on an atemporal reading of the novel. They did not go through the book with an openness that would have disclosed, in the process of reading, the persistence with which actuality bursts through the barriers erected by the aesthetic ironist. Rather, these critics looked at the book from the end; they distanced themselves, as Stephen so often does, to see the book "as a whole."

This distanced posture was adopted and recommended by John Quinn in his review for *Vanity Fair*, which is really a general essay on Joyce and not a detailed discussion of *Dubliners* and *A Portrait*. He praised Joyce lavishly, ranking him a "star of the first magnitude," and placed him in the august company of Yeats, Synge, and others in the "firmament of Irish letters." Quinn was struck by the young novelist's "great sincerity" and "special inventiveness." He attributed to Joyce "a new style" in which "there is no ornament, no rhetoric, nothing declamatory, no compromise, complete realism, and great sincerity." The novel produced by this new style has to be read in a special way. "The book must not be read line by line as a pedant would read it, or as a conventional reviewer would read it, but as a whole, and then one will realise what a fine, hard, great piece of work it is."[59] Quinn's use of the adjective *hard* is worthy of note. T. E.

Hulme insisted that the hard geometric lines of the Byzantine mosaics and paintings were the appropriate models for twentieth-century art, and he prophesied that "a period of dry, hard, classical verse is coming."[60] Worringer, who detected in modern art a movement towards abstraction and away from naturalism, used similar vocabulary. He quoted from Schmarsow's *Grundbegriffe der Kunstwissenschaft* to describe the artist's (in this case the monumental artist's) rendition of pure abstraction. "Forcible accommodation to the framework of cubic form is the first maxim of this monumental endeavour, once the artist has become conscious that it is a matter not of imitating reality, not of representing the living creature in its actions and activities, in its relation to nature, but, on the contrary, of abstracting the constant, of transcribing the living into an immobile, rigid, cold and impenetrable—of recreating it in another, an inorganic nature."[61] Of the urge to abstraction, Worringer wrote that it "finds its beauty in the life-denying inorganic, in the crystalline or, in general terms, in all abstract law and necessity."[62]

The similarity of the vocabulary employed by Worringer, an art historian and critic, and Quinn, a literary critic, sheds light on another feature of the standard definition of Modernism. The distinction among literature, painting, and the plastic arts is blurred. Within literature itself the distinction between fiction and poetry is also blurred, as prose assumes a secondary role. It is not accidental that Quinn hails Joyce as a poet, maintaining that "both Yeats and Joyce are poets."[63] In prose, the unfolding process of language is not very congenial to the sense of instantaneousness assiduously cultivated by the advocates of spatialization and aesthetic irony. The short poem comes much closer to the fixed and graspable wholeness of a framed painting or an immobile statue, and comparisons between literature and the other arts abound in Modernist writing. Stephen Dedalus never stops to reflect on the differences between the movement of language and the fixity of the Venus of Praxiteles. He concentrates on the beauty of individual words or phrases and never dwells on the discursive quality of prose. He also talks of "forging" his work, as if he were a blacksmith or a goldsmith. Yeats's references to the plastic arts in conjuction with literary composition are numerous and well-known. T. E. Hulme's constant references to Byzantine art are consistent with his elevation of the Image and his relegation of "crawling" prose to "a museum where all the old weapons of poetry are kept."[64] More recent critics betray the same tendency. In his essay on "Literary Criticism as a Science", John V. Hogopian equates language with the raw material used by a plastic artist. He points out that "literature is an art whose material is *language*. And just as the other arts radically transform the raw materials with which they work, so literature radically transforms ordinary language. Brancusi's *Bird in Flight* has as much relation to a lump of metallic ore as T. S. Eliot's *Waste Land* has to a lump of ordinary language."[65]

John Quinn himself drew an analogy between Joyce's work and painting. "Joyce's book is like a series of etchings." Further, "to read Joyce is like being in a room hung with noble paintings by Puvis de Chavannes."[66] H. G. Wells similarly resorted to a parallelism with the visual arts. His description of *A Portrait* calls to mind Hulme's association of modern art with Byzantine art, and anticipates the importance attached by Wimsatt to the iconic structure. "Mr. Joyce's book . . . is by far the most living and convincing picture that exists of an Irish Catholic upbringing. It is a mosaic of jagged fragments that does altogether render with extreme completeness the growth of a rather secretive, imaginative boy in Dublin. The techinque is startling, but on the whole it succeeds."[67] By referring to Joyce's novel as a mosaic, Wells distinguishes it from the linear progressive narratives of novelists like himself, Bennett, and Galsworthy, all of whom Virginia Woolf classifies as "materialists." In spite of Joyce's departure from this traditional fictional mode, Wells expressed a favorable opinion of him because he found *A Portrait* had a definite form. Nothing seemed to matter more than form to the reviewers of Joyce's novel. Those who did not find it condemned the novel; those who praised the novel insisted on its formal coherence. Among the latter group was the *Manchester Guardian* reviewer. "Nor for its apparent formlessness should the book be condemned. A subtle sense of art has worked amidst the chaos, making this hither-and-thither record of a young mind and soul . . . a complete and ordered thing."[68]

The comparison with the mosaic is particularly felicitous, for it suggests both the fragments of which the work is made up and the unity which is imposed on the disparate constitutive parts. Its lack of depth implies an emphasis on rigid space and an elimination of movement. The mosaic, especially the icon, also carries strong connotations of a spiritual or religious nature. If Joyce is to be placed in the pantheon of Modernist poets, his work must be shown to possess these iconic qualities. Some of the early reviewers pointed the way and later critics followed. Joseph Frank, the author of the influential essay "Spatial Form in Modern Literature," is representative of the latter group. He finds in Joyce's writings, as in Proust's, Pound's, and Eliot's, a complete spatialization of time.

> Time is no longer felt as an objective, causal progression with clearly marked-out differences between periods; now it has become a continuum in which distinctions between past and present are wiped out. And here we have a striking parallel with the plastic arts. Just as the dimension of depth

has vanished from the sphere of visual creation, so the dimension of historical depth has vanished from the content of the major works of modern literature. Past and present are apprehended spatially, locked in a timeless unity that, while it may accentuate surface differences, eliminates any feeling of sequence by the very act of juxtaposition. . . .

What has occurred, at least as far as literature is concerned, may be described as the transformation of the historical imagination into myth—an imagination for which historical time does not exist, and which sees the actions and events of a particular time only as the bodying forth of eternal prototypes. . . . And it is this timeless world of myth, forming the common content of modern literature, that finds its appropriate aesthetic expression in spatial form.[69]

One must hasten to add that the religious implications suggested by myth are not missed by Joseph Frank. He concludes a brief survey of Worringer's ideas, in an earlier part of the same essay, with the observation that "non-naturalistic styles like Byzantine and Romanesque are produced during periods dominated by religion that rejects the natural world as a realm of evil and imperfection. Instead of depicting the profane vitality of nature with all its temptations, the will-to-art turns towards spatialization; it eliminates mass and corporeality and tries to approximate the eternal, ethereal tranquillity of otherworldly existence."[70]

A more accurately applicable description of Stephen's will-to-art is hard to come by. But when it is applied to Joyce himself one can hardly fail to notice the distortion on which such an application rests. If anything emerges clearly out of *A Portrait* it is the fact that Stephen's spiritualizing of his will-to-art is a hollow glorification of his escapism. In order to place *A Portrait* in the context of an other-worldly iconic art, one has either to ignore in the novel the forceful representation of actuality which constantly drags the reader down from Stephen's rarified aesthetic heights, or to develop the hardness of heart and insensitivity which enable Stephen to look down upon the natural world with the contempt of an ironist. Yet, several critics somehow manage to refer in the same essay to Joyce's sensitivity to the real world and to his sense of the spiritual (by which they mean a gnostic spirituality which regards the world as little better than hell). Virginia Woolf, for instance, finds Joyce's work "most notable" for its "attempts to come closer to life," but she also adds that "Mr. Joyce is spiritual."[71] Ford Madox Ford offers a similar baffling contradiction. He asserts that "Mr. Joyce, the supreme artist, regards with an equal composure—all things." Also, "Mr. Joyce's work is a voyaging on a much higher spiritual plane [than Miss Dorothy Richardson's]." But in the same essay Ford praises *A Portrait* for being a book "of such beauty of writing, such clarity of perception, such a serene love and interest in life, and such charity."[72] Ford claims for Joyce two incompatible characteristics: aloof and indifferent composure and charity. Stephen Dedalus lacks the latter because he strove to attain the former. His aesthetics of ironic indifference require Stephen to forego love and charity. Ford, intent on finding in *A Portrait* a confirmation of his own aesthetics, remains blind to the challenge offered by Joyce's critique of aesthetic distance.

The spirituality frequently discovered in *A Portrait* tends to be little more than a glorified aestheticism. Thus, whenever aestheticism and spirituality are indiscriminately lumped together, the sympathies are always on Stephen's side, and the sources of these sympathies are not examined. This is what leads Hart Crane to his exaggerated approbation of Stephen.

> The character of Stephen Dedalus is all too good for this world. It takes a little experience—a few reactions on his part to understand it, and could this have been accomplished in a detached hermitage, high above the mud, he would no doubt have preferred that residence. *A Portrait of the Artist as a Young Man,* aside from Dante, is spiritually the most inspiring book I have ever read. It is Bunyan raised to art and then raised to the ninth power.

One would find it very difficult to produce a better example of a reader locked in a vicious circle of interpretation. Hart Crane, given all the time till Doomsday, would still find in Stephen a paradigm of the artist, unless in the intervening period he stopped to reflect on his own predisposition to approve of all attempts to get away from the mud of the earth. Crane's aesthetics is very similar to Stephen's and, therefore, he cannot but applaud detachment and aloofness, which for him are not the manifestations of pride but the aspirations of a refined spirit. That is why he pays no attention to and casually dismisses "the most nauseating complaint . . . of immorality and obscenity"[73] made against the book. He does not even deign to look seriously at the most mundane elements in the novel.

The source of such complaints, however, deserves attention. They were uttered by many, including several of those who found merit in *A Portrait*. Virginia Woolf, for one, wondered whether "the emphasis laid perhaps didactically upon indecency contribute[s] to this effect of the angular and isolated."[74] H. G. Wells declared that "Mr. Joyce has a cloacal obsession. He would bring into the general picture of life aspects which modern drainage and modern decorum have taken out of ordinary intercourse and conversation."[75] Those that disapproved of the novel were even more vituperative. The unsigned review in *Everyman* was headlined "A Study in Garbage" and described the novel as "an astonishingly powerful and extraordinary dirty study of the upbringing of a young man by Jesuits." And, "Mr. Joyce is a clever novelist, but we feel he would be at his best in a treatise on drains."[76] According to the anonymous reviewer for *Irish Book Lover*, Joyce's "realism and his violent contrasts—the brothel, the confessional—jar on one's feelings." The same reader put his finger on the very core of the problem presented by Joyce's ostensible obscenity: "Above all, is it Art? We doubt it."[77] This observation is symptomatic of a general inclination to regard art as belonging to a sphere untainted by the least pleasant aspects of the life of the body. It emanates from that same contempt of the world which lies at the heart of Stephen's aesthetic irony. The objections to Joyce's obscenity stem from the realization that he, unlike Stephen, does not make it possible for his reader to assume a safe distance from the work. The desire and loathing which Stephen insists must be stilled by the work of art are roused by Joyce in such a way as to disturb his reader, to jar his expectations, to make him reconsider his views on art and life.

There is a very close connection between the problem of obscenity and the problem of form, as they are raised by *A Portrait*. There is a further connection between these two problems and the treatment of the transcendental impulse behind aesthetic irony in the novel. The unusual handling of these fundamental issues in the same novel is largely responsible for the disarray it caused among the critics. *A Portrait* was found hard to classify, and even harder to analyze conventionally. It is not surprising, therefore, that some critics resorted to comparisons between Joyce and the Russian novelists who were increasingly attracting attention during the early decades of the century. But such comparisons were never elaborate, for it must be recalled that the Russian novels remained for quite some time a great source of bafflement. The Russian novelists did not, of course, receive universal acclamation and Henry James's unfavorable assessment of Tolstoy and Dostoyevsky was by no means idiosyncratic. Interestingly, many of the critics who excoriated Joyce for his poor handling of form seem to echo the sentiments expressed by James in a letter he wrote Hugh Walpole in 1912 on the two great Russian novelists—a similarity which supports the view that the concern with form amounted to an almost blind obsession.

> Form alone *takes*, and holds and preserves, substance—saves it from the welter of helpless verbiage that we swim in as in a sea of tasteless tepid pudding, and that makes one ashamed of an art capable of such degradations. Tolstoi and D. are fluid puddings, though not tasteless, because the amount of their own minds and souls in solution in the broth gives it savour and flavour, thanks to the strong rank quality of their genius and their

experience. But there are all sorts of things to be said of them, and in particular that we see how great a vice is their lack of composition, their defiance of economy and architecture, directly they are emulated and imitated; *then*, as subjects of emulation, models, they quite give themselves away.[78]

Andre Gide, in a lecture on Dostoyevsky, noted that "throughout French literature we find a horror of the formless, a certain impatience with what is not yet formed."[79] That horror is not peculiar to the French, or at least it was not during the latter half of the nineteenth and the early part of the twentieth centuries. Henry James's dissatisfaction with the two Russian novelists is one example of its pervasiveness and the effect it exercised on literary interpretation. There was, of course, nothing startlingly original about this concern with form. Universality and formal structural coherence had been, for as long as one could remember, very basic criteria in the evaluation of art. James distrusted the novels of Tolstoy and Dostoyevsky because their wealth of detail and their concentration on the particular distracted him and frustrated his search for substance. He was not interested in the uniqueness of individual characters or the particularity of situations; he was in search of a still point, some stable "essence" at the center to hold the particulars together. For this reason, he also had a low opinion of Dickens. He considered Dickens inferior to Turgenev (a Russian author James admired immensely), "because his figures are particular without being general; because they are individuals without being types."[80] James, it seems, searched in vain for a metaphysical "substance" in Dickens's works. He elaborated his ideas on Dickens in an essay on *Our Mutual Friend*, where he calls the Victorian writer "the greatest of superficial novelists." Dickens did not "see beneath the surface of things" (that is to say he lacked an ironic vision) and, therefore, James thought it would be "an offense against humanity to place Mr. Dickens among the greatest novelists. . . . He has added nothing to our understanding of human character. . . . Mr. Dickens is a great observer and a great humorist, but he is nothing of a philosopher. . . . a novelist very soon has need of a little philosophy. . . . He must know *man* as well as *men*, and to know man is to be a philosopher."[81]

Obviously, it is not merely Dickens's great penchant for observing and recording trivial minutiae that disturbed James but his supposed failure to make the universal shine through the particular, the failure to move from the fallen world to the sphere of metaphysical truth/beauty. In a work of art, as conceived by James, fragmentariness should give way to significant form. The erratic incidentality of the world of appearance should be transformed by means of aesthetic irony into a formal structure with a metaphysical essence at its core. In this way, the work of art resides in the metaphysical realm of the universal, cut off from even the particular history of its production. This view is not fundamentally different from that expressed by Aristotle in his discussion on the relative values of history and literature and on the kinship between literature and metaphysical philosophy. Stephen Dedalus, arguing along similar lines, distinguishes between a journalistic account of a fatal accident and the work of the "dramatic" writer. Indeed, Stephen's aesthetics and his ironic posture would have received Henry James's blessing. The young artist has a great deal of the philosopher in him, he displays an ironist's contempt for "the surface of things," and he thinks he knows all about man and the human character, even though he appears to know next to nothing about men and human characters. It is his lack of knowledge about the latter that makes his ironic aesthetics cold and dehumanized. He searches so hard beneath the surface of things that he forgets all too readily the things themselves. The bright radiance of the *quidditas* (Stephen's analogue to James's "substance") of things blinds and robs him of any sympathy for the worldly corruptibility of the "source material" of his imagination.

A similar quest by the reader for a Thomistic resplendent form also causes blindness. It induces the interpreter to look at *A Portrait* as "a complete harmonious image,"[82] which is the same way Stephen looks at the world from his detached aesthetic perch. The interpreter, presumably, apprehends this "harmonious image" instantaneously, conveniently bypassing the process of reading which might lead him elsewhere, or nowhere. It is an apprehension which forgets, all too easily, that "A crude grey light, mirrored in the sluggish water, and a smell of wet branches over their heads seemed to war against the course of Stephen's thought" (*P*, 207). The search for form, which has locked so many interpreters of literary texts in a vicious circle, is frequently a manifestation of the metaphysical urge that has governed the direction of Western thought since the ascendancy of post-Socratic metaphysics. It is an urge which stems from man's discomfort in the face of temporality; it is Stephen's urge and that of many of his sympathizers and detractors.

The originality of *A Portrait of the Artist as a Young Man*, and the force with which it breaks loose from the mainstream novelistic and aesthetic tradition cannot strike the reader who is not prepared to place his ingrained metaphysical desires and interpretive criteria in a situation of risk. One has to come out of the comfort and security offered by long-held, crystallized habits and break out of the vicious circularity of one's thinking. The first step in this direction consists of the examination of the tradition on which one's preconceptions are based; that is, the Western tradition which in its craving for stability and permanence constantly resorts to an ironic interpretation of the world and to the spatialization of time. Only then will it be possible to encounter in *A Portrait* that overwhelming awareness of temporality and of the existential human condition grounded in dread-full time which conflicts so sharply with the comforting but dehumanizing posture of aesthetic irony. Joyce points the way throughout his novel by constantly placing before the reader those worldly elements which "war against the course of Stephen's thought" (*P*, 207).

4

The Religious Context:
Catholic Doctrine and Jesuit Spirituality

Religion and Aesthetics

The presence of the Catholic Church in *A Portrait* is obvious. Equally obvious is the presence of a particular aspect of Catholicism: Jesuit thought. The influence exercised over Stephen by the Catholic Church in general, and by the Jesuits in particular, is so enormous that one cannot start to unravel his thoughts and his progress through the novel without taking a close look at Catholic doctrine and Jesuit spirituality. Nor is this an easy task, for Stephen's religion is not an element one can isolate from a myriad of others. Religion is woven, as it were, into the very fabric of his intellect, and to pull it out as a thread would involve a warping of that fabric. The aesthetic theory depends to a very large extent on the religious vocabulary in terms of which it is formulated. Likewise, Stephen's views on religion, the Church, and the Jesuits are filtered through his aesthetic frame of mind. The young artist's aesthetics is as supersaturated with religion as his religion is imbued with aestheticism. A close look at Stephen's aesthetics necessitates an equally careful consideration of the religious ideas which permeate his mind, and *vice versa*.

The inseparability of religion and aesthetics is not peculiar to Stephen Dedalus's theorizing. One is not faced here with a case of synthesis whereby one set of beliefs is made to accommodate or is grafted upon another. The connection between religion and aesthetics goes as far back in intellectual history as one would care to go. At the turn of the century, the context within which Stephen develops, religion and aesthetics were as inextricably intertwined as they had ever been. One encounters in the writings of such diverse writers as Poe, Baudelaire, Pater, Mallarmé, Yeats, T. S. Eliot and others a serious interest in religion and a pervasive use of religious vocabulary. "What had started as a disparagement of the old religion two decades before, ended in the 1870's and 1880's as a conservative clinging to its remains," writes U. C. Knoepflmacher.[1] The "clinging" went on for quite some time. Religion assumed different guises as it was closely associated, not to say identified, with myth, hermeticism, ritual, and aestheticism in its widest sense. As traditional religion was rejected, art was made to replace it. Religion had for long offered a guidance through life, an explanation of the chaotic world humans inhabit, and an assurance of final reward and rest. Once it crumbled, mostly as a result of rationalism and the scientific intellectualism of the eighteenth and nineteenth centuries, one was faced with the choice of either a doubt-ridden existence, or else the erection of a substitute to religion. Not unexpectedly, the latter option proved the more attractive. "The romantic movement," according to W. H. Auden, "has been *au fond* an attempt to find a new nonsupernatural Catholicism, and because art is a shared thing and so in this sense Catholic, one of the romantic symptoms has been an enormous exaggeration of the importance of art as a guide to life, and within art itself, an emphasis on the unconscious, the childish, and the irrational in hope that in these lie human unity."

Auden contrasts "Catholicism" with "Protestantism" in order to expound an idea central to Kierkegaard's thought. According to Auden, the "attempt to find in art a bolster or substitute for faith in which people no longer believe" is illustrative of "the romantic revolt against Protestantism." He clarifies his meaning with a quotation from Kierkegaard's *Journals.*

> Luther set up the highest spiritual principle: pure inwardness. It may become so dangerous that . . . in Protestantism a point may be reached at which worldliness may be honoured and highly valued as—piety. And this—as I maintain—cannot happen in Catholicism. But why can it not happen in Catholicism? Because Catholicism has the universal premise that we men are pretty well rascals. And why can it happen in Protestantism? Because the Protestant principle is related to a particular premise: a man who sits in the anguish of death, in fear and trembling and much tribulation—and of these there are not many in any one generation.[2]

Art, then, does not simply replace religion or bolster it. Rather, art substitutes or supports a particular kind of religion, a religion which is otherworldly, is based on the principle that the world is despicable, and which tranquilizes man's existential anguish. It is of this type of religion, which Kierkegaard calls "Catholic," that art and aestheticism are allies. Auden, under the strong influence of Kierkegaard, "is proscribing that fundamentally unserious attitude which attempts to elevate aesthetics into religion—the attitude which encourages a great *interest* in the 'necessities' of life as the material of art, but will not allow itself to be embarrassed by them. The error is particularly common among the more intelligent: they confuse the aesthetic with the spiritual and, when they begin to think about religion, they run the converse risk of regarding the spiritual life as a kind of aesthetic performance."[3]

The confusion of the aesthetic with the spiritual is, undoubtedly, one of Stephen Dedalus's most salient characteristics. He not only makes a religion out of an aesthetic theory, but from his youngest days he looks at religion and its rites with the eyes of an aesthete. Whether he is going through a religious or an aesthetic phase (if one could ever be distinguished from the other, in his case) Stephen always looks for the same thing: a tranquilizing of the dread which threatens his peace of mind. He always seeks to take leave of the humdrum world and its constant reminders of mortality, change, instability. If he thinks of death he removes its sting by distancing himself from it. When, as a young boy, he is feverishly ill in the infirmary and he thinks of his own death, Stephen is far from terrified. He does not reflect on his own passage through that most dreaded moment. Instead, he imagines a scenario of melancholy beauty and assigns himself the role of a detached spectator. The only person to suffer any discomfort would be Wells, the unfriendly fellow who shoved Stephen into the dirty water.

> He might die before his mother came. Then he would have a dead mass in the chapel like the way the fellows had told him it was when Little had died. All the fellows would be at the mass, dressed in black, all with sad faces. Wells too would be there but no fellow would look at him. The rector would be there in a cope of black and gold and there would be tall yellow candles on the altar and round the catafalque. And they would carry the coffin out of the chapel slowly and he would be buried in the little graveyard of the community off the main avenue of limes. And Wells would be sorry then for what he had done. And the bell would toll slowly.
>
> He could hear the tolling. He said over to himself the song that Brigid had taught him.
>
> > *Dingdong! The castle bell!*
> > *Farewell, my mother!*
> > *Bury me in the old churchyard*
> > *Beside my eldest brother.*
> > *My coffin shall be black,*
> > *Six angels at my back,*
> > *Two to sing and two to pray*
> > *And two to carry my soul away.*

How beautiful and sad that was! How beautiful the words were where they said *Bury me in the old churchyard!* A tremor passed over his body. How sad and how beautiful! He wanted to cry quietly but not for himself: for the words, so beautiful and sad, like music. The bell! The bell! Farewell! O Farewell! (*P*, 24)

Stephen uses his imagination to gain revenge against his rival. His weapons are words and irony, which he employs in such a way as to transform his humiliation into a victory. Needless to say, he distorts reality in the process. The details of his imagined script are derived from his observations, but he transforms them and endows them with qualities which they do not possess. Furthermore, he changes some of the actual details of the liturgical ceremony in order to obtain a more poignant dramatic effect. In fact, Stephen transforms the ritual into a drama of which he is both the author and the sole spectator. This transformation also enhances his own stature, for it enables him to identify with Parnell. He does this by means of distortion. He envisions the rector wearing "a cope of black" for the "dead mass in the chapel." A priest does not wear a cope at mass but a chasuble. The cope, however, is a much more dignified and impressive vestment, and Stephen wants to embellish the scene with all the trappings of dignity he can muster. For the same reason he uses the "catafalque" as a prop. When a mass is said *presente cadavere* no catafalque is used. The coffin is placed on a low platform some distance down the aisle.[4] A catafalque, which is used during a *Requiem* mass in the absence of a coffin, consists of a wooden skeletal framework covered with a black cloth. It is somehow more imposing, and to the mind of a child more mysterious than a normal coffin. More important, Stephen associates the catafalque with Parnell as becomes clear in another feverish dream in which he imagines Brother Michael sorrowfully announcing Parnell's death.

> He saw him lift his hand towards the people and heard him say in a loud voice of sorrow over the waters:
> —He is dead. We saw him lying upon the catafalque. A wail of sorrow went up from the people.
> —Parnell! Parnell! He is dead! They fell upon their knees, moaning in sorrow. (*P*, 27)

Even when practicing his religion Stephen gets caught up in aesthetic reveries which have the effect of annihilating all sense of guilt and religious anguish. As prefect of the sodality he leads his peers in prayers to the Blessed Virgin. His state of sin disturbs him and the hypocrisy of his position nags him. But by immersing himself in the incantatory beauty of

Latin and the exotic Marian imagery, and by assigning himself the chivalric role of a knight dedicated to the Virgin he rids himself of anxiety.

> The falsehood of his position did not pain him. . . . The imagery of the psalms of prophecy soothed his barren pride. The glories of Mary held his soul captive: spikenard and myrrh and frankincense, symbolising the preciousness of God's gifts to her soul, rich garments, symbolising her loyal lineage, her emblems, the lateflowering plant and lateblossoming tree, symbolising the agelong gradual growth of her cultus among men. When it fell to him to read the lesson towards the close of the office he read it in a veiled voice, lulling his conscience to its music.
>
> *Quasi cedrus exaltata sum in Libanon et quasi cupressus in monte Sion.* . . .
>
> If ever he was impelled to cast sin from him and to repent the impulse that moved him was the wish to be her knight. If over his soul, reentering her dwelling shyly after the frenzy of his body's lust had spent itself, was turned towards her whose emblem is the morning star, *bright and musical, telling of heaven and infusing peace,* it was when her names were murmured softly by lips whereon there still lingered foul and shameful words, the savour itself of a lewd kiss. (*P,* 104–105)

His devotion to the Virgin is hardly distinguishable from his adulation of the fictional Mercedes. Both figures have the same effect on him—they are images by means of which he assigns himself a role larger and better than life.

When he takes his solitary walks and meditates on Mercedes, Stephen feels "even more keenly than he had felt at Clongowes, that he was different from others" (*P,* 64–65). His soul yearns not for an earthly encounter but after an "insubstantial image." In the presence of this image "he would be transfigured. He would fade into something impalpable under her eyes and then in a moment he would be transfigured. Weakness and timidity and inexperience would fall from him in that magic moment" (*P,* 65). He obtains a taste of the same magic just by thinking about it, for as he strolls in the peaceful gardens, away from all human companions and alone with his thoughts of Mercedes, "a tender influence [poured] into his restless heart" (*P,* 64). He experiences the same tranquilizing influence with the evocation of the image of the Virgin Mother. Her emblem infuses him with peace and anaesthetizes his conscience—effects which are more aesthetic than religious. For, whereas Stephen is ready to kneel like a humble knight at the feet of the Virgin Mary, he remains unwilling to purge himself of his pride. The solace he finds in the chapel emanates from his imagination and bears no relation to his behavior toward others. The congregation which fills the church inspires Stephen with contempt rather than charity. "Their dull piety and the sickly smell of the cheap hairoil with which they had anointed their heads repelled him from the altar they prayed at" (*P*, 104). The only altar that attracts Stephen is that of his imagination, an altar that sets him apart from the rest, and at which he feels purified of his corporeal corruptibility and relieved of his worldly desires and loathings.

This is the "Catholicism" Kierkegaard and Auden write about. It is a religion which shuns the fallen world and refuses to be embarrassed by it, a religion which hankers so intensely after the eternal and the perfect that it forgets or dismisses as irrelevant the existential condition of man caught up in dread. Its adherents find in it the same kind of solace they derive from art. Their aesthetic experiences and their religious experiences are interchangeable. The calm Stephen obtains in his contemplation of the Virgin is no different from what he gets out of poetry.

> *Art thou pale for weariness*
> *Of Climbing heaven and gazing on earth,*
> *Wandering companionless . . . ?*
>
> He repeated to himself the lines of Shelley's fragment. Its alternation of sad human ineffectualness with vast inhuman cycles of activity chilled him, and he forgot his own human ineffectual grieving. (*P*, 96)

Jacques Maritain, who scrupulously epitomizes Scholastic thought, explains how art because "it rules Making and not Doing . . . stands outside the human sphere; it has an end, rules, values, which are not those of man, but those of the work to be produced." His observations on the implications of the autotelic nature of art are of particular interest because they could be seen as a perfect summary of Stephen Dedalus's aestheticism.

> Hence the tyrannical and absorbing power of Art, and also its astonishing power of soothing; it delivers one from the human; it establishes the *artifex*—artist or artisan—in a world apart, closed, limited, absolute, in which he puts the energy and intelligence of his manhood at the service of a thing which he makes. This is true of all art; the ennui of living and willing ceases at the door of every workshop.[5]

Art, for Maritain, belongs to a transcendent sphere, and aesthetics to the realm of metaphysics. This is a point of special interest because it sheds light on the foundations of Stephen's aesthetic theory and on the close association of religion and aesthetics. Since Maritain is an excellent guide through the complexities of Scholastic philosophy, it would be expedient to pursue some of his ideas a little further.

Maritain draws a distinction between the arts that "tend to make a *beautiful* work" and those arts the work of which "is itself ordered to the service of man, and is therefore a simple means."[6] The former type constitute the fine arts. A similar distinction is made by the dean of studies at the outset of his rather disjointed discussion with Stephen on aesthetics. The priest, who is lighting a fire, greets Stephen with a trite observation.

> —One moment now, Mr. Dedalus, and you will see. There is an art in lighting a fire. We have the liberal arts and we have the useful arts. This is one of the useful arts. (*P*, 185)

The dean asks Stephen whether, given Aquinas's dictum "*Pulcra sunt qui visa placent,*" the fire could be said to be beautiful. Stephen's answer is a subtle reinforcement of the initial distinction: he separates the beautiful from the good: the first is absolute, the second relative, the one autotelic, the other a means to an end.

> —In so far as it is apprehended by the sight, which I suppose means here aesthetic intellection, it will be beautiful. But Aquinas also says *Bonum est in quod tendit appetitus*. In so far as it satisfies the animal craving for warmth fire is good. In hell however it is an evil. (*P*, 186)

Aesthetic pleasure is different from physical comfort in that it belongs to the intellect rather than the body. "The work to which fine arts tend," writes Maritain, "is ordered to beauty; as beautiful, it is an end, an absolute, it suffices itself, and if, as work-to-be-made, it is material and enclosed in a genus, as beautiful it belongs to the kingdom of the spirit and plunges deep into the transcendence and the infinity of being." Furthermore, this contact of fine art with the beautiful discloses some of its salient characteristics, "above all its intellectual character and its resemblance to the speculative virtues."[7]

Maritain also discovers "a curious analogy between the fine arts and wisdom. Like wisdom, they are ordered to an object which transcends man and which is of value in itself, and whose amplitude is limitless, for beauty, like being, is infinite." Art, moreover, although it pursues beauty, also reveals being, for art is transcendental and "the moment one touches a transcendental, one touches being itself, a likeness of God, an absolute, that which ennobles and delights our life; one enters into the domain of the spirit." And art, according to Scholastic theory, belongs to this domain. "Like the one, the true and the good, the beautiful is being itself considered from a certain aspect; it is a property of being."[8] Since all being emanates from divine beauty,[9] not only is the beauty of all things caused by God, but it participates in the beauty of God and points to it. According to this view, then, art emanates from and leads to the contemplation of a transcendental and absolute Beauty which does not belong to the physical order. Indeed the physical order, being imperfect, is abandoned in favor of a reaching out for the spiritual and the permanent. Art, although fashioned out of matter by mortal man, surpasses the created world and through the manifestation of beauty it asserts the supremacy of the spiritual realm. The being which art reveals, therefore, is not the same as the mutable phenomena of the world perceived by the senses. Art, in the context of this theory, aims, like Poe's "prose poem" *Eureka*, "less at physical than at metaphysical order."[10] The artist, like Stephen Dedalus, contemplates and presents for contemplation the intangible and radiant *quidditas*.

This conception of art and of the artist's role is not peculiar to Scholastic philosophy and theology. Several aspects of it are echoed by a variety of writers. Carlyle, for example, in *Sartor Resartus*, maintained that true works of art enable one, by means of symbols, to perceive the Eternal and the Godlike. Maritain himself refers to Baudelaire, whole *L'Art Romantique* he quotes by way of corroborating his own position. He finds in Baudelaire, as he does in Poe, that close connection between aesthetics and religion so obviously present in Scholastic thought.

> Beauty, therefore, belongs to the transcendental and metaphysical order. This is why it tends of itself to draw the soul beyond the created. Speaking of the instinct for beauty, Baudelaire, the *poète maudit* to whom modern art owes its renewed awareness of the theological quality and tyrannical spirituality of beauty, writes: " . . . it is this immortal instinct for the beautiful which makes us consider the earth and its various spectacles as a sketch of, as a *correspondence* with, Heaven. . . . It is at once through poetry, through and *across* music, that the soul glimpses the splendors situated beyond the grave; and when an exquisite poem brings tears to the eyes, these tears are not proof of an excess of joy, they are rather the testimony of an irritated melancholy, a demand of the nerves, of a nature exiled in the imperfect and desiring to take possession immediately, even on this earth, of a revealed paradise."[11]

Man is seen by Baudelaire as forever pining after the perfect and, therefore, perpetually unhappy with his lot. Like Hulme's, Baudelaire's theory highlights the mortality and the limitations of man. Man's art is itself a revelation of his unfortunate condition. Clearly, Baudelaire's aesthetics is unworldly as well as antihumanistic, and so is Maritain's. The latter although wary of the *contemptu mundi* which normally accompanies transcendental aesthetics, still strikes a very patronizing and condescending tone in conceding that "the creature is deserving of compassion, not contempt."[12] In similar fashion, and with hollow magnanimity, Stephen Dedalus is not contemptuous of the dean, but has pity for him—the privileged pity of an ironist.

> Leaning against the fireplace Stephen heard him greet briskly and impartially every student of the class and could almost see the frank smiles of the coarser students. A desolating pity began to fall like a dew upon his easily embittered heart for this faithful servingman of the knightly Loyola, for this half-brother of the clergy, more venal than they in speech, more steadfast of soul than they, one whom he would never call his ghostly father: and he thought how this man and his companions had earned the name of worldlings at the hands not of the unworldly only but of the worldly also for having pleaded, during all their history, at the bar of God's justice for the souls of the lax and the lukewarm and the prudent. (P, 190)

The dean of studies, as seen by Stephen, is most manifestly an average person. He has none of the qualities which, in Stephen's eyes, would set him apart from the common run of humankind. A "faithful servingman" rather than a knight, the dean is no hero. The causes he pleads before God are anything but grandiose; his dedication to his vocation is "steadfast" in a quiet and unspectacular way. In some of the most basic respects, the dean is a true imitator of Christ: he serves rather than rules, he is lowly and unpretentious. Stephen, who himself identifies with Christ, does not see the dean as carrying out the missives of his master. For Stephen, Christ is not the most lowly of human beings but a hero of the highest magnitude, like Napoleon but even greater. Stephen's imagination does not meditate on the Christ who by becoming human gave up his privileged position and rendered man's fall from paradise a *felix culpa*. He has no sense of the historical Christ, so strongly emphasized by Ignatius Loyola in his *Spiritual Exercises*. Stephen's image of Christ points away from the human towards the eternal; it is an image made familiar by a systematic theology which places little weight on the unfolding of the history of salvation in human time. The insistence on doctrine highlights eternal truths and absolutes. Within such an orientation the concept of Christ as the sanctifier of time remains hidden behind the radiant image of Christ the son of God, coequal with the Father and the Holy Ghost. His divine nature obscures his human nature, although in orthodox theology there never has been any question regarding the fact that Christ is both

God *and* man—the ascendancy of one aspect over the other is a matter of emphasis, but nonetheless a crucial feature of Christology and Christian thought generally.

The image of Christ as it emerges from doctrinal principles has a stronger appeal for Stephen than the historical figure of the biblical Christ. The doctrine of trinitarian consubstantiality, the eternal immutability and remoteness of the deity, and the analogy between God the creator of perfect order and the creative artist all figure prominently in Stephen's aesthetics. Stephen's adoption of these concepts for his purpose is not, in any significant way, idiosyncratic. He follows a well-established tradition that finds expression in the writings of the early fathers, scholastic and neoscholastic, as well as subsequent, theologians. Within this tradition Christ is seen for the most part as a perfect reflection of the Father, a flawless being in whom the divine manifests itself through a human form. To quote Maritain again:

> In the Trinity, St. Thomas adds, the name Beauty is attributed most fittingly to the Son. As for integrity or perfection, He has truly and perfectly in Himself, without the least diminution, the nature of the Father. As for due proportion or consonance, He is the express and perfect image of the Father: and it is proportion which befits the image as such. As for radiance, finally, He is the Word, the light and the splendor of the intellect, "perfect Word to Whom nothing is lacking, and so to speak, art of Almighty God."[13]

In short, Christ is the perfect embodiment of the three things required for beauty: *integritas, consonantia,* and *claritas.* Seen in this light, the Son is as remotely removed from the imperfections of mortal man as possible. His radiance emanates from his divinity. Once this perspective is adopted, it becomes extraordinarily difficult to approach the more human side of Christ without emphasizing his divinity to the extent of upsetting the perilous balance. Thus, Maritain, even while explaining that "Christ willed to be an artisan in a little village . . . because he wanted to assume the common condition of humanity," ends up pointing out how the Son is a perfect image of the eternal Father, an observation which places Christ *outside* "the common condition of humanity."[14]

Those who, like Maritain, pursue this approach divert their attention from the historical reality of Christ and concentrate instead on an abstract understanding of him. In Kierkegaardian terms they tend toward an intellectual and aesthetic approach. The existential reality of Christ in time provides them with the raw material from which they abstract doctrinal principles. This tendency is, according to Kierkegaard, inimical to faith for it fosters indifference towards the individual thinker, in this case

Christ as a historical person as distinct from Christ as the image of the Father. This is how Kierkegaard distinguishes between intellectual abstraction and faith:

> The maximum of attainment in the sphere of the intellectual is to become altogether indifferent to the thinker's reality. . . . A believer is one who is infinitely interested in another's reality. This is a decisive criterion for faith, and the interest in question is not just a little curiosity, but an absolute dependence upon faith's object.
>
> The object of faith is the reality of another, and the relationship is one of infinite interest. The object of faith is not a doctrine, for then the relationship would be intellectual, and it would be of importance not to botch it, but to realize a maximum intellectual relationship. The object of faith is not a teacher with a doctrine; for when a teacher has a doctrine, the doctrine is *eo ipso* more important than the teacher, and the relationship is again intellectual, and it again becomes important not to botch it, but to realize the maximum intellectual relationship. The object of faith is the reality of the teacher, that the teacher really exists. . . . The object of faith is hence the reality of the God-man in the sense of his existence. . . . The object of faith is thus God's reality in existence as a particular individual, that fact that God has existed as an individual human being.
>
> . . . Faith constitutes a sphere all by itself, and every misunderstanding of Christianity may at once be recognised by its transforming it into a doctrine, transferring it to the sphere of the intellectual. The maximum of attainment within the sphere of the intellectual, namely, to realize an entire indifference as to the reality of the teacher, is in the sphere of faith at the opposite end of the scale. The maximum of attainment within the sphere of faith is to become infinitely interested in the reality of the teacher. (*CUP*, 290–291)

Yet, the intellectual doctrinal approach has remained dominant in Catholic theology, at least until quite recently. The priority attributed to faith during the Reformation brought in its wake a counter movement which insisted ever more vehemently on doctrine. In 1566, as a result of the deliberations of the Council of Trent, Pope Pius V promulgated an official Catechism which remained, until about two decades ago, the basic model for all Catholic Catechisms. Among the most dedicated disseminators of the Tridentine brand of theology were the Jesuits. Nevertheless, the Council of Trent did not really initiate anything new; its teachings were solidly based on Thomas Aquinas's thought. Indeed, as Harry C. Staley demonstrates in his valuable essay on "Joyce's Catechisms," the translation of "the content of faith into philosophical ideas" dates at least as far back as Origen in the third century.[15] It is certainly no coincidence that Origen, like Augustine, was well-grounded in Platonism, and that

Aquinas was steeled in the school of Aristotle. The Greek philosophers held history in low regard; their primary interest focused on metaphysics which is concerned not with the concrete and the mutable, but with the ideal, the universal, the first cause, and the *telos*. Their philosophical inquiries provided the foundations of Christian theology which quickly adopted Hellenic thought for the purpose of formulating a systematic theology. As a result, even though the Bible remained theoretically the source of God's revelation to man, the Christian (and most particularly the post-Tridentine Catholic) was frequently more familiar with some simplified philosophic theological exposition of doctrine than with the Scriptures. This was certainly the case at the time when Joyce was educated, and it comes as no surprise that Stephen Dedalus quotes more freely from Aquinas than he does from the Bible, and that he seems to have little feeling, if any, for the overwhelming importance of Christ's existential reality. Fr. Michael Tynan (quoted by Staley in the essay on "Joyce's Catechisms") describes the imbalance between doctrine and history perpetuated by the traditional methods of religious teaching in Ireland.

> Perhaps the most striking evidence of our catechism-minded religion training is to be found in the syllabus for the very small children . . . The emphasis from the very beginning is on the *doctrinal* rather than the *historical* concept of religion, the faith being introduced more as a system than a story . . . Our Lord's life is compressed into the catechism formulae which they are endlessly repeating: Christ was born on Christmas Day, Christ was crucified on Mount Cavalry, Christ arose glorious and triumphant . . . The very term Christ, the anointed one, so often used in classroom instruction instead of the sweet name of Jesus, the Saviour, is significant enough.[16]

Harry Staley attaches great importance to this pedagogical stress on doctrine which, he maintains, must have characterized Joyce's early religious training and later influenced his writing. He rightly believes that a solid understanding and a good familiarity with the style and structure of the catechisms are very valuable to the reader of Joyce's work.

> The faith of the catechisms, then, represents Joyce's first formal teleology, and explanation of nature, of all existence, in terms of divine purpose. The catechism was the simple repository of the Roman Catholic response to the turbulent currents of the theological controversy that came to the surface during the Renaissance and culminated in the Reformation. Its radical view of the world is Thomistic and Tridentine; it offers a tripartite formula for individual salvation consisting of belief, obedience, and ritual, or, put another way, through faith, the commandments, and the means of grace.[17]

This is especially true in view of the fact that Joyce's and Stephen Dedalus's educators, the Jesuits, were in the forefront of the theological controversy spurred by the Reformation. They were the most militant counterreformists. Ignatius Loyola, moreover, wrote the Constitutions for his Society of Jesus during the period when the Council of Trent was in session. The idea of calling an Ecumenical Council originated with Pope Paul III, who in 1540 issued the bull *Regimini militantis Ecclesiae* approving Ignatius's "First Sketch of the Institute of the Society of Jesus." The Council of Trent first convened in 1545, by which time Ignatius had started working on the Constitutions. They were officially approved in 1550 by Pope Julius III in his bull *Exposcit debitum*. The authoritativeness accorded the theological writings of Thomas Aquinas by the Council of Trent is paralleled by Ignatius's instructions. He not only stresses the importance of correct doctrine, but he also specifies the use of Aquinas in Jesuit training.

> In general, as was stated in the treatise on the colleges, in each faculty those books will be lectured on which are found to contain more solid and fine doctrine; and those which are suspect, or whose authors are suspect, will not be taken up. But in each university these should be individually designated.
> In theology there should be lectures on the Old and New Testaments and on the scholastic doctrine of St. Thomas; and in positive theology those authors should be selected who are more suitable for our end.[18]

The careful choice of texts applies also to the humanities and other disciplines, for in the Ignatian mode of education all instruction must be directed towards the goal of imparting a systematic body of doctrine. All subjects are therefore regarded as ancillaries to theology, and, to be more exact, to Scholastic theology in particular.

> Likewise, since the arts or natural sciences dispose the intellectual powers for theology, and are useful for the perfect understanding and use of it, and also by their own nature help towards the same ends, they should be treated with fitting diligence and by learned professors. In all this the honor and glory of God our Lord should be sincerely sought.[19]

Works that do not directly contribute to the attainment of this end have to be avoided. Anything that threatens the hegemony of solid, orthodox doctrine should have no place in Jesuit education.

> The doctrine which they ought to follow in each branch should be that which is safer and more approved, as also the authors who teach it. The

rectors will take care of this, by conforming themselves to what is decided in the Society as a whole for the greater glory of God.

In the books of humane letters by pagan authors, nothing immoral should be lectured on; and what remains can be used by the Society like the spoils of Egypt. In the case of Christian authors, even though a work may be good it should not be lectured on when the author is bad, lest attachment to him be acquired. Furthermore, it is good to determine in detail the books which should be lectured on and those which should not, both in the humanities and in the other faculties.[20]

Carried to an extreme these instructions could easily become ludicrous, as is made evident by two incidents in *A Portrait*. Stephen's fellow students, for example, rebuke him severely for preferring Byron to Tennyson. Their high estimation of Tennyson has nothing to do with their critical judgement.

> —In any case Byron was a heretic and immoral too.
> —I don't care what he was, cried Stephen hotly.
> —You don't care whether he was a heretic or not? said Nash.
> —What do you know about it? shouted Stephen. You never read a line of anything in your life except a trans or Boland either.
> —I know that Byron was a bad man, said Boland.
> —Here catch hold of this heretic, Heron called out. In a moment Stephen was a prisoner.
> —Tate made you buck up the other day, Heron went on, about the heresy in your essay.
> —I'll tell him tomorrow, said Boland.
> —Will you? said Stephen. You'd be afraid to open your lips.
> —Afraid?
> —Ay. Afraid of your life.
> —Behave yourself! cried Heron, cutting at Stephen's legs with his cane.
> (*P*, 81)

In their cruel jest the young students reflect the rigid orthodoxy inculcated in them by their teachers; they can conceive of very few more shocking things than the perpetration and support of heresy. The reference to Stephen's heretical statement in his essay recalls the previous scene in which Mr. Tate most scrupulously corrects his precocious student's departure from strict orthodox doctrine.

> Mr. Tate withdrew his delving hand and spread out the essay.
> —Here. It's about the Creator and the soul. Rrm . . rrm . . . rrm . . . Ah! *without possibility of ever approaching nearer*. That's heresy.
> Stephen murmured:

—I meant *without a possibility of ever reaching.*

It was a submission and Mr. Tate, appeased, folded up the essay and passed it across to him, saying:

—O . . . Ah! *ever reaching.* That's another story.

But the class was not so soon appeased. Though nobody spoke to him of the affair after class he could feel about him a vague general malignant joy. (*P*, 79)

Later on, during his conversation with the spiritual director about his vocation, Stephen recollects another instance when his Jesuit educators tried to coerce their literary judgement to fit their beliefs.

One day when some boys had gathered round a priest under the shed near the chapel, he had heard the priest say:

—I believe that Lord Macauly was a man who probably never committed a mortal sin in his life, that is to say, a deliberate mortal sin.

Some of the boys had then asked the priest if Victor Hugo were not the greatest French writer. The priest had answered that Victor Hugo had never written half so well when he had turned against the church as he had written when he was a catholic.

—But there are many eminent French critics, said the priest, who consider that even Victor Hugo, great as he certainly was, had not so pure a French style as Louis Veuillot. (*P*, 156)

Stephen remembers how such "judgements had sounded a little childish in his ears and had made him feel a regret and pity as though he were slowly passing out of an accustomed world and were hearing its language for the last time" (*P*, 156). Still, Stephen never abandons the language of his teachers, nor does he leave behind him their systematic thinking. His revolt against the tyranny of the Catholic Church is not accompanied by a rejection of its methodology. Even his preference for Byron over Tennyson is part of a system. He likes Byron because he fits into Stephen's system as well as Tennyson fits into that of his conformist peers. His aesthetic theory is as closed and coherently formed as the doctrinal system he is made to learn. What Stephen desires above everything else is order; his religious training provides him with a perfectly ordered system, and although he rejects its content he still remains attached to its form as well as to its vocabulary.

When asked by the sculptor August Suter about his Jesuit education, Joyce is reported to have stated: "I have learnt to arrange things in such a way that they become easy to survey and to judge."[21] Jesuit spirituality and pedagogy is, indeed, characterized by the systematic way in which it presents a picture of man's place in the scheme of creation. This is particularly evident in two texts with which Joyce was undoubtedly familiar, namely Ignatius Loyola's *Spiritual Exercises* and the German Jesuit Deharbe's *A Full Catechism of the Catholic Religion*. The slim volume of the *Spiritual Exercises*, although rather sketchy in its form and in the presentation of the material it deals with, constitutes the cornerstone of Jesuit spirituality. Together with the *Constitutions of the Society of Jesus* it is the most important document of spiritual teaching Ignatius bequeathed to his numerous followers. Since their earliest days the Jesuits regarded these works as the repositories of Ignatian thought. From them they derived not only a way of life, a method of prayer, inspiration for their work, and the guiding principles of their Order, but also a distinctive brand of spirituality which, while remaining in the mainstream of orthodox Catholic theology and religious practice, sets them apart and provides them with an orientation which is unmistakably their own. This orientation is evident in the various Jesuit spheres of activity: missionary work, spiritual guidance, theological and ascetical writing, and above all education.

In *A Portrait of the Artist as a Young Man*, Joyce provides a superb illustration of the effectiveness of Jesuit education by showing how thoroughly it influenced Stephen's intellectual development. Diego Angeli was right, even if somewhat hyperbolic, when he argued that one cannot truly understand *A Portrait* unless one is also familiar with Jesuit ways. "One must have passed many years of one's own life in a seminary of the society of Jesus, one must have passed through the same experiences and undergone the same crises to understand the profound analysis, the keenness of observation shown in the character of Stephen Dedalus." Angeli goes further and attributes to Joyce a thorough comprehension of Ignatius Loyola's *Spiritual Exercises*. "No writer, so far as I know, has penetrated deeper in the examination of the influence, sensual rather than spiritual, of the society's exercises."[22] Since the significance and importance of the literary influence of the *Spiritual Exercises* have been noted by several Joyce scholars as well as by other critics, this seminal Ignatian text requires some special consideration.

Excursus: Ignatius Loyola's *Spiritual Exercises*

The *Spiritual Exercises* was composed over a protracted period of time, and the history of its composition closely parallels Ignatius Loyola's spiritual progress from his "conversion" to the foundation of the Society of Jesus. Perhaps, it may be most accurately described as the "periplus" of Ignatius's spiritual journey.

In 1521, after receiving a severe leg wound in a minor battle at Pamplona, Ignatius returned to his homestead in Loyola where, during a rather long and painful convalescence, he spent a considerable amount of time reading spiritual books. One of those books was to exercise a lasting influence on him. It was the *Life of Christ*, written by Ludolph of Saxony, a fourteenth-century German Carthusian, which inspired Ignatius to undertake a pilgrimage to Jerusalem and retrace the steps of Jesus. On his way to Jerusalem, however, he stopped at Manresa. He remained there for almost a year. From March of 1522 till February of 1523 Ignatius led a very solitary life dedicated entirely to prayer. It was a period of ascetic apprenticeship for Ignatius whose enthusiasm and fervor far exceeded his discernment and spiritual wisdom at the time. He learned by trial and error. So, the *Spiritual Exercises* was not a text according to which Ignatius guided his own spiritual development; rather, it was the result of his painful spiritual journey through the uncharted and bewildering regions of the spirit. Through his gradual enrichment by practice and experience the germs of the *Exercises* at Manresa grew into the refined and polished formulation of the final version.

The major incentive for Ignatius to organize his *Spiritual Exercises* into a more or less coherent format came from the occasions he had of giving spiritual guidance to others. Even before he gathered around him the nucleus of men who were to become the first Jesuits, Ignatius had given the *Exercises* to a number of individuals. Later, as the Society of Jesus began to take shape, the *Spiritual Exercises* formed the basis for the Jesuits' spiritual training. All prospective members had to go through them, and this procedure was formalized by an explicit injunction in the *Constitutions of the Society of Jesus* which requires every novice to go through the *Exercises* for one whole month prior to taking vows. From every candidate or aspirant "before he enters the house or college, or after his entrance, six principal testing periods are required . . . The first experience consists in making the Spiritual Exercises for one month or a little more or less."[23]

There are, then, two aspects of Ignatian spirituality. On the one hand, there are Ignatius's own explorations, full of blunders and successes, as he developed from a soldier into a genuinely religious man. On the other hand, there is Ignatius the map-maker, the plotter of a spiritual journey designed to lead his followers to the love and service of God. The presence of these two distinct elements is not exclusively peculiar to Ignatian thought. Joseph de Guibert considers it a recurrent phenomenon. "In general this experience which gives birth to a new school of spirituality is twofold: the founder's experience in the interior life, and his experience in the spiritual training of his first disciples."[24] The distinction is, nevertheless, important for it indicates the complex nature of the *Spiritual Exercises* which is not written as a book to be read, but as a manual to be used; hence its sketchy form. The exercitant has to go through an encounter with God and he has to decide, alone, which way of life to choose for the greater glory of his creator. But, whereas Ignatius lived through a process of discovery with no idea of where his experience would lead him, the peruser of the *Spiritual Exercises* is kept constantly aware of the ultimate purpose of the *Exercises*. Ignatius was an explorer; his *Spiritual Exercises* is, when taken as a whole, a map. Whenever somebody undertakes to do the *Exercises*, he is placed in the privileged position of having a bird's-eye view, a vantage point which Ignatius attained only after his travails by retrospection. Going through the *Exercises*, it is true, one can retrace the steps of Ignatius, but one does so in an ordered and systematic fashion with little or none of the confusion and uncertainty which Ignatius himself experienced. The element of authentic discovery is consequently diluted for the exercitant, since he is always aware of his position in the scheme of things. Ignatius himself was aware of this, and he must have seen it as problematical. He knew and appreciated the individuality of every person and he realized that everyone must go through one's own particular process of discovery.

Ignatius's attention to the uniqueness of every individual is manifest throughout his text. In the directions which precede the *Exercises* proper, he reminds the preacher or director of the *Exercises*: "It may happen that some exercitants are slower than others in finding the contrition, sorrow, and tears for their sins that they are seeking. In like manner some may be more diligent than others, or be more disturbed or tired by different spirits. It may be necessary sometimes to shorten the week and on other occasions to lengthen it."[25] Later, in the "Additional Directions" he suggests: "When I find that which I desire, I will meditate quietly, without being anxious to continue further until I have satisfied myself" (*SE*, 61). Similarly, he concludes his rather detailed instructions regarding penance with the admission that in the final analysis each individual should, with the help of God, find what is best for him. "Since God our Lord knows our nature infinitely better than we do, often in such changes He grants to each of us to understand what best suits him" (*SE*, 63). One of Ignatius's most explicit statements, revealing the emphasis he placed on individual experience, is found in a direction aimed at the preacher of the *Exercises*.

> The one who is giving instruction in the method and procedure of meditation or contemplation should be explicit in stating the subject matter for the contemplation or meditation. He should limit his discourse to a brief, summary statement of its principal points; for then the one who is making the contemplation, by reviewing the true essentials of the subject, and by personal reflection and reasoning may find something that will make it a little

more meaningful for him or touch him more deeply. . . . This is a greater spiritual satisfaction and produces more fruit than if the one who is giving the Exercises were to discourse at great length and amplify the meaning of the subject matter, for it is not an abundance of knowledge that fills and satisfies the soul but rather an interior understanding and savoring of things. (*SE*, 37)

The flexibility which Ignatius allows in the application of his spiritual method is a clear indication of his awareness of the particularity of each situation. But it might also be taken to betray a deeply rooted desire to formulate and crystallize a correct and all-embracing form within which could be accommodated all possible details and variations. It is possible to look at the form of the *Exercises* as contrived, calculatingly and ingeniously tailored to guide the experience of individuals much as a map guides a traveller. Every contingency is planned for and anticipated. Everything has its place in a larger scheme. In spite of its brevity the *Spiritual Exercises* is surprisingly comprehensive, and has virtually no loose ends. This characteristic was noted and emphasized by the Jesuit General Roothaan in his letter of December 27, 1834, to all the members of the Society of Jesus. It was entitled *The Study and Use of the Exercises* and, as de Guibert points out, "It would be difficult to exaggerate its importance for the history and spirituality of the Jesuits."[26] In that letter Roothaan exhorted the members of his Order to make extensive use of the *Exercises* and to regard it as a central source of both their prayer and activity. He found in the Ignatian text "the principal teachings of the spiritual life presented in an admirable order."[27]

John Roothaan was elected General of the Jesuits on July 9, 1829, and he governed the Society till his death on May 8, 1853. He was one of the most influential generals in Jesuit history, but he is chiefly remembered for the high degree of importance he attached to the *Exercises* which for him represented the quintessence of the Ignatian and, therefore, the Jesuit spirit. He even prepared a new and very faithful Latin translation of the text, accompanied by thorough annotation. The Jesuits who educated Joyce were, in all probability, still strongly affected by the great influence Roothaan exerted during his long and vigorous generalship. Joseph Deharbe, whose *Full Catechism of the Catholic Religion* Joyce had to memorize at Clongowes,[28] was a member of the Society throughout Roothaan's entire generalship. He first published his Catechism in 1849, while Roothaan was general and after Roothaan's letter of 1834 which called attention to the *Spiritual Exercises* as an indispensable source book for Jesuits.

The influence of the *Exercises* on Deharbe's work is detectable. Like every other catechism, Deharbe's is carefully ordered and systematic. Its structure is a proof of the lasting influence of the Council of Trent. The presence of Ignatius's spirit is most evident in the introductory section "On the End of Man" which vividly brings to mind the "Principle and Foundation" in the opening part of the *Spiritual Exercises*. The very first question in Deharbe's Catechism asks: "For what end are we in this world!" The answer: "We are in this world that we may know God, love Him, and serve Him, and thereby attain Heaven."[29] At the very beginning man's purpose is categorically stated and his position within the universe is clearly defined. Once the end is established, everything else becomes a means towards that end. Happiness consists of reaching the predetermined end. Given this perspective, everything that follows must necessarily be seen in terms of how it fits into the large scheme. It is therefore obvious that "the things of this world cannot possibly make us happy," for the simple reason that "all earthly things are vain and perishable" whereas "man is made for God and for everlasting happiness in Heaven." Created things, that is, neither should nor could be ends in themselves. Man must use the rest of creation in order to attain his own end. Indeed, according to the *Catechism*, all the things of the world were given to man so that he "may use them for the purpose of knowing and serving God."[30]

The preoccupation with defining the end at the very outset is a hallmark of Ignatian thinking. It can be observed in the *Constitutions* as well as in the *Spiritual Exercises*. The latter opens with an introductory section providing a set of directions for the user. The *Exercises* proper starts with the section entitled "The First Week" which contains three opening items of paramount importance. The first is a one-sentence declaration of the "Purpose of the Exercises." This is followed by a brief section under the heading of "Presupposition." Then comes the "Principle and Foundation" which in practice is frequently used as the subject of the first meditation of the *Exercises*. It is made up of two paragraphs. The first one defines man's purpose, much in the same words as the *Catechism*, while the second derives an obvious conclusion and asserts what is undoubtedly the very core of Ignatian spirituality. The "Principle and Foundation" in its entirety:

> Man is created to praise, reverence, and serve God our Lord, and by this means to save his soul. All other things on the face of the earth are created for man to help him fulfill the end for which he is created. From this it follows that man is to use these things to the extent that they will help him to attain his end. Likewise, he must rid himself of them in so far as they prevent him from attaining it.
>
> Therefore, we must make ourselves indifferent to all created things, in so far as it is left to the choice of our free will and is not forbidden. Acting

accordingly, for our part, we should not prefer health to sickness, riches to poverty, honor to dishonor, a long life to a short one, and so in all things we should desire and choose only those things which will best help us attain the end for which we are created. (*SE,* 47–48)

The "Principle and Foundation" comprises two elements which, together with Ignatius's method of meditation based on the technique of the "composition of place," has proved very attractive to litterateurs. First, it presents an ordered picture of the universe in which every creature has a meaningful function by virtue of being governed by an ultimate *telos.* Second, it proposes the virtue of indifference. Man must stand apart from creation so as to be able to use it detachedly for the fulfillment of his end. In so using the creatures around him, man not only reaches his goal, but he also brings about the fulfillment of nature's purpose which happens to be that of leading man towards the attainment of that end for which God created him. The whole of creation thus resembles an intricate poem or a huge mosaic in which all the parts are held together by their common interdependent *telos.* God is the author of this poem or vast mosaic. The traditional human artist attempts to emulate the creator by producing works of rich complexity and flawless order. His task is to encompass in an ordered fashion as much diversity as possible, and to make his work the object of contemplative joy. Ignatius was not, of course, interested in aesthetics and never imagined that his text would become a literary model. But there are aspects of it which have triggered the imaginations of many, even though, for the most part, this has entailed a narrow approach that ignored some of the most central ideas propounded in the *Spiritual Exercises.*

In *The Poetry of Meditation* Louis Martz has described the widespread knowledge and usage of the Ignatian meditative mode by the Metaphysical poets, particularly John Donne. In his study, Martz points out that the essential quality of Ignatian meditation is its ability to "produce hitherto unparalleled integration of feeling and thought, of sensuous detail and theological abstraction."[31] The meditator attains what Coleridge's ideal poet does, namely "a tone and spirit of unity, that blends, and (as it were) *fuses,* each into each, by that synthetic magical power, to which we have exclusively appropriated the name of imagination."[32] T. S. Eliot, echoing Coleridge, states in his essay "The Metaphysical Poets" that "when a poet's mind is perfectly equipped for its work, it is constantly amalgamating disparate experience."[33] Donne, for Eliot, was a perfectly equipped poet. And what Eliot finds in Donne, Martz finds in Donne's sources. Just as Donne, in Eliot's view, leads his reader through a variety of associations and a mass of heterogeneous material to a final vision of unity, so does Ignatius Loyola, according to Martz, lead the meditator through a carefully plotted process to a final fusion of the abstract and the concrete, the ethereal and the sensuous. In the final analysis, both the Jesuit founder and the Anglican eminent divine aim at a state of static contemplation. The movement of one's meditation and of the other's poem is towards a still point, a total "arrest." In Coleridgean terms, the Ignatian meditation, like the poetry of Donne, "forms all into one graceful and intelligent whole."[34]

It is not hard to find out why the Ignatian mode of meditation proves attractive to someone, such as Martz with a New Critical orientation. It imparts the sense of synthetic unity which was highly valued by I. A. Richards and which made Metaphysical poetry so attractive to T. S. Eliot, it aims at the fusion of the abstract and the concrete to which Allen Tate ascribed the highest importance, and it possesses that quality of "drama" which for Cleanth Brooks was the hallmark of poetic achievement. Martz finds in the Ignatian meditation a dramatization of abstract theological ideas which follows well-thought-out lines of development and progresses by means of a "sequence of articulated, climactic structure"[35] to "the end foreseen"[36] at the very outset of the meditation. Through this dramatization, Ignatius and other meditative writers place the meditator in the position of "feeling theological issues as part of a concrete dramatic scene."[37] Herein lies the "subtle fusion of passion and thought, of concrete imagery and theological abstraction."[38] This fusion, of course, is possible only because the end is always in view, or at the very least it is presupposed. As Martz does not fail to point out, Ignatius requires the meditator "to ask God our Lord for what I want and desire" (SE, 54) prior to launching into his meditation. There is an undeniable pattern, a carefully structured one, in an Ignatian meditation and Martz describes it as well as anybody could. But having revealed the pattern Martz proceeds no further in his analysis of Ignatian spirituality.

There is, however, that element in Ignatian spiritual thought which, in a sense, contradicts the grand design so ably outlined by Louis Martz. It is a contradiction which, as has been pointed out, seems to reside in Ignatius's mind and which is inherent in his writing. While he takes great pains to plot the progress of his meditator and to lead him to a predetermined end, he also goes to great lengths to ensure that each meditator (and, more important, each person undertaking the full month's course of the Spiritual Exercises) goes through a personal process of discovery. While he provides the meditator with a chart, he would like him to venture into the spiritual realm in the same way an explorer gropes into virgin land. Thus, the "composition of place," prescribed by Ignatius as the first prelude to a meditation, performs two distinct and apparently irreconcilable functions. On the one hand, it renders the abstract concrete. It lays out the matter of the meditation in a scene, as on a stage. The "composition of place" enables the meditator to visualize things dramatically, but in so doing it also distances him by objectifying and spatializing the matter at hand. At the same time, however, the "composition of place" positions the meditator in the midst of a very particular situation and, therefore, reduces the distance between him and the subject of the meditation. The meditator may thus feel the immediacy of the events upon which he meditates. In order to facilitate a sense of involvement, Ignatius asks the meditator to make full use of all his senses, and not just sight. The fifth contemplation of the opening day of the second week of the *Spiritual Exercises* is devoted entirely to the application of the five senses to a meditation on the mysteries of the Incarnation and Nativity. The Ignatian "composition of place," then, tends in two directions: it may make of the meditator either a spectator or a participant.

The dichotomous nature of Ignatius's work stems from his attempt to achieve two separate ends. He would like the meditator to see himself in the great plan of salvation, to see the whole of creation with God at its center. But, simultaneously, he would also like him to discover God personally, to experience the mystery of God, to be open to it, and to enter into a dialogue with that mystery. He wants his meditator to develop a relationship with God based on faith rather than on rational understanding.

Whether the Ignatian meditation becomes a tapestry presenting the viewer with a picture of a vast but ordered creation within which he has a definite role, or involves the meditator in a personal exploration of the mysterious relationship between God and himself, depends entirely on the way the text of the *Spiritual Exercises* is approached. Treated as a work to be read and studiously analyzed it becomes a teleological document, or a kind of poem in which all the parts cohere to form a unified whole. This is the aesthetic approach which demands that the reader retain his distance from the text so as to be able to view it as a whole. In this case Ignatius's work yields a sense of pleasure; its order could be said to be beautiful as well as reassuring. But when the individual meditator goes through the *Exercises* as a process, the pleasant order which delights the aesthetic imagination vanishes. Certitude gives way to doubt. The text ceases to be an object of contemplation and it comes disconcertingly to life. It also becomes unpredictable because the meditator who is going through the process does not have the advantage of viewing his progress from the end. If he follows Ignatius's instructions, the exercitant will not even wait anxiously for the end, or anticipate it in any way.

> It is to be observed that during this week and the following weeks, I should read only the mystery concerned with the contemplation that I am on the point of making. Thus, for the time being, I should not read any mystery which I am not going to consider on that day or that hour, so that the consideration of one mystery may not interfere with the consideration of another. (*SE*, 73)

The critic or scholar who lays out the whole text of the *Spiritual Exercises* before him and then proceeds to describe its structural unity violates the religious intent of the work. He indulges in an aesthetic exercise which smothers the religious character of the book and deprives it of its kinetic quality. Aesthetics and religion are two areas which cannot be confused without a falsification of either one.

Imitatio Dei: The Aesthetic Religion of Ironic Detachment

The distinction between religion and aesthetics is vitally important. One must insist upon it because it has been largely ignored with the consequence that much confusion normally obfuscates discussions of either religion or aesthetics. Too often, an aesthetics discourse is taken to possess religious qualities, and religion is considered to have an ally in aesthetic discourse. In many of his writings Kierkegaard endeavored to unscramble this confounding knot. One of his lengthy notes in *Concluding Unscientific Postscript* helps clarify the issue considerably.

> The clergy preach *about* faith, and recount the exploits of faith—and are either aesthetically indifferent as to whether we who listen are believers or not, or aesthetically polite enough to suppose that we are. In this manner faith becomes a sort of allegorical figure, and the clergyman a troubadour, and a sermon about faith becomes a sort of analogy to the story of St. George and the dragon. The scene is in the air, and faith overcomes every difficulty. And so likewise with hope and love. The religious address becomes something in the same *genre* with the first medieval essays in the dramatic art, the so-called Mysteries, when religious material was treated dramatically, and comedies were played precisely on Sundays and precisely in the church. Because there is discourse about faith, hope, and love, and about God and Jesus Christ, presented in a solemn tone (whether this be more artistic, or the course bass of an awakened despiser of all art) and in a church, it does not follow that it is a godly discourse by any means. What counts in this connection is the manner in which the speaker and the listener are related to the discourse or are presumed to be related. The speaker's relation to the discourse must not be merely through the imagination, but as himself being what he speaks about, or striving toward it in his own experience and continuing to have his own specific mode of experience in

relation to it. The listeners must be informed and assisted in becoming that of which the discourse speaks. . . . In godly discourse concerning faith, the important thing is that the question of how you and I (particular individuals) become believers is illuminated, that the speaker assists us in becoming emancipated from illusions, and knows all about the long and toilsome way, the dangers of relapse and so forth. If it is described as easy to become a believer (as for example by being baptized in childhood) and if the discourse is merely *about* faith, then the whole underlying relationship is merely aesthetic, and we are attending a comedy—in church. For a mere bagatelle we receive admittance to the clergyman's dramatic spectacle, where we sit in contemplation of what faith can do—not as believers, but as spectators of the exploits of faith, just as in our age we do not so much have philosophers, as we have spectators of the exploits of philosophy. . . . (*CUP*, 374n)

The sermons of Father Arnall in *A Portrait* do not qualify as religious discourses in the Kierkegaardian sense. It is true that he evokes very vividly the reality of hell and the despicability of sin. He employs various techniques suggested by Ignatius in the *Spiritual Exercises*—he also ignores some of the most important instructions—and succeeds in terrifying the young Stephen and driving him to confession. But Arnall does not deal with the realities of Christian faith, which has to be lived from day to day. His vision is panoramic. He presents the young students with a large and detailed canvas depicting the magnificent order of God's creation. Sin, for him, is ugly because it mars the beauty of the picture and impairs the great providential order. The remedy for this disruption is also made to look easy. One has to repent and go to confession. Nothing is said about the difficulties of *living* a life of faith. Christianity is made to look simple. He does not deal with "the long and toilsome way, the dangers of relapse," nor does he assist Stephen and his peers in "becoming emancipated from illusions." Rather, he fosters illusions by employing an aesthetic stance of omniscience; he speaks with certitude, as if he has an all-encompassing vision. He even persuades Stephen, though indirectly, to entertain aesthetic visions which makes faith comforting rather than challenging. Fr. Arnall illustrates in a brief vignette how the faithful Christian is spared the dread which plagues the sinner.

Death, a cause of terror to the sinner, is a blessed moment for him who has walked in the right path, fulfilling the duties of his station in life, attending to his morning and evening prayers, approaching the holy sacrament frequently and performing good and merciful works. For the pious and believing catholic, for the just man, death is no cause of terror. Was it not Addison, the great English writer, who, when on his deathbed, sent for the wicked young earl of Warwick to let him see how a christian can meet his end. He it is and he alone, the pious and believing christian, who can say in his heart:

> O grave, where is thy victory?
> O death, where is thy sting? (P, 114–115)

It is only natural that after the sermon Stephen is soothed by a vision of ethereal beauty, which in spite of its religious content has nothing to do with religious faith.

> In the wide land under a tender lucid evening sky, a cloud drifting westward amid a pale green sea of heaven, they stood together, children that had erred. Their error had offended deeply God's majesty though it was the error of two children, but it had not offended her whose beauty *is not like earthly beauty, dangerous to look upon, but like the morning star which is its emblem, bright and musical.* The eyes were not offended which she turned upon them nor reproachful. She placed their hands together, hand in hand, and said, speaking to their hearts:
> —Take hands, Stephen and Emma. It is a beautiful evening now in heaven. You have erred but you are always my children. It is one heart that loves another heart. Take hands together, my dear children, and you will be happy together and your hearts will love each other. (P, 116)

After his conversion Stephen's attitude towards religion remains misguided in the same way. He turns to it for comfort. When it fails him as a source of solace he gives it up for another aesthetic system which might prove more reliable in protecting him from the unpleasantness of the world and in providing him with visions of unearthly quality.

In spite of its affinity to many of the points raised in the *Spiritual Exercises*, Fr. Arnall's series of sermons is not truly Ignatian. For one thing, he impresses upon his congregation an image of a remote, even if merciful, God. He hardly touches upon the historical reality of Christ. In the *Spiritual Exercises* the second and third week are devoted almost exclusively to meditations on the life of Christ. (One must not forget it was the reading of *The Life of Christ* that, more than anything else, brought about Ignatius's conversion. His overwhelming passion was to imitate Christ, to follow in his footsteps and at one time he even thought of doing so physically and literally. When he named his Order "The Society of Jesus" he demonstrated his abiding concentration on the historical aspect of Christ.) The Christ Arnall alludes to is an abstract figure, Christ the redeemer, the Saviour of the catechism books. The Christology of Ignatius is different; it concentrates on the humanity of Christ, and it insists on the difficulties and hardships attending all those who make the serious and existential choice of following him. It is towards this choice that the efforts of the *Spiritual Exercises* are directed, and it is a choice that leads to action. Arnall's sermons move to a dead end. He pursues his goal relentlessly. He wants the students to go to confession. But after confession, what? Ignatius, too, aims his meditations at a goal. While going through the process of the *Exercises* the meditator is, indeed, being led carefully to a predetermined end, namely the contemplations of the fourth week when the *Exercises* culminates with the "Contemplation to Attain Love." But this ending is not a *terminus ad quem*; it is rather and very definitely a *terminus a quo*. The *telos* of the *Spiritual Exercises* is a starting point, and yet it is a *telos* nonetheless.

Since the *Spiritual Exercises* has been used to throw light upon certain literary works and since it has been analyzed in the same manner as literary works, it is absolutely essential to distinguish between the *telos* of the *Spiritual Exercises* and that of a poem. The importance of such a distinction is heightened by the fact that it has been, to a large extent, ignored in most literary approaches to the Ignatian text. Nowhere is this more evident than in Thomas Van Laan's study "The Meditative Structure of Joyce's *Portrait.*" Following in Martz's footsteps, Van Laan sees in "the Ignatian spiritual exercise, a ready made system already containing the introspective focus in a pattern which gives shape to miscellaneous units and organizes them into a highly integrated and meaningful whole." Van Laan finds in Joyce's use of Ignatius's work a "fusion of religious pattern with aesthetic discipline" which "parallels Stephen's own fusion of Aquinas and Aristotle in his theory of art." Moreover, this structural parallelism, in Van Laan's view, "helps to define the double source of Stephen's maturity and to re-affirm the religious basis of his ultimate dedication."[39] This analysis glosses over the fundamental difference between Stephen's aesthetic theory and Ignatius's spiritual views. The former aims at stasis; his "ultimate dedication" is to a life of utter detachment. Ignatius, on the other hand, leads his exercitant to the inevitability of choice, the necessity of involvement. The difference between Ignatius and Stephen resides ultimately in their incongruent concepts of *telos*.

There are, of course, many similarities between Stephen's aesthetics and Ignatius's spirituality, but in drawing comparisons one is often tempted to ignore the incongruities. Two ideas which, for example, appear to have a close resemblance are Ignatius's notion of indifference and Stephen's concept of detachment. These ideas parallel each other in many respects, but when one looks closely enough one discovers that they are irreconcilable. Ignatius's indifference and Stephen's detachment are aimed at distinctly different goals. An indiscriminate association of the two leads to a distortion of both and lays down false foundations for the formulation of the relationship between the religious attitude and aesthetics.

The concept of indifference lies at the very center of Ignatian thought. Indifference, in this case, must not be mistaken for passivity. In order to attain the end for which he was created, according to Ignatius, an individual must first learn to be free of all kinds of attachments to earthly things. The whole universe is created to help man attain his end, but this can be achieved only if all creatures remain a means and never become an end. The moment things become attractive in themselves they become positive hindrances to man's progress towards the fulfillment of the end for which God created him. Man must, therefore, protect himself against the materialistic tendency which naturally drives him in the direction of created things and away from God. In making decisions he should be careful to weigh the alternatives, not in the light of what attracts him at the moment of choice, but from the perspective of the end for which he was created. It is the main aim of the *Exercises*, as designed by Loyola, to help one do exactly this. "The purpose of these Exercises is to help the exercitant to conquer himself, and to regulate his life so that he will not be influenced in his decisions by any inordinate attachment" (*SE*, 47).

There is in this concept a heavy residue of the age-old stance of *contemptu mundi*, a stance which, though not particularly salient during the humanistic revival of the Renaissance when the *Exercises* was written, is consonant with other medieval elements manifest in Ignatian thought. The idea of the retreat from the world for periods of prayer and examination of conscience, on which Ignatius placed great emphasis, is akin to that impulse which led to the establishment of monastic orders. (One must add, however, that Ignatius did not envisage his religious order as a group of men protected from this world by the walls of a cloister, but rather as a society of contemplatives in action.) Similarly, Ignatius's insistence on the observance of poverty by the members of his order parallels that of the mendicant orders. The importance of poverty lies in the actual as well as in the symbolic rejection of and detachment from all worldly goods. From the same desire for total detachment stems the vow of obedience taken by all the members of every religious order. Through obedience the religious assures himself of fidelity to his ultimate end. By following his inclinations an individual might be serving his own best interests. Obedience to one's superiors, through whom Christ's will is ostensibly transmitted, ensures indifference to all personal gain and total commitment to God's plan.

The Jesuits' strict adherence to the rule of obedience is notable. All members of the Society take vows of obedience and many of them take an additional vow pledging special obedience to the Pope. The language which Ignatius uses in the *Constitutions* leaves no room for any doubts about the great significance he attached to obedience.

> We ought to be firmly convinced that everyone of those who live under obedience ought to allow himself to be carried and directed by Divine Providence through the agency of the superior as if he were a lifeless body which allows itself to be carried to any place and to be treated in any manner desired, or as if he were an old man's staff in which the holder wishes to use it. For in this way the obedient man ought joyfully to devote himself to any task whatsoever in which the superior desires to employ him to aid the whole body of the religious Institute; and he ought to hold it as certain that by this procedure he is conforming himself with the divine will more than by anything else he could do while following his own will and different judgment.[40]

It is also clear from this passage that underlying the concept of obedience is the much larger and more comprehensive notion of indifference.

J. Mitchell Morse, in *The Sympathetic Alien*, sees this doctrine as a form of "moral passivity" and a "disavowal of personal responsibility" which in his view "militated against the development of the artist."[41] Indeed, Stephen himself appears to regard the dean of studies at University College unfavorably precisely because of his avowal of obedience. In this passage the dean is compared to Loyola whom he resembles in his lameness.

> As he came to the hearth, limping slightly but with a brisk step, Stephen saw the silent soul of a Jesuit look out at him from pale loveless eyes. Like Ignatius he was lame but his eyes burned no spark of Ignatius's enthusiasm. Even the legendary craft of the company, a craft subtler and more secret than its fabled books of secret subtle wisdom, had not fired his soul with the energy of apostleship. It seemed as if he used the shifts and lore and cunning of the world, as bidden to do, for the greater glory of God, without joy in their handling or hatred of that in them which was evil but turning them, with a firm gesture of obedience, back upon themselves: and for all his silent service it seemed as if he loved not at all the master and little, if at all, the ends he served, *Similiter atque senis baculus*, he was, as the founder would have had him, like a staff in an old man's hand, to be left in a corner, to be leaned on in the road at nightfall or in stress of weather, to lie with a lady's nosegay on a garden seat, to be raised in menace. (*P*, 186)

Stephen does not reflect so much on the idea of indifference which is the source of the dean's obedience. He dwells rather on the lowliness and the lack of dignity which seem to render the dean lifeless. He disapproves of what he believes to be a lack of involvement on the part of the dean, and he views his strict adherence to obedience as an estrangement from reality. The apparent dissociation of religion from the real world is, in fact, the purported cause of Stephen's disenchantment with the Church.

Stephen does not appear to be struck by the parallelism that can be drawn between the Ignatian idea of indifference and his own aesthetic theory. The absence of joy and hatred which Stephen finds reprehensible and pitiable in the dean resembles in certain respects (but only in certain respects) the absence of desire and loathing which Stephen considers of the essence in his aesthetic theory. He explains to Lynch that desire and loathing are kinetic feelings roused by bad art. "Desire urges us to possess, to go to something; loathing urges us to abandon, to go from something. These are kinetic emotions. The arts which excite them, pornographic or didactic, are therefore improper arts" (*P*, 205). Even more pertinent is Stephen's subsequent remark to Lynch that desire and loathing belong to the realm of the physical, whereas beauty is metaphysical. "The desire and loathing excited by improper esthetic means are really unesthetic emotions not only because they are kinetic in character but also because they are not more than physical. Our flesh shrinks from what it dreads and responds to the stimulus of what it desires by a purely reflex action of the nervous system" (*P*, 206).

The dean at University College does not, of course, practice obedience because of an aesthetic theory. The limp Jesuit, like the founder of his Order, is emotionally detached from the world because he has been trained to disdain the physical in order to be better able to attain his supernatural end. Ignatius, in the first week of his *Exercises*, seeks to inculcate a deep suspicion, and even aversion, for the world of the flesh. The early section of the *Exercises*, commonly referred to as the purgative stage, consists of a series of meditations which concentrates on man's "corruption and foulness of body." In the second exercise the meditator is instructed to see himself "as a sore and an abscess from whence have come forth so many sins, so many evils, and the most vile poison" (*SE*, 57). The purpose of these meditations is to encourage the exercitant to free himself from all worldly attachment and thus dispose his soul to the promptings of the spirit. The "soul imprisoned in its corruptible body" cannot reach its creator who is its end and fulfillment, unless the chains which hold it as an "exile among brute beasts" are broken. Man must therefore transcend his animal state in order to reach the *summon bonum*. There is never any suggestion, however, that this purgation occurs easily. It is a lifelong struggle and no man is ever so freed into transcendence as to look down with disdain upon his unpurged fellow human beings.

For Stephen the highest good is beauty, and beauty shares many of the qualities of the soul. It is a "soaring impalpable imperishable being" (*P*,

169). The artist fashions this being out of the "sluggish matter of the earth," and yet his artifact must possess something that is both immaterial and atemporal. Stephen, therefore, considers it imperative that the artist be free of all earthly tendencies which prevent the soul from soaring. The physical world, in Stephen's aesthetic theory, should be used only as a means toward an end. It provides the artist with the raw material, but the artist must not be attached to it because his aim is to transform it, transubstantiate it. Stephen, like Ignatius, has a grave distrust of the tendency of the flesh to get attached to creatures. They are both afraid lest things become an impediment to the attainment of their ends. In the "Contemplation to Attain Love" which occurs in the fourth week of the *Exercises*, Ignatius instructs the exercitant to "consider how God dwells in His creatures: in the elements, giving them being; in the plants, giving them life; in the animals, giving them sensation; in men giving them understanding" (*SE*, 104). God's creatures, then, are not to be enjoyed for themselves; they are supposed to lead to something beyond them. In Ignatius's writing, however, one looks in vain for the cultivated contempt for the contradictory, mortal physical world, such as is harbored by Stephen. Nor does one find in Ignatius Stephen's flight from the immediate and the concrete. The opposite is true, as de Guibert amplifies.

> One consequence of this place given to the humanity of Christ, as it appears to us in the Gospels, is the eminently concrete character of the whole book of the Exercises. . . . Hence comes the importance given to what Ignatius calls the composition of place, and to the application of the senses which is to be made each evening to the mysteries contemplated during the day. Wholly on his guard as he was against the infatuation for imaginative visions, Ignatius seems to have feared much less than did St. John of the Cross, that in prayer this recourse to the imagination might become a source of illusion. Perhaps he counted on the reactions springing from the active and apostolic life as a means to prevent all confusion between the free play of the imagination and visions or words of a preternatural order.[42]

Stephen's tendency is to follow a route that leads him away from the immediate and the concrete and to give free play to his imagination. He constantly takes the tangible details that surround him and transforms them into abstractions, or symbols. He repeatedly arranges the discrete units of reality which he encounters in his everyday experience to form coherent and pleasant fictions. Stephen succeeds in doing this because of his ability to detach himself from his physical surroundings and to view everything from his ironic perch, with indifference. What he gains by adopting this ironic attitude is some degree of security, the kind of security that comes when one is able to make sense out of the multifarious and disconnected phenomena which one encounters. Stephen reacts to the constant flux around him by imaginatively creating a world at once patterned and significant. Just as Ignatius in his "Principle and Foundation" offers the exercitant a coherent picture of the universe, a picture within which the actions of the individual obtain a context and therefore meaning, so Stephen constantly strives to fit all the pieces together into a structure which is not only not absurd but also infuses his own existence and actions with significance.

Stephen's earliest explicit and systematic attempt to figure out his position in the scheme of things takes place at Clongowes. He writes his cosmic address on the flyleaf of the geography book. To this Fleming adds a statement of purpose: "And heaven my expectation" (*P*, 16). In spite of Fleming's teleological contribution, however, Stephen remains troubled; and what really bothers him is "Nothing." He feels uneasy because he does not have God's power "to think everything and everywhere" (*P*, 16). When confronted by nothingness Stephen feels uncomfortable, not so much because he is overwhelmed by his diminutiveness, but because he cannot understand or master it, as only God can. The fact that he understands his position in the universe through the hierarchical address affords him some consolation. But his address is not complete because he does not know what comes after "The Universe." It is this lack of knowledge that makes him feel "small and weak," and not his relative puny stature. "It pained him that he did not know where the universe ended. He felt small and weak" (*P*, 17). The knowledge sought by Stephen is possessed only by God. What Stephen desires most is to see things as God sees them.

Distancing allows Stephen to observe himself from outside his immediate, historical context. In order to describe his own position to himself he has to objectify his being. His mind, in other words, no longer remains earthbound; it hovers high above the whole of creation by ridding itself of its temporality, and when it looks down it sees its own embodiment. An inescapable dichotomy thus ensues between the real situation of Stephen Dedalus and the imaginary station assumed by the disembodied mind. A chasm separates the two positions. Stephen is inclined towards the loftier stance and he increasingly relies on his imagination to escape the real world in favor of the ethereal. In this regard Stephen differs from Ignatius, although the latter uses the same technique as Stephen. In the second exercise of the first week of the *Exercises* he offers the following consideration:

1. What am I in comparison to all men?

2. What are men in comparison with the angels and saints in heaven?
3. What is all creation in comparison with God? Then myself alone, what can I be? (*SE*, 57)

In order to meditate on these points the exercitant must allow his imagination to hover high above the physical world and view himself as an object in a scheme larger than is normally perceivable. Ignatius, however, unlike Stephen, wants the dichotomy to stand out vividly, for it instills in the individual an awareness of his misdirected tendencies. Such awareness holds one's worldly tendencies in check; it is conducive to humility; it makes one's desires subordinate to the end for which one was created. Ignatius employs the imagination to gain a clear view of God's plan of salvation. But that vision itself remains subservient to the ultimate purpose: salvation and unification with God. By contrast, Stephen strives after the aesthetic vision as an end in itself. He wants to be like God and derive pleasure out of his imagination's creation. Stephen, with his creative imagination, could be described in almost the same terms Deharbe uses in his *Catechism* to describe God's relation to His creation. Stephen creates a world of symbols and images and directs everything to form an order determined by him. Ignatius, however, orders all things and directs them towards an end determined by God.

Notwithstanding their many similarities, the visions of Ignatius Loyola and Stephen Dedalus are, ultimately, irreconcilable since that of the Spanish saint is theotelic while Stephen's is autotelic. They differ in their purpose; they pursue mutually exclusive ends. Ignatius, in spite of his distrust of the world and his spiritual detachment from it, still dedicates himself to living in it. The emphasis placed in the first week of the *Exercises* on the revulsion of the tangible world is counterbalanced by the subsequent emphasis on the Incarnation. Faith does not assure Ignatius of an easy life. It plunges him into a life of persistent struggle. There is no escape from the world for the individual who goes through the *Exercises*. The resolutions he arrives at commit him to a total involvement in the world around him. He must not look for comfort or for reward, and in pledging allegiance to Christ he affirms "that it is my wish and desire, and my deliberate choice, provided only that it be for Thy greater service and praise, to imitate Thee in bearing all injuries, all evils, and all poverty both physical and spiritual, if Thy most Sacred Majesty should wish to choose me for such a life and state" (*SE*, 68). If the Christian desires the kingdom of heaven he can reach it only by first going through the painful journey which is his human life, as Christ did. During this life he should find no rest, for he is *on the way*. Ignatian spirituality is a spirituality of passage.

> Whatever else this Ignatian itinerary was in the secret depths of his soul, it
> was without doubt a way of abnegation growing ever greater, and of a
> mastery growing constantly more complete over his passions and the en-
> tire sensible part of his soul. But it was not in any manner a way of gradual
> disengagement with the sensible, nor a flight ever more complete from the
> corporeal. In this regard it was completely different from the type of mysti-
> cism which can be called "Dionysian."[43]

Temporal existence, in Ignatian spirituality, is the only context within
which man can imitate Christ.

Stephen Dedalus is different. Temporality, for him, is the source of
disorder and discontent; he does everything in his power to escape it. If
Ignatius preaches a religion of passage, Stephen embraces an aesthetics
of ironic transcendence. He takes refuge in what William F. Lynch calls
"the special irony of the elite."

> This kind of irony is often used to create a sense of identity; it marks people
> off from the everyday run of people. (Only masses will accept the ordinary
> meaning.) It is clear that it is divisive. It does not *pass through* a lesser or literal
> meaning to get to a higher. It refuses to pass through the smaller line. It
> translates the lesser or the lower or the literal away; it is cabalistic and
> secret. It does not give any power to the lower to move into the higher
> meaning. It does not want to move through the lower, but to transcend it.
> Secretly, therefore, it has no use for the human and is never really funny. It
> rejects that fundamental act of the imagination which is passage through
> reality. For such an elite there is no real relationship, in their images of
> faith, between the smaller and larger line. In the past they have also usually
> shown themselves as fearful of historical fact and event.[44]

The aesthetics spawned by this type of irony is stamped by several identifiable characteristics: the privileged position accorded the artist who is
set above the human mass and is privy to recondite and mysterious
knowledge, the contempt for the lowly world of existential actuality, the
transformation of the concrete into the abstract which stills the calls for
involvement and care, the erasure of ethical distinctions between good
and evil, the flight to the other-worldly that willfully blinds itself to history. All these elements are present in Stephen's theory, but he is by no
means the first one to formulate them. Stephen's views are highly deriv-
ative; far from being original, they are firmly entrenched in the mainstream of what Heidegger calls the ontotheological tradition.

"Art," Stephen informs Lynch, "is the human disposition of sensible or
intelligible matter for an esethetic end" (*P*, 207). He then proceeds to
quote Aquinas, and Lynch provides him with the Latin version: "*Pulcra*

sunt quae visa placent" (*P*, 207). Stephen had used the same phrase in his discussion with the Jesuit college dean. On that occasion he had also referred to another Aquinian dictum: *"Bonum est in quod tendit appetitus"* (*P*, 186). In his conversation with Lynch, however, he purposely leaves this particular statement out of the discussion. He wants to "keep away good and evil" (*P*, 207) from the discussion, for that would entail taking into consideration desire and loathing, which in Stephen's view have no place in the concept of beauty. For beauty, like truth, is static. Indeed, "beauty is the splendour of truth" (*P*, 208), says Stephen with due acknowledgement to Plato. He also uses Aristotle to buttress his argument. These references to classical and other authors are frequently inaccurate, as Don Gifford points out in *Notes for Joyce*. In spite of these inaccuracies, however, Stephen does not seriously misrepresent his sources. His view of beauty as static, his connection of beauty with truth, and his presentation of the aesthetic in terms analogous to the religious, place him, in many ways, in a direct line of descent from Plato, Aristotle, Aquinas and Kant.

Stephen equates quidditas with *claritas*, and *claritas* is, for him, the only "logical and esthetically permissible" synthesis of *integritas* and *consonantia*. He also describes quidditas as a radiance, "the supreme quality of beauty" (*P*, 213). *Claritas* is, according to Stephen, "the clear radiance of the esthetic image." This radiance "is apprehended luminously by the mind which has been arrested by its wholeness and fascinated by its harmony." In this apprehension lies the "luminous stasis of esthetic pleasure" which, to Stephen, is "a spiritual state," an "enchantment of the heart" (*P*, 213). Stephen seeks to bolster this theory by claiming Aquinas as his source and by referring to Shelley's *A Defence of Poetry*. His fidelity to Aquinas, though, has been questioned. William T. Noon, for instance, in *Joyce and Aquinas*, maintains that the "identity which Stephen establishes between *claritas* and the Scholastic *quidditas* . . . is . . . questionable if Stephen claims Aquinas as his authority." Noon further suggests that Stephen's *claritas* is closer to Duns Scotus's *haecceitas* than to Aquinas's *quidditas*.[45] This has led to speculation about the lingering influence of Gerard Manley Hopkins at University College. Yet, while Hopkins could well have left behind him a genuinely strong interest in Scotus, Kate Harrison is probably right in asserting that "the identification of 'claritas' with 'haecceitas' is of limited value, and should perhaps remain tentative."[46]

Regardless of the accuracy with which Stephen handles his sources, one salient characteristic of Stephen's aesthetic theory is consistently adhered to. The necessarily static quality of art and of aesthetic pleasure is repeatedly insisted upon and uncompromisingly upheld. Apart from the frequent use of the word *stasis* one encounters terms like *wholeness* and *harmony* and *arrest*—terms which reinforce the same idea. The verb *apprehend* is also a careful and suggestive choice. Stephen intelligently avoids giving the impression that the perception of the radiance of an aesthetic image is an experience, for *experience* connotes process and trial. There is a sense of movement in *experience* totally absent in *apprehension* which implies the seizing, the capture, the arrest, the mental encompassment of something. *Apprehension*, however, can also suggest anxiety and dread, nuances which Stephen clearly and most ironically overlooks in his use of the word. The irony of this oversight rests on the fact that Stephen's elaboration of the aesthetic theory is rooted in a desire to purge his mind of the human tendencies of desire and loathing. He regards such tendencies as kinetic, and in his sense dread and anxiety would be kinetic, too. Anxiety has no place in Stephen's concept of aesthetic apprehension. The "enchantment of the heart" is untrammelled and perfectly at peace; it does not reach after anything nor is it repelled by anything; it refers to a spiritual or intellectual state. The mind rests in the unperturbed contemplation of beauty, in the "luminous silent stasis of esthetic pleasure" which, as William T. Noon—like many others before and after him—observes, "comes very close to the concept of 'detachment' or 'distance' of Kantian 'disinterest' and students of St. Thomas have not failed to point out the resemblance and the priority of St. Thomas's formulation. 'Motus et quies reducuntur in causalitatem pulchri,' says St. Thomas." But Noon finds in Aquinas's words the "possibility to argue on Thomist grounds of beauty that the dramatic emotion is as much an instance of psychological involvement as it is of aesthetic distance."[47]

Since Stephen's view does not seem to allow for psychological involvement, Noon catches the young artist diverging from genuine Thomism. Noon draws the distinction between Stephen's idea of aesthetic stasis and Aquinas's *"motus-quies* polarity." He quotes Stephen: "The Tragic emotion, in fact, is a face looking two ways, towards terror and towards pity, both of which are phases of it." And he comments that "from this approach we might have expected him to point to art as a resolution, at least in symbolic terms, of the complexities and contradictions of experience."[48] But Stephen's remark points toward precisely such a resolution of complexity and contradiction. It certainly does not aim at a positivistic resolution, but offers instead a resolution through aesthetic irony. Nevertheless, the resolution envisaged by Stephen is static, and Noon's intention is to show that even rigorously Thomistic thought does not have to "repudiate all kinetic elements in art." Indeed, according to Noon, "the most supremely intellective act of which Thomas can conceive is the Beatific Vision which, as he thinks of it, is highly kinetic and has an abundant resonance in the affective nature." He supports his contention by citing

Contra Gentes (Lib.III.c.63): "*Qualiter in illa ultima felicitate omne desiderium hominis completur.*" It appears that for Noon there lies a significant difference between Stephen's anaesthetizing aesthetic and Aquinas's ideal of contemplation vibrant with love. "The Aquinian contemplation is as much kinetic as it is static, and Stephen might have made a better formulation of pity and terror as the essentially tragic emotions had he realized that when the mind is arrested by the artistic vision of conflict and collision it is very much in action and not static at all."[49] This distinction may be valid, but it conceals a very real similarity between Stephen's aesthetic vision and the mystics' Beatific Vision. In fact, Stephen's description of the relationship between the mind and the beauty it beholds is strongly reminiscent of the communion between the mystic's soul and God. His assertion that the aesthete's enchantment of the heart is a "spiritual state" does not simply elevate aesthetic pleasure above the natural physical order, but it also forms part of the general parallelism between aesthetics and religion found throughout the novel. The "luminous silent stasis of esthetic pleasure" bears a strong resemblance to the ideal of mystical union with God.

It is possible to miss the overwhelming importance of Stephen's insistence on rising above desire and loathing and finding in it little more than an anaesthetizing drive, a hardening of the heart against all feeling. But it is not feeling that Stephen wants to banish; what he is set against is emotional involvement with the corruptible forms of being. Stephen does not stifle the affective nature; he seeks to sublimate his affections. Miserable in his existential condition, Stephen strives towards a higher good, a source of permanent joy. For Aquinas the only possible source of such joy is God, and man is restless until he reaches his creator; for Stephen, Beauty is the ultimate goal. There is more than a touch of Platonism in Stephen's theory and aspirations, but there is also a heavy dosage of transposed Scholastic thought. That these two elements should coexist is not entirely surprising when one remembers that Renaissance neo-Platonic Christian theology could accommodate Thomistic doctrine on the subject of man's ultimate purpose of union with God. Marsilio Ficino's use of Thomism in his *Theologia Platonica* has been amply demonstrated by Adris B. Collins in *The Secular is Sacred*. Collins's paraphrastic account of the Ficinian and Thomasitic positions regarding man's restlessness in his search for God may help shed some light on Stephen's predicament.

> . . . man is frustrated, unhappy, and dissatisfied with his lot. His very nature thrusts him far beyond the human. His desire for God is intense and unavoidable; it is a necessity of nature. Yet he cannot by his own power achieve the object, since the object is beyond his nature. But natural desire

cannot be frustrated without involving the creator in contradiction and absurdity. Therefore, Ficino, following Aquinas, concludes that man is destined for a perfect union with God in which God will carry the human soul beyond its limitations not through an image or representation, but through direct presence. Thus man's dissatisfaction with his present condition and his desire for a more perfect contemplation manifests his immortality and justifies the claim that philosophy cannot be separated from religion. All human knowledge is a search for God and hence is necessarily related to the worship of its object.[50]

Stephen's knowledge is a search for Beauty. He tries to find it in the contemplation of himself; his self is also the subject of his aesthetic worship. Stephen, of course, is not humble enough to believe that he cannot attain the object of his desire by himself. He tries to go beyond his human limitations on his own, and in this manifestation of pride he is Satanic. He is more obviously Satanic in his usurpation of God's prerogative. He does not allow God to elevate him above his human limitations; he purports to do it singlehandedly. In so doing he refuses to accept his humanity. In order to be consistent he must also reject desire, or the state of desiring. "The inclination and inadequacy of human nature are brought together in desire," Collins explains, for "desire reveals the object only enough to create dissatisfaction with the present state of affairs."[51] Stephen, the God-like artist, stands above desire as he fashions the work of art in which he brings Stephen, the creature, to his fulfillment, that is the union with Stephen the creator. Thus, Stephen's recollections move Stephen, the subject of the recollections, towards a point of rest, a state of contemplation, a union of the aspiring artist with his goal, the full-fledged aesthete—an ironic union of subject and object. In this respect, Aquinas's description of the Beatific Vision may be seen as a most apt parallel to Stephen's aesthetic vision. Aquinas's phrases *"ultima felicitate"* and *"omne desiderium hominis completur"* are strongly indicative of a sense of ending, the final and complete attainment of *telos*—as both termination and goal. There is nothing beyond the *"ultima felicitate"*; it constitutes the fulfillment of man's purpose, and consequently desire is laid to rest. This *telos* is most unambiguously a *terminus ad quem*, and in this sense the Beatific Vision is static, not unlike the state of *eudaimonia* and Plato's highest contemplation of the absolute form of Good.

Stephen's embracement of the artistic vocation follows closely upon his rejection of the Jesuit calling. As he looks "northward towards Howth" (*P*, 170) and wades in the stream, he becomes ecstatic, in the fundamental sense of the word *ekstasis*—that is, "standing apart from." Stephen stands apart from himself and sees not only "the end he had been born to serve" (*P*, 165) but also his entire life as a movement towards and an embodiment of that end. He soars above time; he transcends his immediate existential situation. Even while his peers hail him on the beach, he stands "apart from them and in silence" (*P*, 168). Their mockery fails to offend him as he is caught up in a trance. "So timeless seemed the grey warm air, so fluid and impersonal his own mood, that all ages were as one to him" (*P*, 168). At this point, when he is most removed from the vulgar world of temporality, when he is most detached from "the dull gross voice of the world of duties and despair" (*P*, 169), Stephen becomes vividly aware of "a prophecy of the end he had been born to serve and had been following through the mists of childhood and boyhood, a symbol of the artist forging anew in his workshop out of the sluggish matter of the earth a new soaring impalpable imperishable being" (*P*, 169). What Stephen beholds is his *telos*—the end and the purpose of life. He sees his life as a story, as a work of art both unified and complete. But he is also the author of this life, the one who gives it purpose and infuses it with meaning. Stephen, insofar as he is the *telos*-giving creator of his own lifestory, resembles God the creator. Stephen, the protagonist of the story who contemplates the essence of his own being, resembles God in His eternal contemplation of Himself. Stephen Dedalus, the aesthete, orders his life in the same way as, in Deharbe's catechetical description, God governs the world. "He takes care of all things, orders all things, and in his wisdom and goodness, directs all things to the end for which He has created the world."[52] The similarity is even stronger and more subtle. For, according to Catholic trinitarian doctrine, the self-contemplation of God the Father eternally generates the Son. As Deharbe explains in his *Catechism*, "the Father begets the Son by the knowledge of Himself, wherefore the Son is also called the essential 'Image,' the eternal 'Word' of the Father."[53] Stephen's familiarity with this doctrine is explicitly mentioned in *A Portrait*.

> The imagery through which the nature and kinship of the Three Persons of the Trinity were darkly shadowed forth in the books of devotion which he read—the Father contemplating from all eternity as in a mirror His Divine Perfections and thereby begetting eternally the Eternal Son and the Holy Spirit proceeding out of Father and Son from all eternity—were easier of acceptance by his mind by reason of their august incomprehensibility than was the simple fact that God had loved his soul from all eternity, for ages before he had been born into the world, for ages before the world itself had existed (*P*, 149).

But the Father and the Son, though distinct, are also one and the same. Stephen begets Stephen in his own image; Stephen the creator begets Stephen the *logos*. Out of Stephen's self-knowledge and self-contemplation emanates the "word" which is his own "image." In mythological terms, Stephen is both Daedalus and Icarus. The old artificer and his ill-fated son, however, are not identical in the way God the Father and the Son are. Yet, Stephen, employing the labyrinthine complexities of Catholic trinitarian theology, identifies himself simultaneously with the winged creature and his creator.

In his ecstasy during which he experiences a symbolic Christ-like resurrection (he sheds the "cerements, the linens of the grave"), Stephen also rejects or ignores an essential element of Ignatian Christology and eschatology. By transforming religion into an aesthetic theory (or, at the very least, by incorporating it into his aesthetic vision) Stephen self-servingly dodges the insistence with which religion pushes him towards a view of himself as an existential being. Stephen turns a blind eye to the terrestial implications of Christian belief and instead embraces the transcendent goal of mysticism. Thus, he rejects a religion which forces him to make real choices and replaces it with a metaphysical aestheticism which places him in a false but privileged position above the realm of engagement. The importance of this privileged position for Stephen is underlined by his insistence on stasis. To use another set of terms, Stephen abandons *chronos* in favor of *kairos*. In other words, he bypasses his human situation caught up in "passing time" (i.e., temporality) and stands above it in "a point in time filled with significance, charged with a meaning derived from its relation to the end." To see things from the end necessitates a divine posture of eternality. From this position it is possible to regard at once, both beginning and end, and to see the beginning infused with meaning by the end. To see things from the end is to see them as God does. Frank Kermode, in his discussion of *chronos* and *kairos*, remarks that "the divine plot is the pattern of 'kairoi' in relation to the End."[54] Stephen, then, is a divine plotter; with supreme arrogance he shoves aside the Ignatian idea of *imitatio Christi* and fashions for himself a transcendent existence *in imitatio Dei*.

The divergence of Stephen from the imitation of Christ and his calculated attempt to imitate God does much more than illustrate his pride; it points to the very center of the irreconcilable difference which separates Stephen's concept of religion from that of his Jesuit educators. Ignatian spirituality is, in many respects, markedly down-to-earth. It takes full cognizance of man's existential situation and enjoins a Christology which is both concrete and immediate. The humanity of Christ emerges from the *Spiritual Exercises* with a vigor virtually unsurpassed and rarely matched in Catholic asceticism. It is precisely this vital feature of Jesuit spirituality that Stephen deftly avoids. As closely as possible the Ignatian road to salvation follows the road traced by the historical Jesus in the course of his earthly sojourn.

The contemplation of the mysteries of Christ's earthly life constitutes by far the greatest part of the material in the text of the *Exercises*. If Christ appears less in the first week, He is there nevertheless . . .—Christ in his concrete human actions with the most humble of their sensitive details, Christ portrayed by the narratives and conversations in the Gospels rather than the Christ of theological speculation. Ignatius wishes us to exhaust all the aids which the Incarnation has brought to our sentient and intellectual nature—intellectual indeed but setting out from the sentient—in order to raise us up by this loving contemplation of the vesture of the flesh with which the Word has clothed Himself. There, as in his mystical life, if he [Ignatius] preaches a rigorous, pitiless abnegation of all that is love of self or worldly outlook, he does not seek in any way to withdraw us from our integral human life which is simultaneously sentient and intellectual.[55]

Stephen's movement is diametrically opposed to the Ignatian program. In his aesthetic mysticism Stephen betrays no abnegation of self and he *does* withdraw from his integral human life. Stephen's movement is from flesh to *logos*—he moves away from the Incarnation, away from the sentient (both the physical senses and the longings of the heart) towards the abstract, the ethereal. Stephen's ideal is his own dehumanization. Insofar as he imitates Christ, Stephen does so in order to single himself out from the rest of humanity. The ignominy of the cross, the ostracism suffered by Christ as he degraded himself are inverted by Stephen Dedalus when he uses them to exalt his ego in his arrogant *imitatio Dei*.

Stephen is irritated by the impingement of the material world and the desires of his body; and so he does his best to minimize and even neutralize his humanity. Like Icarus he reaches for the heavens, but Icarus is brought down to earth by those natural realities so carefully depicted by the "Old Masters" in Auden's *"Musee des Beaux Arts."*

> They never forgot
> That even the dreadful martyrdom must run its course
> Anyhow in a corner, some untidy spot
> Where the dogs go on with their doggy life and the
>   torturer's horse
> Scratches its innocent behind on a tree.[56]

In similar fashion Stephen's attempt to fly away from existence cannot result in his salvation; his escape will not redeem him from his temporal condition fraught with suffering, restlessness, desire, and loathing. Stephen's manner of shaking off his fallen state will lead only to another fall because the only way open to man-in-the-world is to embrace his human condition.

NOTES

CHAPTER I: A Modernist Classic in a Postmodern Age

1. Alexander Pope, "The First Epistle of the Second Book of Horace Imitated," lines 35–36, 115–118 and 131–134, in *The Poems of Alexander Pope*, ed. John Butt (London: Methuen, 1965), pp. 626, 628.

2. Harry Levin's "What Was Modernism?" was first published in 1960 in *The Massachusetts Review*. It was republished with a substantial prefatory note in Harry Levin, *Refractions: Essays in Comparative Literature* (New York: Oxford University Press, 1966), pp. 271–95 (hereafter cited as *WWM*).

3. John Dryden, "To my Dear Friend Mr. Congreve," lines 1–19, in *The Poems and Fables of John Dryden*, ed. James Kinsley (London: Oxford University Press, 1958), p. 489.

4. Friedrich Nietzsche, *The Use and Abuse of History*, trans. Adrian Collins (Indianapolis, Ind.: Bobbs-Merrill, 1957), p. 17 (hereafter cited as *UAH*).

5. *Selected Prose of T. S. Eliot*, ed. Frank Kermode (New York: Harcourt Brace and Farrar Straus, 1975), p. 177.

6. *Selected Prose of T. S. Eliot*, p. 176.

7. In *Literary Theory and Structure: Essays in Honor of William K. Wimsatt*, ed. Frank Brady, John Palmer and Martin Price (New Haven, Conn.: Yale University Press, 1973), p. 375.

8. R. P. Blackmur, *Eleven Essays in the European Novel* (New York: Harcourt Brace, 1964), p. 27.

9. Hans-Georg Gadamer, *Truth and Method* (New York: Seabury, 1975), p. 253.

10. Hans Robert Jauss, "Literary History as a Challenge to Literary Theory," *New Directions in Literary History*, ed. Ralph Cohen (Baltimore, Md.: The Johns Hopkins University Press, 1974), p. 15.

11. Jauss, "Literary History as a Challenge to Literary Theory," p. 30.

12. *James Joyce: The Critical Heritage*, ed. Robert H. Deming (London: Routledge & Kegan Paul, 1970), vol. 1, pp. 64, 62.

13. James Joyce, *Ulysses* (New York: Vintage, 1961), p. 34 (hereafter cited as *U*).

14. Martin Heidegger, *Being and Time*, trans. John Macquarrie and Edward Robinson (Oxford: Blackwell, 1967), pp. 43, 44.

15. Wyndham Lewis, *Time and Western Man* (New York: Harcourt Brace, 1928), pp. 91, 100.

16. See, for example, Geddes MacGregor, "Artistic Theory in James Joyce," *Life and Letters*, 54 (1947), pp. 18–26; Haskell Block, "The Critical Theory of James Joyce," *Journal of Aesthetics and Art Criticism*, 8 (1950), pp. 172–84; Marvin Magalaner, *Time of Apprenticeship* (London: Abelard-Schuman, 1959); and Robert S.

Ryf, *A New Approach to Joyce* (Berkeley, Cal.: University of California Press, 1966).

17. W. K. Wimsatt, *The Verbal Icon* (The University Press of Kentucky, 1954), pp. 268, 270–71.

18. Morris Beja, *Epiphany in the Modern Novel* (Seattle, Wash.: University of Washington Press, 1971), p. 22. Irene Hendry Chase in "Joyce's Epiphanies," *Sewanee Review*, 54 (1946), pp. 1–19 argues that the epiphanic theory lies at the heart of all Joyce's work.

19. See, for example, Robert Klawiter, "Henri Bergson and James Joyce's Fictional World," *Comparative Literature Studies*, 3 (1966), pp. 429–37; and Shiv. K. Kumar, "Joyce's Epiphany and Bergson's 'L'Intuition Philosophique,' " *Modern Language Quarterly*, 20 (1959), pp. 27–30.

20. T. E. Hulme, *Speculations*, ed. Herbert Read (New York: Harcourt Brace, 1924), especially pp. 141–214. See also "Notes on Bergson" in T. E. Hulme, *Further Speculations*, ed. Sam Hynes (Lincoln, Neb.: University of Nebraska Press, 1962), pp. 28–63.

21. W. K. Wimsatt, *The Verbal Icon*, pp. 272–73.

22. Roger Fry, *Vision and Design* (London: Chatto and Windus, 1925), p. 29.

23. Clive Bell, *Art* (New York: Capricorn, 1958).

24. William York Tindall, *James Joyce: His Way of Interpreting the Modern World* (New York: Scribner's, 1950), p. 119. Tindall makes a similar observation in *A Reader's Guide to James Joyce* (New York: Noonday, 1959), pp. 95–96. "Stephen's theory, announced in 1902, is formalist. A theory of art for art's sake, it suitably follows Oscar Wilde's and anticipates Clive Bell's."

25. Frederick J. Hoffman, *The Imagination's New Beginning* (Notre Dame, Ind.: Univ. of Notre Dame Press, 1967), pp. 28–29.

26. Herbert M. McLuhan, "Joyce, Aquinas, and the Poetic Process," *Renascence* 4 (1951), p. 7.

27. Jane H. Jack, "Art and *The Portrait of the Artist*," *Essays in Criticism*, 5 (1955), p. 355.

28. Bernard Benstock, "A Light from Some Other World: Symbolic Structure in *A Portrait of the Artist*," *Approaches to Joyce's PORTRAIT*, ed. Thomas F. Staley and Bernard Benstock (Pittsburgh, Pa.: University of Pittsburgh Press, 1976), p. 185.

29. Hugh Kenner, "The Cubist *Portrait*," *Approaches to Joyce's PORTRAIT*, p. 173.

30. For literary analogues to cubism in the plastic arts, see Hugh Kenner, *The Pound Era* (Berkeley, Cal.: University of California Press, 1971). An influential essay on the spatialization of time as a distinguishing feature of modern literature is Joseph Frank's "Spatial Form in Modern Literature," *The Widening Gyre* (Bloomington, Ind.: Indiana University Press, 1968), pp. 3–63.

31. William T. Noon, S. J., "*A Portrait of the Artist as a Young Man*: After Fifty Years," *James Joyce Today: Essays on the Major Works*, ed. Thomas F. Staley (Bloomington, Ind.: Indiana University Press, 1966), p. 60. Touching on the same issue, S. L.

Golberg correctly observes that "to view Joyce's own art through the theory in the *Portrait* could lead to just that kind of formalist analysis and evasion of judgement it has received from some of its commentators." *The Classical Temper: A Study of James Joyce's ULYSSES* (London: Chatto & Windus, 1961), p. 46.

32. Grant H. Redford, "The Role of Structure in Joyce's *Portrait*," *Modern Fiction Studies*, 4 (1958), p. 30. Cf. also A. D. Hope, "The Esthetic Theory of James Joyce," *Australasian Journal of Psychology and Philosophy*, 21 (1943), pp. 93–114; and Eugene M. Waith, "The Calling of Stephen Dedalus," *College English*, 18 (1957), pp. 256–61.

33. William V. Spanos, "Modern Literary Criticism and the Spatialization of Time: An Existential Critique," *Journal of Aesthetics and Art Criticism*, 29 (1970), p. 97.

34. Ibid.

35. Edward W. Said, *Beginnings: Intention and Method* (New York: Basic Books, 1975), pp. 380, 378.

CHAPTER II: Joyce *Redivivus*: A Meditation

1. James Joyce, *Dubliners* (New York: The Viking Press, 1958), p. 176 (hereafter cited as *D*).

2. Don Gifford, *Notes for Joyce* (New York: Dutton, 1967), p. 74.

3. Herbert Gorman quotes Joyce as saying that he "chose Dublin for the scene [of *Dubliners*] because that city seemed to me the centre of paralysis." Gorman, *James Joyce* (New York: Farrar & Reinhart, 1939), p. 150.

4. James Joyce, *Finnegans Wake* (London: Faber, 1964), p. 486.

5. Samuel Beckett, *Proust* (New York: Grove Press, 1931), pp. 9–12.

6. Quoted by Maurice Beebe in "Joyce and the Meanings of Modernism" in *Litters from Aloft*, ed. Ronald Bates and Harry J. Pollock (University of Tulsa Department of English Monograph Series, no. 13, 1971), p. 15; and in "Ulysses and the Age of Modernism," *James Joyce Quarterly*, 10 (1972), p. 172.

7. Leslie Fiedler, "Bloom on Joyce; or, Jokey for Jacob," *Journal of Modern Literature*, 1 (1970); and in *New Light from the Dublin Symposium*, ed. Fritz Senn (Bloomington, Ind.: Indiana University Press, 1972).

8. The place of Joyce, or at least of *Ulysses*, his last manageable work, in the body of Modernist literature was felt to be assured at least as far back as 1956. A work has to be managed, grasped, possessed; i.e., the critic must be habitualized to it (the word *habit* comes from the Latin habere, to possess) before he can "place" it and determine its position in the literary canon. According to Marvin Magalener and Richard Kain, "the position of *Ulysses* in modern letters [now seems to] be entrenched." Magalener and Kain, *Joyce: The Man, the Work, the Reputation* (New York: New York University Press, 1956), p. 214. Five years before Magalener and Kain's assertion, however, Patrick Kavanagh

was enquiring about the death not of Modernism but of Joyce and his work. His essay "Who Killed James Joyce?" appeared in the Irish periodical *Envoy*, the May 1951 issue of which was devoted to Joyce. The same essay appears in *A Bash in the Tunnel: James Joyce by the Irish*, ed. John Ryan (London: Clifton Books, 1970). Kavanagh concludes his brief and witty piece with some verse:

> Who killed James Joyce?
> I, said the commentator,
> I killed James Joyce
> For my graduation.
>
> What weapon was used
> To slay mighty Ulysses?
> The weapon that was used
> Was a Harvard thesis.
>
> How did you bury Joyce?
> In a broadcast Symposium.
> That's how we buried Joyce,
> To a tuneful encomium.
>
> . . .
>
> Who killed Finnegan?
> I, said a Yale-man,
> I was the man who made
> The corpse for the wake man.
>
> And did you get high marks,
> The Ph.D.?
> I got the B. Litt.
> And my master's degree.
>
> Did you get money
> For your Joycean knowledge?
> I got a scholarship
> To Trinity College.
>
> I made the pilgrimage,
> In the Bloomsday swelter,
> From the Martello Tower
> To the cabby's shelter.

9. Beebe, "*Ulysses* and the Age of Modernism," p. 174.

10. Beebe, "Joyce and the Meanings of Modernism," p. 16. It is worth noting that among the "Modernist artists still alive and active in the Post-Modernist, Neo-Romantic age in which we are now groping our way," Beebe lists Beckett, Nabokov, Durrell, Warren and Bellow. He also fails to draw any significant distinction between "Postmodernism" and "Neoromanticism." Beebe, "*Ulysses* and the Age of Modernism," p. 174.

11. Ibid.

12. Ibid.

13. James Joyce, *A Portrait of the Artist as a Young Man* (New York: The Viking Press, 1964), p. 212 (hereafter cited as *P*).

14. Beebe, "*Ulysses* and the Age of Modernism," p. 175.

15. "First, Modernist literature is distinguished by its formalism. It insists on the importance of structure and design—the esthetic autonomy and independent whatness of the work of art . . . Secondly, Modernism is characterized by an attitude of detachment and noncommitment which I would put under the general heading of 'irony' in the sense of that term as used by the New Critics. Third, Modernist literature makes use of myth . . . as an arbitrary means of ordering art. And, finally . . . there is a clear line of development from Impressionism to reflexivism. Modernist art turns back upon itself and is largely concerned with its own creation and composition." Ibid.

16. Ibid., p. 174.

17. Beebe, "Joyce and the Meanings of Modernism," p. 16.

18. Jean-Paul Sartre, *What is Literature?* (New York: Harper and Row, 1965), pp. 22–23.

19. Beebe, "*Ulysses* and the Age of Modernism," p. 176.

20. Richard Ellmann, *Ulysses on the Liffey* (New York: Oxford University Press, 1972); Saul Field and Morton P. Levitt, *Bloomsday* (Greenwich, Conn.: New York Graphic Society, 1972); Phillip F. Herring, ed., *Joyce's ULYSSES Notesheets in the British Museum* (Charlottesville, Va.: University Press of Virginia, 1972); Erwin R. Steinberg, *The Stream of Consciousness and Beyond in ULYSSES* (Pittsburgh, Pa.: University of Pittsburgh Press, 1972).

21. *Etudes Anglais: ULYSSES Cinquante Ans Apres*, 53 (1974); *James Joyce Quarterly*, 10 (1972); *Mosaic*, 6 (1972). The essays in the *James Joyce Quarterly* special issue had been read at a colloquium on Joyce held at the University of Tulsa in July, 1972.

22. A. Walton Litz, "Pound and Eliot on *Ulysses*: The Critical Tradition," in *Ulysses: Fifty Years*, ed. Thomas F. Staley (Bloomington, Ind.: Indiana University Press, 1974), pp. 5–18. The pagination is identical to that in *James Joyce Quarterly*, 10 (1972).

23. For a detailed discussion of the influence of *Ulysses* on T. S. Eliot's composition of *The Waste Land* see Robert A. Day, "Joyce's Waste Land and Eliot's Unknown God," in *Literary Monographs*, vol. 4, ed. Eric Rothstein (Madison, Wis.: University of Wisconsin Press, 1971).

24. A. Walton Litz, "*The Waste Land* Fifty Years After," in *Eliot in His Time: Essays on the Occasion of the Fiftieth Anniversary of THE WASTE LAND*, ed. A. Walton Litz (Princeton, N.J.: Princeton University Press, 1973), p. 3.

25. James Boswell, *Life of Johnson*, ed. R. W. Chapman (London: Oxford University Press, 1970), p. 696.

26. T. S. Eliot, *Selected Essays* (New York: Harcourt Brace, 1950), p. 4.

27. Richard Poirier, *The Performing Self: Compositions and Decompositions in the Language of Contemporary Life* (New York: Oxford University Press, 1971), p. 49.

28. Samuel Beckett, *Proust*, p. 17.

29. Beckett, *Proust*, pp. 19–20.

30. Hugh Kenner has argued quite convincingly that Frank was deceiving Eveline all along and that Frank "skilfully shaped his yarn by the penny romances from which [Eveline] derives her sense of the plausible." *Joyce's Voices* (Berkeley, Cal.: University of California Press, 1978), p. 81. So, Eveline is choosing between two fictions. Still, this does not alter the reasons why Eveline opts for one fiction rather than the other.

31. Beckett, *Proust*, p. 19.

32. Beckett, *Proust*, pp. 20–21.

33. T. S. Eliot, "Tradition and the Individual Talent," *Selected Essays*, p. 4.

34. Martin Heidegger, *Being and Time*, trans. John Macquarrie and Edward Robinson (Oxford: Blackwell, 1962), p. 43.

35. See W. K. Wimsatt, Jr., *The Verbal Icon* (University Press of Kentucky, 1954) pp. 272–73.

36. Hugh Kenner, "The *Portrait* in Perspective," *James Joyce: Two Decades of Criticism*, ed. Seon Givens (New York: Vanguard Press, 1948), pp. 158, 159. For another articulation of Kenner's position see his essay "The Cubist Portrait."

37. E. H. Gombrich, "*Icones Symbolicae*," *Journal of the Warburg and Courtauld Institutes*, 9 (1948), p. 187.

38. Hugh Kenner, "The *Portrait* in Perspective," pp. 158–59.

39. An influential work which traces themes found in *A Portrait* through their growth and evolution in Joyce's later works is Edmund L. Epstein's *The Ordeal of Stephen Dedalus* (Carbondale, Ill.: Southern Illinois University Press, 1971).

40. Robert S. Ryf, for example, asserts that "the entire history of Joyce scholarship has been the gradual revelation of the organic interrelationship of his works. It is now generally agreed that in theme, imagery, symbolism, and rhythm, his writings are all of one piece. In a sense, he wrote but one book." Consequently, "the *Portrait*, properly understood, occupies a central position in the Joyce canon. It is a nuclear work, and may properly be considered a guidebook to the rest of his writings." Ryf, *A New Approach to Joyce*, pp. 2, 5.

41. Bernard Benstock, "A Light from Some Other World: Symbolic Structure in A Portrait of the Artist," in *Approaches to Joyce's PORTRAIT*, p. 185.

42. Benstock, "A Light from Some Other World," p. 210.

43. Ibid.

44. Paul Bovè, "The Poetics of Coercion: An Interpretation of Literary Competence," *boundary 2*, 5 (Fall 1976), pp. 273–74.

45. Immanuel Kant, *Critique of Pure Reason*, trans. Norman Kemp Smith (New York: St. Martin's Press, 1965), p. 20.

46. Jacques Derrida, "Structure, Sign and Play in the Discourse of the Human Sciences," *The Structuralist Controversy*, ed. Richard Macksey and Eugenio Do-

nato (Baltimore, Md.: The Johns Hopkins University Press, 1972), p. 252.

47. Helene Cixous, *L'Exil de James Joyce, ou l'art du remplacement* (Paris: Grasset, 1968).

48. Cixous, *The Exile of James Joyce*, trans. Sally A. J. Purcell (New York: David Lewis, 1972).

49. Francois Van Laere, rev. of *L'Exil de James Joyce*, by Helene Cixous, *James Joyce Quarterly*, 7 (1970), p. 260.

50. Charles Rossman, rev. of *The Exile of James Joyce*, by Helene Cixous, *James Joyce Quarterly*, 10 (1973), p. 360

51. Van Laere, rev. of *L'Exil de James Joyce*, p. 266.

52. Van Laere, rev. of *L'Exil de James Joyce*, pp. 264–65.

53. Robert Scholes, "*Ulysses*: A Structuralist Perspective," in *ULYSSES: Fifty Years*, p. 161.

54. Norris, *The Decentered Universe of FINNEGANS WAKE: A Structuralist Analysis* (Baltimore, Md.: The Johns Hopkins University Press, 1976), p. 1.

55. *Tel Quel*, 32 (Winter, 1967), p. 22, n. 17. Derrida's essay can also be found in a somewhat modified version in his *La Dissemination* (Paris: Editions du Seuil, 1972).

56. Robert M. Adams, "The Bent Knife Blade: Joyce in the 1960's," *Partisan Review*, (1962), p. 512.

57. Among the most interesting innovative approaches to Joyce see Colin Mac-Cabe, *James Joyce and the Revolution of the Word* (New York: Barnes and Noble, 1979); MacCabe (ed.), *James Joyce: New Perspectives* (Bloomington, Ind.: Indiana University Press, 1982) and D. Attridge and D. Ferrer (eds.), *Post-structuralist Joyce: Essays from the French* (Cambridge: Cambridge University Press, 1984). For an extremely well-argued reconsideration of the definition of Modernism and Joyce's place within it see William A. Johnsen, "Joyce's 'Dubliners' and the Futility of Modernism" in W. J. McCormack and Alistair Stead (eds.), *James Joyce and Modern Literature* (London: Routledge & Kegan Paul, 1982), pp. 5–21. This collection includes other essays which suggest interesting new avenues for Joycean studies. The persistence of old habits is still evident, however, in much recent Joyce scholarship, even though passing allusions to "postmodern" critics are frequently thrown in. See, for example, R. F. Peterson, A. M. Cohn and E. L. Epstein (eds.), *Work in Progress: Joyce Centenary Essays* (Carbondale, Ill.: Southern Illinois University Press, 1983).

58. Edward Said, *Beginnings: Intention and Method* (New York: Basic Books, 1975), pp. 379.

CHAPTER III: The Demystification of Irony

1. See *James Joyce: The Critical Heritage*, ed. R. H. Deming (New York: Barnes & Noble, 1970), vol. 1, pp. 114–16 from which subsequent quotations are taken.

2. Allen Tate, *On the Limits of Poetry, Selected Essays: 1928–1948* (New York: Swallow Press, 1948).

3. Cleanth Brooks, *The Well Wrought Urn: Studies in the Structure of Poetry* (New York: Harcourt Brace, 1947), p. 266.

4. W. K. Wimsatt, *Hateful Contraries: Studies in Literature and Criticism* (Lexington, Kentucky: University of Kentucky Press, 1966), p. 48.

5. Paul A. Bovè, *Destructive Poetics: Heidegger and Modern American Poetry* (New York: Columbia University Press, 1980), p. 95.

6. Paul de Man, *Blindness and Insight: Essays in the Rhetoric of Contemporary Criticism* (New York: Oxford University Press, 1971), pp. 8–9.

7. Paul A. Bovè, *Destructive Poetics*, pp. 96–97.

8. Paul Ricoeur, *The Philosophy of Paul Ricoeur: An Anthology of His Work*, ed. Charles E. Reagan and David Stewart (Boston: Beacon Press, 1978), pp. 234–35.

9. Michel Foucault, *Language, Counter-Memory, Practice*, ed. and introd. Donald F. Bouchard; trans. Donald F. Bouchard and Sherry Simon (Ithaca, New York: Cornell University Press, 1977), p. 142.

10. Robert W. Stallman, "The New Critics" in *Critiques and Essays in Criticism: 1920–1948*, ed. R. W. Stallman (New York: Ronald Press Co., 1949), p. 488.

11. Robert W. Stallman, "The New Critics," pp. 488, 489.

12. T. S. Eliot, "A Commentary," *The Criterion*, 2 (1924), p. 231.

13. Robert W. Stallman, "The New Critics," p. 493.

14. Cleanth Brooks, "Metaphor and the Function of Criticism," in *Spiritual Problems in Contemporary Literature*, ed. Stanley Romaine Hopper (New York: Harper and Row, 1952), p. 136.

15. T. E. Hulme, *Speculations*, p. 71 (hereafter cited as *S*).

16. *The Second Book of the Rhymers' Club* (London, 1894), p. 90.

17. Rupert Brooke, *Collected Poems* (New York, 1923), p. 38.

18. Clive Bell, in *Art* (pp. 68–69), adopts the same attitude. "Art and religion are, then, two roads by which men escape from circumstance to ecstasy. Between aesthetic and religious rapture there is a family alliance. Art and religion are means to similar states of mind. And if we are licensed to lay aside the science of aesthetics and, going behind our emotion and its object, consider what is in the mind of the artist, we may say, loosely enough, that art is a manifestation of the religious sense."

19. *A Casebook on Ezra Pound*, ed. William Van O'Connor and Edward Stone (New York: Thomas Crowell, 1959), p. 45.

20. *A Casebook on Ezra Pound*, pp. 91.

21. Cleanth Brooks, *The Well Wrought Urn*, p. 266.

22. Robert W. Stallman, "The New Critics," p. 503.

23. Soren Kierkegaard, *Concluding Unscientific Postscript*, trans. David F. Swenson, introd. Walter Lowrie (Princeton, N.J.: Princeton University Press, 1941), p. 397 (hereafter cited as *CUP*).

24. Soren Kierkegaard, *The Concept of Irony*, trans. and introd. Lee M. Capel (Bloomington, Ind.: Indiana University Press, 1968), pp. 312–13.

25. Edmund Wilson, *Axel's Castle: A Study in the Imaginative Literature of 1870–1930* (London: Collins, 1961), p. 210.

26. Edmund Wilson, *Axel's Castle*, p. 211.

27. Soren Kierkegaard, *The Concept of Irony*, p. 303.

28. Alasdair MacIntyre and Paul Ricoeur, *The Religious Significance of Atheism* (New York: Columbia University Press, 1969), pp. 94–95, 97.

29. Wilhelm Worringer, *Abstraction and Empathy*, trans. M. Bullock (New York: International University Press, 1953), pp. 16–17.

30. Clive Bell, *Art*, p. 126.

31. "Sailing to Byzantium," *Selected Poems and Two Plays of W. B. Yeats*, ed. M. L. Rosenthal (New York: Collier, 1962), p. 96.

32. Martin Heidegger, *Being and Time*, p. 230.

33. J-P. Sartre, *Nausea*, trans. L. Alexander (New York: New Directions, 1969), p. 39.

34. Worringer, *Abstraction and Empathy*, p. 134.

35. Ibid.

36. Ibid., p. 133.

37. W. Y. Tindall, *A Reader's Guide to James Joyce* (New York: Noonday Press, 1959), p. 69.

38. R. J. Andreach, *Studies in Structure* (New York: Fordham University Press, 1964), p. 68.

39. *The Critical Writings of James Joyce*, ed. E. Mason & R. Ellman (New York: Viking Press, 1964), p. 111.

40. *A Reader's Guide to James Joyce*, p. 96 and p. 72.

41. *The Concept of Irony*, p. 306.

42. Ibid., p. 308n.

43. *A Reader's Guide to James Joyce*, pp. 67–68.

44. *The Concept of Irony*, p. 312–13.

45. M. Heidegger, *Being and Time*, p. 183.

46. *The Concept of Irony*, p. 316.

47. Ibid., pp. 340–41.

48. Ibid., p. 295.

49. Ibid., p. 300.

50. William F. Lynch, *Images of Faith* (Notre Dame: Notre Dame University Press, 1973), p. 153.

51. James Joyce: *The Critical Heritage*, 1. p. 110.

52. James Joyce: *The Critical Heritage*, 1. pp. 81–82.

53. *Metaphysics*, iv. 4, 1015^a, 10–11 (*ousia* can also be translated as "substance").

54. Cf. *Metaphysics*, vi. 7, 1032^b, 15–17.

55. *James Joyce: The Critical Heritage*, 1. pp. 107–8.

56. Ibid., 1. p. 98.

57. Ibid., 1. p. 102.

58. Ibid., 1. p. 98.

59. Ibid., 1. pp. 103 and 105.

60. Quoted from *Speculations* by Glenn Hughes in *Imagism and the Imagists* (Stanford: Stanford University Press, 1931), p. 17.

61. *Abstraction and Empathy*, p. 87.

62. Ibid., p. 4.

63. *James Joyce: The Critical Heritage*, 1. 105.

64. Quoted by Hughes, *Imagism and the Imagists*, p. 21.

65. *Topic*, 21 (1966), p. 52.

66. *James Joyce: The Critical Heritage*, 1. p. 104.

67. Ibid., 1. p. 87.

68. Ibid., 1. p. 92.

69. Joseph Frank, *The Widening Gyre*, pp. 59–60.

70. *The Widening Gyre*, p. 54.

71. *James Joyce: The Critical Heritage*, 1. p. 125.

72. Ibid., 1. p. 128.

73. Ibid., 1. p. 124.

74. *James Joyce: The Critical Heritage*, 1. p. 126. Woolf is here referring primarily to *Ulysses*. But what seems to trouble her, namely the ostensible uncouthness of Joyce, is also present to some extent in *Dubliners* and quite pronouncedly in *A Portrait*.

75. *James Joyce: The Critical Heritage*, 1. p. 86.

76. Ibid., 1. p. 85.

77. Ibid., 1. p. 102.

78. *Theory of Fiction: Henry James*, ed. J. E. Miller (Lincoln: University of Nebraska Press, 1972), pp. 266–67.

79. Andre Gide, *Dostoyevsky* (New York: New Directions, 1961), p. 109.

80. *Theory of Fiction: Henry James*, p. 202.

81. Ibid., pp. 213–14.

82. Ibid., 1. 12.

CHAPTER IV: The Religious Context: Catholic Doctrine and Jesuit Spirituality

1. U. C. Knoepflmacher, *Religious Humanism and the Victorian Novel* (Princeton: Princeton University Press, 1965), p. 7.

2. W. H. Auden, "Mimesis and Allegory" in *English Institute Annual: 1940* (New York: Columbia University Press, 1941), pp. 16–17.

3. Richard Hoggart, *Auden: An Introductory Essay* (London: Chatto & Windus, 1965), p. 141.

4. This platform is sometimes also called a "catafalque," but in the old Catholic liturgy *catafalque* refers more precisely to that structure which is used as a replacement for the coffin.

5. J. Maritain, *Art and Scholasticism and the Frontiers of Poetry*, trans. Joseph W. Evans (Notre Dame: Notre Dame University Press, 1974), p. 9.

6. J. Maritain, *Art and Scholasticism*, p. 33. In his essay "Art and Intellectual Virtue" in the same book, Maritain makes a very interesting observation regarding the division of the different arts into separate categories:

> It is curious to note that in their classifications the ancients did not give a separate place to what we call the fine arts. They divided the arts into servile arts and liberal arts, according as they required or did not require the labor of the body, or rather—for this division, which goes deeper than one thinks, was taken from the very concept of art, *recta ratio factibilium*—according as the *work to be made* was in one case produced in matter (*factibile* properly speaking), in the other a purely spiritual construction remaining in the soul. In that case, sculpture and painting belonged to the servile arts, and music to the liberal arts, where it was next to arithmetic and logic. (p. 21)

7. *Art and Scholasticism*, p. 33.

8. Ibid., pp. 32–33.

9. Maritain (*Ibid.*, p. 31) quotes from Aquinas's *Commentary* (lect. 5): "*Ex divina pulchritudine esse omnium derivatur.*"

10. *The Complete Works of Edgar Allan Poe* (New York: AMS Press, 1965), vol. 16, p. 276.

11. *Art and Scholasticism*, p. 32.

12. Ibid., p. 36n.

13. Ibid., pp. 31–32. Maritain is referring to Aquinas's *Summa Theologiae* 1. 39, 8. His quotation is from Augustine's *De Doctrina Christiana* 1, 5.

14. Ibid., pp. 20–21.

15. *James Joyce Quarterly*, 6. 2 (Winter '68); cf. especially pp. 137–38.

16. "Joyce's Catechisms," p. 142. Quoted from "Teaching the Bible in School," in *The World of Life* (Dublin, 1959), pp. 77–78.

17. Ibid., p. 151.

18. *The Constitutions of the Society of Jesus*, trans. with Introduction and Commentary by George E. Ganss S. J. (St. Louis: Inst. of Jesuit Sources, 1970), p. 219. In his note the translator provides the background for this rule.

> Until well into the 1500's, Peter Lombard's *Sentences* was the most widely used textbook on theology. But in the first half of the sixteenth century the use of

> St. Thomas' *Summa Theologiae* was much furthered by Dominicans Cajetan in
> Italy, Vitoria and others in Spain, and Crockaert, Vitoria, and Peter of Nijme-
> gen at Paris from about 1504 to 1526. . . . Ignatius was within this influence
> during his study of theology under the Dominicans at Paris in 1534 . . . Ever
> afterwards he and the early Jesuits, especially Nadal, had the esteem of St.
> Thomas manifested in the legislation. . . . though they were not slavishly
> bound to his opinions. . .

19. *The Constitutions of the Society of Jesus*, p. 214.

20. Ibid., pp. 189–90.

21. Richard Ellmann, *James Joyce* (New York: Oxford University Press, 1959), p. 27.

22. *James Joyce: The Critical Heritage*, 1. p. 115.

23. *Constitutions of the Society of Jesus*, pp. 95–96.

24. J. de Guibert, *The Jesuits: Their Spiritual Doctrine and Practice*, trans. William J. Young (Chicago: Inst. of Jesuit Sources, 1964), p. 10.

25. *The Spiritual Exercises of St. Ignatius*, trans. Anthony Mottola (New York: Image Books, 1964), p. 38 (hereafter cited as *SE*).

26. *The Jesuits*, p. 467.

27. Quoted by de Guibert, *The Jesuits*, p. 530.

28. Cf. Kevin Sullivan, *Joyce Among the Jesuits* (New York: Columbia University Press, 1958), p. 47.

29. Joseph Deharbe, *A Full Catechism of the Catholic Religion*, trans. John Fander, ed. P. N. Lynch (New York: Catholic Pub. Soc., 1886), p. 67.

30. J. Deharbe, *A Full Catechism*, p. 67.

31. Louis Martz, *The Poetry of Meditation* (New Haven: Yale University Press, 1962), p. 79.

32. S. T. Coleridge, *Biographia Literaria*, ed. J. Shawcross (Oxford: Oxford University Press, 1907), 2. p. 12.

33. T. S. Eliot, *Selected Essays*, p. 247.

34. *Biographia Literaria*, 2. p. 13.

35. L. Martz, *The Poetry of Meditation*, p. 83.

36. Ibid., p. 33.

37. Ibid., pp. 29–30.

38. Ibid., p. 83.

39. T. Van Laan, "The Meditative Structure of Joyce's *Portrait*," *James Joyce Quarterly*, 1. 3, pp. 12–13.

40. *The Constitutions of the Society of Jesus*, pp. 248–49.

41. J. Mitchell Morse, *The Sympathetic Alien* (New York: New York University Press, 1959), p. 70.

42. *The Jesuits*, p. 136.

43. de Guibert, *The Jesuits*, p. 59. This is not to suggest that Stephen, in contrast to

Ignatius, entertained a Dionysian impulse. The ideal novel Stephen envisages is an "Apollonian" novel, a novel which according to Thomas Mann:

> . . . keeps its distance from things, *has* by its very nature distance from them; it hovers over them, smiles down upon them, regardless of how much, at the same time, it involves the hearer or reader in them by a process of weblike entanglement. The art of the epic is Apollonian art as the aesthetic term would have it, because Apollo, distant marksman, is the god of distance, of objectivity, the god of irony. Objectivity is irony and the spirit of epic art is the spirit of irony. (Thomas Mann: "The Art of the Novel" in *The Creative Vision*, eds. Haskell M. Block and Herman Salinger [New York, 1960], p. 89).

44. W. F. Lynch, *Images of Faith*, pp. 98–99.
45. W. T. Noon, *Joyce and Aquinas* (New Haven: Yale University Press, 1957), pp. 49 and 51.
46. K. Harrison, "The *Portrait* Epiphany," *James Joyce Quarterly*, 8 (1970/71), p. 150.
47. *Joyce and Aquinas*, pp. 38–39.
48. Ibid., p. 80.
49. Ibid., p. 37.
50. A. B. Collins, *The Secular Is Sacred* (The Hague, 1974), p. 109.
51. *The Secular Is Sacred*, p. 109.
52. J. Deharbe, *A Full Catechism*, p. 90.
53. Ibid.
54. F. Kermode, *The Sense of an Ending* (New York: Oxford University Press, 1967), p. 47.
55. de Guibert, *The Jesuits*, p. 135.
56. W. H. Auden, *Collected Poems*, ed. E. Mendelson (New York: Random House, 1976), p. 147.

INDEX